Equal Opportunity

Equal Opportunity

EDITED BY

Norman E. Bowie

WESTVIEW PRESS
Boulder & London

Copyright © 1988 by Westview Press, Inc., except Chapter 2 (© Brian Barry) and Chapter 8 (© Owen Fiss)

Published in 1988 in the United States of America by Westview Press, Inc.; Frederick A. Praeger, Publisher; 5500 Central Avenue, Boulder, Colorado 80301

Library of Congress Cataloging-in-Publication Data
Equal opportunity.
  1. Affirmative action programs—United States.
I. Bowie, Norman E., 1942–   .
HF5549.5.A34E7 1988   331.13′3′0973   87-7253
ISBN 0-8133-0567-5
ISBN 0-8133-0568-3 (if published as a paperback)

Printed and bound in the United States of America

The paper used in this publication meets the requirements of the American National Standard for Permanence of Paper for Printed Library Materials Z39.48-1984.

10   9   8   7   6   5   4   3   2   1

Contents

Acknowledgments

The idea for this volume arose from a May 1985 conference, "Equal Opportunity: Legitimate Ideal or Cruel Hoax," sponsored by the Center for the Study of Values and the College of Education at the University of Delaware. Financial support for the conference was provided by the College of Education and the Rockefeller Foundation. The editor expresses his appreciation to the twenty conference participants; to the co-organizer of the conference, Jim Crouse; and to Sandy Manno, who prepared the manuscript for publication.

Norman E. Bowie

Introduction

NORMAN E. BOWIE

We hold these truths to be self-evident; that all men are created equal, that they are endowed by their Creator with certain inalienable rights, that among these are life, liberty, and the pursuit of happiness.

[Upon this moral affirmation a nation was born. But once the Revolution had succeeded, this moral affirmation had to be embodied in the social and political institutions of the new republic—at least if the new republic was to be true to the moral ideals that in part created it. The Declaration of Independence had provided a philosophy of government. A function of the state was to protect and implement these inalienable rights. If the new republic was to have moral legitimacy, it should protect and implement the enumerated rights of the Declaration of Independence.]

Much has been written about the failure of the new republic in this respect. At first, the Articles of Confederation hardly provided a national state. Although the Constitution did provide the basis of a genuine national state, it also institutionalized slavery. Women and blacks were totally without the vote. The various states still had many laws and regulations that effectively disenfranchised large numbers of males. Indeed many have argued that the Constitution was inspired by the desires of the privileged to protect their interests.

Without denying these failures, many historians and social commentators have insisted that the moral affirmations of the Declaration of Independence have guided the development of our social and political institutions—unevenly perhaps but steadily. One could look at U.S. history from the perspective of an attempt to institutionalize the moral ideals that gave birth to the American republic.

Of course it is one thing to assert that individuals have certain inalienable rights and that the states' duty is to respect these rights; it is quite another thing to live and to be governed by these ideals. To succeed in this latter task, the moral ideal obviously must remain alive in the society; it must become part of the ideology of society. And so it did.

[Particularly these individual rights became linked with the notion of equal opportunity. All citizens were to have equal protection of their life and liberty, and all citizens were free to pursue individual happiness. The United States of America was the land of opportunity. In the frontier society it was not class or status that provided success but rather achievement. A person was limited only by ability. Poor people could become rich and a poor boy could even grow up to be president. Although this rags-to-riches ideology may seem hopelessly naive and out of fashion to those who have studied how decisionmaking actually occurs, the belief that most Americans do have unlimited opportunities to better themselves is still widely accepted in American society. People still believe that the United States is the land of equal opportunity.] But is it?

This book will not address that question directly. Rather it will address a logically prior question: Could the United States be the land of equal opportunity? Answering that question will not be easy. First, there is a problem of definition. What does "a land of equal opportunity" mean? Second, there is a problem of consistency. Does it make sense to say that people should not be penalized because of their race or sex since people are not responsible for their race or sex, but people should be penalized for their IQ even though presumably they are not responsible for it. And if that position does not make sense, how can the concept of equal opportunity be redefined so that it does not violate the canons of consistency. Third, there is a problem of coherence. How does the notion of equal opportunity fit with the other aspects of our ideology? Is it consistent with our views of freedom, property, and the sanctity of the family? Fourth, there is a problem about free will—a metaphysical problem. All variations of equal opportunity presuppose that in some respects human beings are sufficiently free to be held responsible for many of their actions, and, if equal opportunity is provided, they are responsible to a significant extent for their station in life. But how free is "sufficiently free" and do we have such freedom or would equal opportunity provide it? Fifth, there is a problem of narrowness. In the American tradition, the term "equal opportunity" applies primarily to individuals. But much decisionmaking and social analysis is carried out in terms of groups. Lobbyists lobby for bankers, farmers, or teachers. Is a rational legislator interested in us as individuals or as members of a group? In the vast majority of cases, the interest is primarily in our group memberships. But do all individuals have an equal opportunity to participate in the political process if that participation is primarily in terms of group activity? Is affirmative action, which is based on group characteristics, consistent with a commitment to equal opportunity? These questions provide both the rationale and the focus of this book.

WHAT DOES EQUAL OPPORTUNITY MEAN?

The chapters in the first part of the book address the issues of definition and consistency. In our society equal opportunity is a necessary condition for fair or just competition. But what counts as equal opportunity in the competitive process? A widespread and popular view is that equal opportunity exists when persons with the same ability and talents, and who expend roughly the same effort, have roughly the same prospects for success. Race, religion, sex, and family background should not be relevant to one's success or failure in the competitive struggle.

The chapters by James Fishkin and Brian Barry challenge this popular understanding. Fishkin argues that the concept of equal opportunity is contradictory in the sense that attempts to achieve it involve us in a trilemma. If a society is to be characterized as supportive of equal opportunity, three conditions should hold: (1) The achievement of desirable positions should be based on merit; (2) the prospects of children to achieve these positions should not be predictable on the basis of arbitrary native characteristics; and (3) society should not interfere with the autonomy of the family.

Although no explanatory comment is necessary for conditions 1 and 3, some might be useful for condition 2. What condition 2 asserts is that in a society characterized by equal opportunity, you should not be able to predict the future income, occupation, or status on the basis of a child's race, sex, religion, ethnic identification, or family background. Those characteristics are not qualifications required by a job and hence are arbitrary. Predictions can be made on the basis of IQ because presumably IQ is relevant to occupation.

Fishkin argues that no society can consistently embody all three principles. Of special interest is the fact that if you try to achieve condition 2, you violate either 1 or 3. Either you have to cancel out the advantages that come with a favorable family background, and hence violate family autonomy, or you have to stop awarding desirable positions on the basis of merit alone.

Fishkin's trilemma becomes even more acute when we consider what counts as an arbitrary characteristic with respect to predicting occupational success. Fishkin seems to consider as arbitrary any characteristic that is not causally relevant to the achievement of desirable positions. But most supporters of equal opportunity go further than that. They argue that the prospects for success should not be based on any characteristic the individual is not responsible for.

In Chapter 2, Brian Barry argues that any attempt to understand equal opportunity in terms of a full-blown principle 2 leads us away from equal opportunity to equality of results. Barry begins his analysis by examining John Rawls's distinctions among various egalitarian systems. In a society with a system of natural liberty, formal equality of opportunity prevails. Under formal equality of opportunity all have the same legal rights of access to advantaged social positions. Rawls and most other supporters of equal opportunity reject formal equality of opportunity as inadequate. Accident, luck, natural assets, and social circumstances that are arbitrary from the moral point of view still play too great a role in the attainment of advantaged social positions.

In a society characterized by liberal equality, corrections are made for social class advantages. Here equal opportunity is identified with the absence of differential environmental effects. A system of public education is the most common and prominent means in such societies to overcome class advantages. However, many other adjustments must be made, as Fishkin points out, to compensate for differential environmental effects.

But why stop with environmental effects? In a system of democratic equality, the effects of genes (the natural distribution of abilities and talents) would be eliminated as well. Why should a society disapprove of environmental inequalities but approve of genetic ones? Both are equally arbitrary from the moral point of view. However, if you try to correct for all environmental and genetic differences, you try to correct for all differentiating characteristics—an impossible ideal. Equal opportunity cannot mean the absence of the ability to predict success on any differentiating personal characteristic.

Hence, philosophical analysis tends to support an argument that equal opportunity is an unrealistic political ideal. Formal equality of opportunity is too impoverished a notion to yield desirable results. Even the attempt to correct for environmental disadvantages creates conflicts with other highly valued social ends such as the autonomy of the family. But in terms of access to favored positions, genetic differences are the best predictors of all. Attempts to correct for genetic differences would create even larger and more numerous conflicts with other highly valued social ends.

Barry and Fishkin differ sharply about the legitimacy of Fishkin's condition that equal opportunity requires equality of life chances. Suppose people identify with the values and attitudes they acquired as they grew up. As Barry points out, if a person grows up in a Methodist family she is more likely to be a Methodist. Does that mean she did not have equal opportunity to be a Catholic or an atheist? Barry argues that such a question cannot be answered on the basis of statistical predictions on the likelihood of her being a Methodist. What counts is whether her choice to become a Methodist was genuinely hers.

Fishkin accepts Barry's argument as it relates to religious choice because "a person's life chances will not, and should not, hang on whether he is, say, Protestant or Jewish." But a person's attitude toward education does affect a person's life chances. Thus, if we can predict that children born in households in which education is not valued are likely to not value it themselves and that as a result their prospect for future occupational success is diminished, shouldn't we intervene—even in the case of a late teen whose dislike of education is genuine. Whether equal opportunity requires a societal attempt to change individual values and if so whether society would be justified in doing so are major items of contention in this book.

Moreover, does the notion of equal opportunity require that we be unable to predict on arbitrary characteristics the chances a child has for obtaining a desirable position? Barry argues that equal opportunity should not carry the whole burden of what counts as a just society. Perhaps it is unrealistic and not morally required that every citizen have an equal opportunity for all favored positions. Having an equal opportunity to genuinely compete for a few of them is sufficient. However, justice requires that such a view of equal opportunity must be supplemented by a guarantee of a minimum standard of living.

WHAT DOES EQUAL OPPORTUNITY REQUIRE IN EDUCATION AND THE WORKPLACE?

If equal opportunity is accepted as a legitimate goal for the just society, what does equal opportunity require? In Chapter 3, Christopher Jencks asks us to imagine a hypothetical Ms. Higgins who is a sixth-grade language arts teacher, committed to providing equal educational opportunity. How should she behave? Jencks argues that she has five equal-opportunity norms that are relevant to the classroom situation. The moralistic view urges Ms. Higgins to reward effort (that is, achievement, as effort is not easily identified). The humane view instructs Ms. Higgins to give extra resources to those with the greatest disadvantages.

Under what Jencks calls the myopic utilitarian view, Ms. Higgins's goal
is to maximize short-run satisfaction. The view tells Ms. Higgins to
distribute her time on the basis of demand. Under what Jencks calls
the enlightened utilitarian view, Ms. Higgins distributes her time so as
to maximize the long-run welfare of society as a whole. Finally, under
democratic equality, every student gets equal time and attention—
period.

What Jencks does is to thoroughly analyze the strengths and weak-
nesses of all five positions. He seems most favorably disposed toward
the fifth norm—democratic equality—in part because of the severe
problems that afflict the four other theories. However, even if some
would reject his choice, all five theories share a common element. If
Ms. Higgins is to treat children unequally, she must justify that treatment
in terms of universally applicable principles that bear directly on the
learning process. All five theories limit favoritism and the use of
irrelevant characteristics.

One might think that five equal-opportunity norms are a sufficient
number to complicate the analysis. Yet the situation may be even more
complex than Jencks points out. Jencks omits any discussion of cultural
equality. If there is a large number of Hispanics, should Spanish be
spoken in the classroom? If there is a large number of blacks should
Frederick Douglass's birthday be celebrated?

It should also be noted that Jencks argues that society is as responsible
for differentials determined by genes as it is for socioeconomic differentials. We can only change the distribution of genes by changing the
members of society. To change the distribution of economic status we
only need to change the workings of society. In that way Jencks must
agree with Barry that Fishkin's principle 2 should be given the full-
blown interpretation. People should not be able to predict a child's
future success on the basis of knowledge of her genes. But wouldn't
such an interpretation require equality of results? Society has not
accepted such an implication, however. Traditionally equal opportunity
in education has been limited to ensuring procedural fairness, so that
favored positions could be rewarded according to merit. Much of the
debate about equal opportunity has centered on what in addition to
formal equality of opportunity should be provided to ensure that rewards
are determined on the basis of merit and not on unfair advantages.

One of the most serious impediments to fair competition in our
society is the overt discrimination against minorities, especially blacks
and native Americans and the more limited and covert discrimination
against women. In Chapter 4, Jennifer Hochschild argues that genuine
equal opportunity for black Americans requires a departure from formal
equality of opportunity. The first step in Hochschild's argument is to

show that race, class, and lack of access to power interact in cumulative ways making it more difficult for black Americans to enjoy equal citizenship. Equal citizenship cannot be achieved merely by having equal rules; people must also have equal equipment—a box of tools, a set of skills. Hochschild refers to this form of equal opportunity as "means-regarding equal opportunity." Genuine equal opportunity requires that "resources must be redistributed so that every child faces adulthood (and every young adult faces maturity) with a similarly middle-class background."

To examine the results of means-regarding equal opportunity for policy, Hochschild distinguishes between external means (the tool box) and internal means (the set of skills). Modern liberals endorse state provision of external means. They quarrel about the size and contents of the box of tools and about who should pay. Such quarrels involve serious philosophical debates, but the end result is that the disadvantaged do not receive enough. Bad as that may be, Americans seem unwilling to provide the internal means. Providing the internal means requires intervening in socialization, which, as Fishkin has pointed out, involves intervening in the family. And if you intervene, where do you stop? As Hochschild says, "If it makes sense to try to change children's ability to read, then why not also seek to change their motivation to learn to read? And if that too makes sense, why not seek to change their desire to become an auto mechanic into a desire to become a college professor?"

As Hochschild points out, this line of questioning can be taken too far. Anything that differentiates children could be a candidate for equalization. At the extreme, equal opportunity would expand to making children absolutely equal. And society should shrink back from that.

Yet cultural and psychological circumstances are causally relevant to success and need to be addressed. Sometimes we are willing to do so. We are willing to try to change the habits and attitudes of welfare recipients. But how far should we go? Hochschild avoids wading into that "bottomless swamp."

In Chapter 5, George Sher defends the view that persons should be hired or admitted to educational institutions on the basis of their qualifications (selected for merit). Sher points out that education and jobs have purposes that will best be accomplished if one hires the most skilled (best qualified). "Similarly the primary purpose of admitting persons to educational institutions will best be accomplished by admitting those who are most able to learn." Hence, the fact that an applicant best enables the purposes of a job to be fulfilled because the applicant has the requisite skill justifies hiring the best qualified applicants from the hiring officer's perspective. But what about from the applicant's point of view? Sher argues that by abstracting from all the facts about an applicant except the applicant's ability to perform, the applicant is treated as an agent whose acts are capable of making a difference in the world. Also by concentrating on abilities that are internally connected to jobs, "we affirm the applicant's involvement in the wider life of the community." Such attitudes regard persons as rational autonomous agents and hence treat persons with respect as required by morality.

Would selection criteria other than qualification treat people with respect and perhaps advance other desirable social goals? Sher thinks not. If an applicant is not hired on the basis of her qualifications, then she is being hired for some reason only incidentally connected to her actions. As such the applicant is not treated as an individual but as a mere bearer "of needs or claims, as passive links in causal chains, or as interchangeable specimens of larger groups or classes." Such an applicant is treated as a means to the ends of another. With respect to education and jobs, selection according to merit is the only way to honor the moral imperative to respect persons. Although Sher admits that the duty to respect persons in these contexts can be overridden by higher moral goals and that his argument is made more complicated by the fact that the prevailing reward structure is morally suspect, he attempts to counter these criticisms and show that his argument is essentially correct. If reward according to merit in education and job selection is morally legitimate, then equal opportunity norms can serve their traditional function of enabling persons to achieve consistent with their ability and effort.

WHAT DOES EQUAL OPPORTUNITY REQUIRE IN TERMS OF POLITICAL REPRESENTATION?

Even if equal opportunity norms have as their sole function sweeping away the arbitrary impediments to the flourishing of ability and effort, there will still be disagreement in society as to what constitutes an impediment and how corrections should be made and at what cost. To the extent that several accepted but competing concepts of equal opportunity are at work in society, the disagreement becomes more intense. Both the choice of an equal opportunity norm and the decisions on its implementation are political questions. The members of society need to make a decision.

The chapters in Part 3 discuss the question, "What does equal opportunity in the political realm amount to?" The question turns out to be astonishingly complex, and the answers to it give inconsistent results in the sense that achievement of equal opportunity in one area tends to sacrifice it in another. In Chapter 6, Jane Mansbridge approaches the question from the perspective of the equal opportunity to exercise power. Equal opportunity in the political context is the equal opportunity to influence political results—to get one's way politically. Mansbridge distinguishes between political activity that seeks to achieve the common interest and political activity by which a person or group tries to achieve aims in conflict with those of another person or group. In the former context equal opportunity is achieved when provision is made for merit. The most meritorious should have the most influence. Because the aim of political activity in these cases is the common interest, it is best for all if the most meritorious have the most influence.

However, in the struggles of day-to-day affairs political activity is generally viewed as adversarial rather than nonadversarial. In such situations, the classical view of formal equal opportunity that permits merit to emerge is inappropriate. The most meritorious would get their way at the expense of the interest of others. In adversarial political contexts, some try to coerce others because they try to force others to sacrifice their interests so that they can achieve their own. Mansbridge argues that in most adversarial political situations, equal opportunity would not permit unequal coercive power.

The traditional device to avoid inequality of coercive power is the one citizen/one vote rule. What legitimates the right of the majority to achieve its interests at the expense of the minority is that the majority won in a fair fight in which each citizen had an equal vote and putatively an equal chance to affect the outcome.

But the one citizen/one vote rule is plagued with both problems of meaning and problems of justification. With respect to justification, Mansbridge points out an exception to a one citizen/one vote rule of equal opportunity in a political context. Sometimes society appropriately wants to reward effort because effort is an indication of the intensity of the desire to achieve a goal. Society can allow for greater intensities of desire when the good is abundant. A paper towel dispenser will yield more towels to the person who makes the greater effort. Unequal coercive power is legitimate, Mansbridge argues, when the inequality is simply the result of differences in effort. However, it is not legitimate when it results from differences in ability or in the costs and benefits of the participatory act itself. Poor people do not have the ability to contribute to political campaigns, and since money affects outcomes and the interests of the poor conflict with the rich, the one citizen/ one vote rule does not permit a fair fight. Mansbridge also points out that the poor are less likely to vote, contact a representative, or get up a petition than the rich. Although Mansbridge seems to assume that these inequalities result from inequalities either in ability or in the cost of participation, others could argue that the differences are attributable to effort. Whether or not effort should be treated as just another ability returns us to the debate in Part 1.

The problem of meaning is especially acute in a representative democracy. If one citizen/one vote is a way of making the adversarial battle fair, then if you reside in a district in which you are a member of a permanent minority and overwhelmingly outvoted, the right to cast one vote is little more than an exercise in futility. Equal opportunity in the political process requires attention to the fairness of voting mechanisms for representation. In our history, as Charles Beitz points out in Chapter 7, partisan and racial gerrymandering, multimember districting, and at-large election systems have all been criticized as being unfair because the chances of electoral success under such systems are unequal.

Beitz argues that any districting scheme will be an advantage to some interests and a disadvantage to others. What is needed is some criterion that tells us which advantages are legitimate and which ones are not. Beitz argues that "a system is qualitatively fair to the extent that it yields political decisions that satisfy everyone's political preferences equally often." Any districting scheme that has a structural bias that systematically produces inequalities in the distribution of preference satisfaction is illegitimate. What this means in practice is that society should try to avoid creating districts where there are likely to be either intense or permanent minorities.

Beitz is arguing that equal opportunity in the political process has two requirements: Citizens must be treated as persons entitled to equal status as participants in politics (equal recognition), and they must also be treated equally as the subjects of public policy (equal consideration). A necessary but not sufficient condition for the first is that each person be entitled to cast an equally weighted vote for a representative who will be entitled in turn to cast an equally weighted vote in the legislature. The second requires a theory of just legislation.

Both Mansbridge and Beitz agree that formal equality in the political realm is insufficient. Both want a more robust concept of equal opportunity. Their perspective is shared by Owen Fiss who urges us to rethink our tradition regarding free speech. Here, as with the equal opportunity to participate in politics, mere freedom has been viewed as sufficient. There should be no artificial barriers. In the free speech tradition the unit of analysis has been the liberty of the street corner speaker. Each citizen has an equal opportunity to influence public opinion as long as the state avoids censorship. The Supreme Court has tolerated regulations on time, place, and manner but has only permitted censorship on content at the last possible moment—by using the so-called clear and present danger test. Taking the Central Broad-casting Station (CBS) as an example, Fiss argues that we must shift the focus of analysis. The decision to fill an hour of prime time with an episode of "Love Boat" means that other programs such as a critique of the president's foreign policy cannot be broadcast. Suppose we think of freedom of speech in the First Amendment as referring to a social state of affairs in which issues upon which public choice depends are fully aired. In that case giving CBS the freedom of the street corner speaker may undermine opportunities for policy issues to be fully aired.

The street corner analogy is flawed because CBS is not like a private individual and there is a problem of scarcity. CBS is a corporate entity licensed by the state; its decisions as to what goes on the air prevent other views from being heard. If the purpose of free speech is to give everyone an equal opportunity to have his or her views about public policy heard, then society must ensure that there is an ample opportunity for opposing viewpoints to be expressed. The state's job is to intervene positively, as it does with the Federal Communications Commission (FCC) fairness doctrine, to ensure that the public is exposed to a wide diversity of opinions. However, as Fiss points out, to view the state as a potential friend of free speech as well as a potential enemy requires a change in our traditional thinking, that sees the state only as a potential enemy.

Fiss points out that if his analysis is correct recent court decisions that give First Amendment protection to corporations may also be mistaken. The key test the court should apply is whether or not corporate free speech will narrow or restrict the quality of public debate about policy issues. If it does, then in that case corporate free speech should be circumscribed.

Nevertheless, to permit the state to intervene so that a wide spectrum of views can be heard does represent some curtailment of corporate free speech. If the media are forced to present opposing sides of a debate, their speech is restricted because they cannot carry "Love Boat," which the public wants to see and they want to provide. Some curtailment of free speech is necessary if the commitment to free speech is to be fully honored.

The discussion of equal opportunity in the political context has led to some extremely interesting results. There seems to be universal agreement that formal equality of opportunity is inadequate. To have equality of opportunity in the political arena, the freedom to vote, seek public office, and engage in political office by itself does not provide equal opportunity to have a candidate elected, to influence public debate, or to achieve political goals. Moreover, there is no simple answer to the question, "What else is needed for there to be genuine equality of opportunity?" Each of the authors in Part 3 has attempted to formulate answers to that question such that the notion of equal opportunity could continue to function as a useful political tool.

CONCLUSION

Several writers in this book have argued that the purpose of a notion like equal opportunity is to ensure fairness in the competition for favored positions and material reward. Considerable debate centers around the differences among individuals that must be corrected for competition to be fair. Although some like John Rawls argue that nearly all differences are morally arbitrary and hence subject to correction, others argue for the correction of environmentally caused differences, and still others argue for the correction of societal-caused environmental differences. The last point of view requires the least in terms of state action.

The authors of the chapters in this book have not resolved the questions about equal opportunity we raised at the beginning of this Introduction. However, they have accomplished much. The traditional view of equal opportunity has been described, and the objections against it clearly raised. If we are to expand the notion, the difficulties that face us are known. Moreover, equal opportunity is a complicated concept that can be used in different contexts in different ways. Correct use of the concept will not provide a just society, but equal opportunity still has a role to play in a just society. Reading the chapters in this book should make that role clearer.

PART 1

An Impossible Goal

1

Do We Need a
Systematic Theory of
Equal Opportunity?

JAMES S. FISHKIN

The recent revival of liberal theory has been premised on the expectation of finding a *systematic solution*—one that solves what Rawls calls the "priority problem." Such a solution provides one or more principles with clear priority rules leaving nothing to "intuition"; its principles never have to be traded off or balanced against one another (or against other considerations). Such a systematic solution is perfectly explicit and determinate in its requirements and, in that sense, it solves the problem.[1]

I argue here that this expectation is misplaced. Liberalism is inevitably full of contradictions in many of its main implications. Furthermore, in the specific area of equal opportunity, systematic solutions define the route to clearly illiberal conclusions. We have been blinded to the difficulties facing a rigorous normative theory of equal opportunity by our neglect of one crucial factor—the family and the issues of liberty surrounding it. Once we take full account of the family, the ideal theory test only yields a pattern of contradictory results—a pattern I call a trilemma.

What I call the trilemma of equal opportunity can be quickly sketched. Let us assume favorable and realistic conditions—only moderate scarcity, with good faith efforts at strict compliance with the principles we propose (both in the present and in the relevant recent past). However, to be realistic, let us also assume background conditions of inequality, both social and economic. The issue of equal opportunity—the rationing of chances for favored positions—would be beside the point if there were no favored positions (if there were strict equality of result throughout the society). Every modern developed country, capitalist or socialist, has substantially unequal payoffs to positions. The issue of equal opportunity within liberal theory is how people get assigned to those positions—by which I mean both their prospects for assignment and the method of assignment (whether, for example, meritocratic procedures are employed guaranteeing equal consideration of relevant claims).

The trilemma consists in a forced choice among three principles:

- Merit: There should be widespread procedural fairness in the evaluation of qualifications for positions.[2]
- Equality of Life Chances: The prospects of children for eventual positions in the society should not vary in any systematic and significant manner with their arbitrary native characteristics.[3]
- The Autonomy of the Family: Consensual relations within a given family governing the development of its children should not be coercively interfered with except to ensure for the children the essential prerequisites for adult participation in the society.[4]

Given background conditions of inequality, implementing any two of these principles can reasonably be expected to preclude the third. For example, implementing the first and third undermines the second. The autonomy of the family protects the process whereby advantaged families differentially contribute to the development of their children. Given background conditions of inequality, children from the higher strata will have been systematically subjected to developmental op-portunities that can reliably be expected to advantage them in the process of meritocratic competition. Under these conditions, the prin-ciple of merit—applied to talents as they have developed under such unequal conditions—becomes a mechanism for generating unequal life chances.

Suppose one were to keep the autonomy of the family in place but attempt to equalize life chances? Fulfilling the second and third prin-ciples would require sacrifice of the first. Given background conditions of inequality, the differential developmental influences just mentioned will produce disproportionate talents and other qualifications among children in the higher strata. If they must be assigned to positions so as to equalize life chances, then they must be assigned regardless of these differential claims. Some process of reverse discrimination in favor of those from disadvantaged backgrounds would have to be applied systematically throughout the society if life chances were to be equalized (while also maintaining family autonomy).

Suppose one were to attempt to equalize life chances while maintaining the system of meritocratic assignment? Given background conditions of inequality, the autonomy of families protects the process by which advantaged families differentially influence the development of talents and other qualifications in their children. Only if this process were interfered with, in a systematic manner, could the principles of both merit and equal life chances be achieved. Perhaps a massive system of collectivized child rearing could be devised. Or perhaps a compulsory schooling system could be devised so as to even out home-inspired developmental advantages and prevent families from making any differential investments in human capital in their children, either through formal or informal processes. In any case, achieving both merit and equal life chances would require a systematic sacrifice in family autonomy.

Implementation of any two of these principles precludes the third. While inevitable conflicts might be tolerated by systematic theorists in the nonideal world, these conflicts arise within ideal theory. This argument is directed at the aspiration to develop a rigorous solution even if it is limited to the ideal theory case. Given only moderate scarcity and strict compliance with the principles chosen, given that there is no aftermath of injustice from the immediate past, we are applying these principles in our thought experiment to the best conditions that could realistically be imagined for a modern, large-scale society.

Of course, liberalism has long been regarded as an amalgam of liberty and equality. And liberals and libertarians have long been fearful of the sacrifices in liberty that would be required to achieve equality of result. Equality of opportunity, by contrast, has been regarded as a weakly reformist, tame principle that avoids such disturbing conflicts.[5] However, even under the best conditions, it raises stark conflicts with the one area of liberty that touches most of our lives most directly. Once we take account of the family, equal opportunity is an extraordinarily radical principle and achieving it would require sacrifices in liberty that most of us would regard as grossly illiberal.

The force of the trilemma argument depends on each of the principles having independent support. Merit makes a claim to procedural fairness. However, as Brian Barry has argued, procedural fairness is a thin value without what he calls "background fairness,"[6] and background fairness would be achieved by equality of life chances. Family autonomy can be rationalized within a broader private sphere of liberty; it protects the liberty of families, acting consensually, to benefit their children through developmental influences. The principle leaves plenty of room for the state to intervene when some sacrifice in the essential interests of the child is in question or when consensual relations within the family have broken down (raising issues of child placement or children's rights, and so on). Without the core area of liberty defined by this narrow principle, the family would be unrecognizably different.

Thus these principles are not demanding by themselves; they are demanding in combination. For each of the trilemma scenarios fully implementing two of the principles leads to drastic sacrifice of the third. To blithely assume that we can realize all three is to produce an incoherent scenario for equal opportunity, even under ideal conditions.

In Chapter 2 of this book, Brian Barry responds to this argument by rejecting equality of life chances, even as an aspiration. He terms the principle an "inadvertent reductio" because it would be fulfilled if a lottery system at birth reassigned children to parents. He presents equal life chances "as satisfying (totally, in Fishkin's view) the requirements of equal opportunity." If we imagine a society with a rigid "caste system" in which an earlier lottery at birth is discovered, Barry argues, we would not react to the discovery by saying that equal opportunity had really been achieved. Note, however, that I present equal life chances as only one of two essential components of the strong doctrine of equal opportunity. Equal life chances and merit together define equal opportunity in the strong sense. Either component without the other is a severe sacrifice (which is why each scenario in the trilemma is thought to be a counterexample). Because a society with "a rigid caste system" grossly sacrifices meritocratic assignment, it cannot be viewed as fulfilling equal opportunity, regardless of whether or not there is a birth lottery. In any case, my own discussion of the birth lottery focused on the objection that it would severely sacrifice family autonomy. Even though it might, from a certain perspective, be viewed as increasing opportunities, it does so only through an unacceptable sacrifice in the liberty of families to raise their children. For this reason, my argument should not, of course, be construed as advocating such a lottery.

Barry offers a second objection, one that raises more fundamental issues. He attacks my position that "I should not be able to enter a hospital ward of healthy newborn babies and, on the basis of class, race, sex, or other arbitrary characteristics, predict the eventual position in society of those children." He notes,

We can predict, in a society like Britain, the eventual distribution among religious denominations (and none) of children raised by Roman Catholics, Methodists, Baptists, members of the Church of England and so on. These distributions will be different for each group and will show a tendency for those brought up in one denomination to stay in it. But there is no reason to suppose that people could not recognize these facts and still feel that their adult religious position was their own—was something for which they took personal responsibility.

Barry goes on to compare the factors determining religious affiliation with "the details of upbringing that make for a greater or lesser thirst for educational attainment and a greater or lesser capacity to give educational institutions what they want," all of which are "part of the constituents of people's personal identity."

I reply that there is nothing pernicious in the fact that we can reliably predict the religious affiliations of newborn babies. In societies that fulfill meritocratic assignment to a substantial degree, religious affiliation will not, by itself, be a basis for the distribution of anything else. A person's life chances will not, and should not, hang on whether he or she is, say, Protestant or Jewish. The account of equal life chances that Barry quotes specifies that one should not be able to predict the "eventual position in society" of these newborns. Being able to predict religious affiliations would not, by itself, be a violation of that principle—in societies in which we can safely view religious affiliation as a private matter. On the other hand, if one imagined a society in which each class had its own distinct religion, and in which mobility was impossible without changes of religion, then the predictability of religious affiliation would violate equal life chances (but this religious-class structure would presumably violate meritocratic assignment as well).

However, Barry could accept this point but argue that the real issue is the analogy between religious affiliation and educational values. Because both may be closely connected to the determinants of personal identity, the implication is that we should not be concerned with differential causal factors that produce unequal life chances—through the development of different values and motivations. They are both elements of personal identity for which the person, in the end, should take responsibility.

On this view, there is no basis for objecting if women aspire to become nurses while men aspire to become doctors, if women aspire to become secretaries while men aspire to become business executives, if members of one race aspire to work with their hands (for low pay) while members of another race aspire to work with their brains (for much higher pay). ⌈These are just aspects of personal identity. Of course, in a sense, they are (or become so). But if we can predict, uniformly and reliably, how these aspects of personal identity will come to be distributed, then we can locate something objectionable about the process by which these values are determined—values which, unlike religion, determine life chances directly through meritocratic assignment. In a sufficiently sexist society a woman may never really have a chance to become a doctor rather than a nurse or an executive rather than a secretary. While the motivations and aspirations that channel her one way rather than another may become deeply rooted components of her identity, the fact that we could reliably predict how her options would turn out shows how equal opportunity has not been fully achieved. If we can take newborn babies and employ arbitrary native charac- teristics—such as race, sex, or ethnic group—and predict (1) that members of those groups will be socialized for comparatively unde- sirable or desirable positions and (2) that the socialization in question will determine their eventual positions in society, then a pattern of grossly unequal opportunities has been perpetuated through the dif- ferential development of motivations and aspirations.⌉

Barry rightly notes that family background plays a role in the differential development of aspirations. He notes the comparative success of certain groups (Jewish, Japanese, Chinese) in motivating their children. His position is that this should not be construed as having any effect whatsoever on equal opportunity. My position, by contrast, is that to whatever extent family background determines differential motivations that affect life chances, there is an effect on equal oppor- tunity. It is, however, an effect that could only be controlled at a cost in family autonomy. Rather than claim that there is no value being sacrificed, I regard it as an example of the pervasive conflict between the claims of liberty constitutive of the family and the claims of equality in the strong doctrine of equal opportunity.

One reasonable but unsystematic response to this pattern of conflict would be to trade off small increments of each principle without full realization of any. But this is to live without a systematic solution. The aspiration fueling the development of ideal theory has been that some single solution in clear focus can be defined for ideal conditions and then policy can be organized so as to approach this vision asymptotically. But if trade-offs are inevitable, even for ideal theory, then we have ideals without an ideal, conflicting principles without a unifying vision.

NOTES

1. Throughout this chapter I rely on arguments I developed more fully in *Justice, Equal Opportunity, and the Family* (New Haven, Conn.: Yale University

Press, 1983). For more on the "priority problem" see John Rawls, *A Theory of Justice* (Cambridge, Mass.: Harvard University Press, 1971), pp. 34–45. See also Bruce Ackerman, *Social Justice in the Liberal State* (New Haven, Conn.: Yale University Press, 1980), p. 14.

2. By "qualifications" I mean criteria that are job related in that they can fairly be interpreted as indicators of competence or motivation for an individual's performance in a given position. Education, job history, fairly administered test results, or other tokens of ability or effort might all be included. Inferences that because one is a member of a group that generally does poorly, one is unlikely to do well would not be included within my account of qualifications; such inferences would constitute statistical discrimination.

3. By a native characteristic, I mean any factor, knowable at birth, that could be employed to differentiate adult persons of at least normal health and endowment. As I noted in *Justice,* these characteristics are not necessarily unalterable. "Even though native characteristics can be ascribed to an individual at birth, they are not necessarily unalterable, as cases of sex change illustrate dramatically" (p. 28, note 20). What do I mean by arbitrary? A native characteristic will be considered arbitrary unless it predicts the development of qualifications to a high degree among children who have been subjected to equal developmental conditions. Race, sex, ethnic origin, and family background are considered arbitrary here. I employ the characteristic liberal assumption that under equal developmental conditions knowledge of these factors would not permit us reliably to predict qualifications of these individuals for desirable positions in the society. I am giving liberalism the benefit of the doubt here since my point is to establish the conundrums of the trilemma under optimistic conditions for a liberal thought experiment.

4. By "essential prerequisites" I mean the physical and psychological health of the child and his or her knowledge of those social conventions necessary for participation in adult society. Literacy, the routines of citizenship, and other familiar elements of secondary education count among the essential prerequisites (absence of which could justify coercive interference by the state).

5. See, for example, John H. Schaar, "Equality of Opportunity and Beyond," in J. Roland Pennock and John W. Chapman, eds., *Equality: Nomos IX* (New York: Atherton Press, 1967).

6. Brian Barry, *Political Argument* (London: Routledge and Kegan Paul, 1965), pp. 98–99.

2

Equal Opportunity and Moral Arbitrariness

BRIAN BARRY

I

This chapter falls into two sections. In the first section I lay out, as accurately as I can, John Rawls's analysis of equal opportunity in *A Theory of Justice*.[1] In the second section I offer some reflections upon it.

Rawls presented a line of argument that is, I think, very powerful. He showed how, starting from commonly accepted premises, one can be led by a progression of moves to the surprising conclusion that the only adequate form of equal opportunity is equality of outcome, measured in terms of income. If we find this a strange conclusion, we must retrace our steps and see what we want to reject in the premises. That is the inquiry I pursue in the second part of the chapter.

Before I get started, there is one preliminary that must be got out of the way. It is by now I suppose notorious that in *A Theory of Justice* Rawls claimed that principles of justice are to be established by making conjectures about the principles that would be chosen to regulate their common life by people in a suitably characterized original position, designed to embody elements constitutive of fairness. (Uncontroversially, this entails the exclusion of the ability to coerce others into a disadvantageous agreement; more controversially, for Rawls it entails the exclusion of the ability to gain any bargaining advantage from the possession of natural or social advantages.) In reading what follows, I ask you to dismiss all this apparatus from your minds. I shall make no use of it, and it is in no way required in order to trace through the course of the argument from equal opportunity to equality.

While it is true that Rawls's official view in *A Theory of Justice* was that all arguments are ultimately made with reference to choice in a suitably specified original position, he did not simply postulate an original position and set about deriving principles from it. The original position is itself to be justified on moral grounds. Thus, it denies people knowledge of their natural and social advantages so as to eliminate their ability to exploit such advantages in the process of bargaining about principles. But the case for thinking that only in that way can a just outcome be secured is itself derived from a deep moral principle: that "morally arbitrary" features are not to count in determining the requirements of justice. To have application this principle requires a specification of what counts as "morally arbitrary" features. And it is precisely to establish what is in the realm of the "morally arbitrary" that Rawls engages in his discussion of equal opportunity. For the principle of equal opportunity is plausibly regarded as a call for the elimination of "morally arbitrary" determinants of success or failure. (I shall pursue this further in the following discussion.)

The structure of Part One of *A Theory of Justice* ("Theory") has, it is worth pointing out, the following form. The first of the three chapters into which it is divided ("Justice as Fairness") contains some introductory ideas about justice (that its subject is the "basic structure of society" and that it is the "first virtue" of social institutions), a discussion of the contractarian foundations of justice, and then (the second half of the chapter) various remarks about methodology in moral philosophy. The second chapter ("The Principles of Justice") sets out the two principles that Rawls intends to argue for and then, in the central sections of the chapter, puts forward a long and intricate argument that starts from equal opportunity and ends up with the difference principle. The second chapter concludes with two sections on "Principles of Individuals." Only after all this do we get to "The Original Position," Chapter three, which contains the well-known and extensively discussed attempt to derive the principles of justice as principles that would be chosen in a suitably constituted original position.

Like the human brain, and unlike a typical computer program, *A Theory of Justice* is replete with redundancy. Some of this redundancy takes the form of mere repetition of the same ideas in different parts of the book (often in almost identical words); but there is also a more interesting and valuable kind of redundancy to be found in it. What I mean by this is that many of the ideas put forward in the book are independent of one another. If one is removed, even the one officially

claimed to be basic, much is still left. Indeed, my claim is that the material provided in the central part of the second chapter of the book provides a self-contained argument for the principles of justice (and particularly the difference principle) that in no wise stands or falls with the argument in Chapter three that derives the principles of justice from the original position.

Lest this sound too good to be true, let me again emphasize that the constraints imposed on the choice of principles in the original position are motivated by the conception of moral arbitrariness developed in chapter two. It need not therefore be too surprising if I suggest that the argument in chapter two might be sufficient to generate the principles of justice by itself. None of this would matter, of course, if the derivation from the original position worked. But there is a virtual consensus (in which I share) that it does not. The argument in the second chapter, on the other hand, seems to me to be valid in its own terms.

What is this argument? It falls into two parts. The first half of the argument starts from equality of opportunity and finishes up with equality. The second half starts from equality and then adds the premise that any state of affairs that makes the members of all representative positions better off than equality should be preferred to it. By an intricate and usually misunderstood chain of reasoning Rawls arrived at the conclusion that the difference principle—that things should be arranged so that the representative of the worst-off social class should be as well off as possible—is the uniquely acceptable specification of the general idea that it is rational to welcome Pareto improvements on a just starting point.[2] In this chapter I shall have nothing further to say about the second half of the argument. I shall, however, have a lot to say about the stage of it that establishes equality as the just baseline to which the Pareto improvement principle is then applied.

The way in which Rawls proceeded was to offer three possible interpretations of the second principle of justice, which he stated in general terms as follows: "Social and economic inequalities are to be arranged so that they are both (a) reasonably expected to be to everyone's advantage, and (b) attached to positions and offices open to all."[3] These alternatives were called by him the system of natural liberty, liberal equality, and democratic equality. As we shall see, they embody increasingly stringent notions of equal opportunity.

The System of Natural Liberty

The first conception corresponds fairly closely to the idea of social justice that one finds in Adam Smith's *The Wealth of Nations*. According to this, any distributive outcome is just if it is arrived at by exchange on a free market. Each person owns his own labor power (there can be no slavery or serfdom) and there are no arbitrary barriers to advancement: There is "a formal equality of opportunity in that all have at least the same legal rights of access to all advantaged social positions."[4]

Rawls was vague about how the initial allocation of property rights is to be made in the system, though in this he did no more than echo advocates of the system themselves. (From John Locke to Robert Nozick there is a long and disreputable tradition of using a fairy story about the way in which acquisition might have occurred as the basis for a defence of the status quo.) However, the important point for him was that once the system has been in operation for some time, the distributive outcomes in any given period will depend on the "initial distribution of assets" at the beginning of the period, and this will be "strongly influenced by natural and social contingencies."[5] As Rawls explained:

> The existing distribution of income and wealth, say, is the cumulative effect of prior distributions of natural assets—that is, natural talents and abilities—as these have been developed or left unrealized, and their use favored or disfavored over time by social circumstances and such chance contingencies as accident and good fortune. Intuitively, the most obvious injustice of the system of natural liberty is that it permits distributive shares to be improperly influenced by these factors so arbitrary from a moral point of view.[6]

Rawls in this passage distinguished "such chance contingencies as accident and good fortune" from "social circumstances." This is in accordance with normal usage, wherein we ascribe some things that work out to people's advantage to fortune but not everything. Very crudely, to say that something is accidental or fortunate is to suggest that almost exactly the same causal sequence might have produced a very different outcome, much better or worse. A close shave is lucky; the less close the shave the less we are inclined to talk of luck. Thus, if a plate glass window falls onto the street from the top of a tall building just seconds after you passed the spot where it lands, you count yourself extremely lucky, but far less so if you passed the same spot an hour before.

It is, however, "arbitrary from a moral point of view" when the window falls. Whether or not it is close enough for its missing you to count as a fortunate accident can scarcely affect that. And in the passage just quoted, we find Rawls including in the realm of the morally arbitrary, along with "accident and good fortune," the distribution of natural assets and the social circumstances that favor or disfavor their use. It is moral arbitrariness, and not any distinction between fortune and other social sources of advantage, that matters here.

Liberal Equality

An alternative conception that closes some of the loopholes in the system of natural liberty was described by Rawls as a system of "liberal equality."[7] This adds to the lack of formal barriers to entrance encompassed in the system of natural liberty "the further condition of the principle of fair equality of opportunity."[8] Thus, according to Rawls,

> assuming that there is a distribution of natural assets, those who are at the same level of talent and ability, and have the same willingness to use them, should have the same prospects of success regardless of the initial place in the social system, that is, irrespective of the income class into which they are born. In all sectors of society there should be roughly equal prospects of culture and achievement for everyone similarly motivated and endowed. The expectations of those with the same abilities and aspirations should not be affected by their social class.[9]

I believe that Rawls was here tracing a quite genuine progression of ideas that is both logical and chronological.[10] The idea of equal opportunity begins, as he said, with the slogan, "careers open to talents."[11] This calls for the abolition of formal barriers to entry: for example, the opening up of positions in the civil service to all who qualify on the basis of competitive examinations instead of their reservation to members of a hereditary aristocracy and, perhaps, their protégés. But it does not include the notion of an equal opportunity to acquire those qualifications.

At the next stage, formal education barriers are attacked: limitations of elite education to members of a certain religious denomination, for example. At this point the focus shifts to the inability of many parents to pay for education for their children, so first schooling becomes free and then there is at any rate some pressure for it to be equally good in all parts of a country without regard to the wealth of the catchment area of any school. Economic limitations on the ability of those who qualify to go on to higher education will also come under fire at this stage. The ideal of equal opportunity at this point was accurately described by Rawls as follows: "Chances to acquire cultural knowledge and skills should not depend on one's class position, and so the school system, whether public or private, should be designed to even out class barriers."[12]

Now in practice there is probably no country that has completely equalized the quality of schooling, measured in terms of the physical facilities and the quality of the instructors, but some have gotten close enough to make it apparent that educational attainment would not be equalized by equalizing the quality of the schooling. Nor, after all, is this surprising since children spend only a fraction of their time in school and are already highly differentiated in relevant ways by the time they start attending school. Moreover, at a cost of some millions of dollars sociologists discovered the rather obvious fact that a large part of the educational environment of a child consists of the other children in the school. Given the tendency of people in a neighborhood within any city to have similar educational and cultural backgrounds, this entails that (at any rate in urban areas) the effects of individual parents on their children's prospects will be multiplied by the likelihood that the other children will have similar parents. Nothing short of scattering children at random over an entire metropolitan area could avoid this.

The ideal of equal opportunity began by being related in a rather obvious way to that of fairness: Given two people one of whom is more qualified for a job than the other, it is unfair that the more qualified should be ruled out in virtue of, say, parentage. We can here talk of the "accident of birth" because we are, in the context, treating the relative qualifications as nonaccidental features of the candidates. We can say that parentage is a "morally arbitrary" fact about them because we have a firm grip on the contrast we want to make with what is "morally relevant," namely their qualifications.

The same distinction between what is morally relevant and morally arbitrary can be traced, though it of course falls in a different place, as we take equally able students at some point in their careers and ask whether they have equally good opportunities to go further. The ability is the "morally relevant" factor, and such things as the parents' income or the location of the school are by contrast "morally arbitrary." However, if we push this idea further and further back, we finish by saying that everything (except genetic endowment) that makes for greater or less success is a denial of equal opportunity. Everything that happens to people during their lifetimes that can affect their subsequent success goes into the "morally arbitrary" side and the only thing that is left as "morally relevant" is the physical human being at the moment of birth—or one should say at conception, since such things as the mother's diet during pregnancy can make a difference. By the age of a few weeks, the more or less stimulating nature of the infant's environment will (according to what I take to be the current thinking) have made more or less of a contribution to the development of its neural processes, and it will be well along the path of the differentiated development that is "morally arbitrary."

Rawls recognized and drew attention to this implication. His initial statement of the conception of justice as liberal equality, which I quoted previously, is not completely explicit. He said that there should be "the same prospects of success" for those who are "at the same level of talent and ability and have the same willingness to use them" and used (apparently as alternative expressions of the same ideas) the phrases "similarly motivated and endowed" and "same abilities and aspirations." One might read this as allowing for parental or more generally social influence on at any rate part of what is to go on the "morally relevant" side, since it seems hard to imagine that willingness to use one's talents, motivation, or aspiration is (entirely) genetically determined.

This would, however, be to misconstrue Rawls's intentions. The passage I quoted began with the words: "assuming that there is a distribution of natural assets. . . . " This is crucial. For on the basis of what he went on to say a little later it becomes clear that Rawls wanted to draw a distinction along the line of "natural assets" versus environmental effects and to identify equality of opportunity with the complete absence of differential environmental effects. We should thus read Rawls as referring to the (assumed) genetic component in willingness to use one's talents, motivation, and aspiration when he said that there should be equal prospects of success for those who are equal in these respects. This becomes clear when Rawls said that

> the principle of fair opportunity can be only imperfectly carried out, at least as long as the institution of the family exists. The extent to which natural capacities develop and reach fruition is affected by all kinds of social conditions and class attitudes. Even the willingness to make an effort, to try, and so to be deserving in the ordinary sense is itself dependent upon happy family and social circumstances. It is impossible in practice to secure equal chances of achievement and culture for those similarly endowed, and therefore we may want to adopt a principle which recognizes this fact and also mitigates the arbitrary effects of the natural lottery itself.[13]

Democratic Equality

Once one has identified equal opportunity with the elimination of all factors except that of genetic endowment, it is fairly easy to see the attraction of the final move, which is to ask why we should regard equality of opportunity so conceived as fair. As Rawls put it, "even if [the liberal conception] works to perfection in eliminating the influence of social contingencies, it still permits the distribution of wealth and income to be determined by the natural distribution of abilities and talents . . . and this outcome is arbitrary from a moral point of view."[14]

Equality of opportunity for zygotes that have the capacity (with identical environments prenatally and postnatally) to become identically successful within the educational system and then in achieving lucrative and rewarding careers is, after all, a bizarre notion of equal opportunity, even though we seem to be driven to it by an inexorable series of steps. At about the time Rawls was writing *A Theory of Justice,* Christopher Jencks expressed much the same idea in his book *Inequality* in relation to educational attainment. I quote him because he brought out more forcefully than did Rawls the underlying idea of equal opportunity and how strange it begins to seem once one reflects on it:

> One inevitable result of eliminating environmental inequality would be to increase the correlation between IQ genotype and IQ scores. Indeed, this is often a conscious objective of educational policy. Most schools try to help students with high "native ability" realize their "potential." In effect, this also means eliminating the unfair advantage of students who have unpromising genes but come from stimulating homes. The idea seems to be that inequality based on genetic advantages is morally acceptable, but that inequality based on other accidents of birth is not. Most educators and laymen evidently feel that an individual's genes are his, and that they entitle him to whatever advantages he can get from them. His parents, in contrast, are not "his" in the same sense, and ought not to entitle him to special favors. For a thoroughgoing egalitarian, however, inequality that derives from biology ought to be as repulsive as inequality that derives from early socialization.[15]

Since we are already dealing heavily in counterfactuals to define equal opportunity, there is an obvious final step: We go to equal opportunity for zygotes irrespective of their genetic potential. But equal opportunity so conceived is, in effect, equal opportunity for beings behind a veil of ignorance with Rawls's specifications: equal opportunity for human beings stripped of all identifying characteristics, either genetic or environmental. As Rawls explained his strategy, his object in going through the alternative conceptions was "to prepare the way for the favored interpretation of the two principles so that these criteria, especially the second one [the conception of "democratic equality"], will not strike the reader as too eccentric or bizarre." Democratic equality is the only one "which does not weight men's share in the benefits and burdens of social cooperation according to their social fortune or their luck in the natural lottery."[16]

But then what exactly does the conception of "democratic equality" come to? It must say that equal opportunity with all morally arbitrary contingencies eliminated amounts to equal success for all human beings. What, after all, can be meant on the present understanding by the slogan "Equal opportunity for zygotes?" We are to rule out, as lying in the realm of the morally arbitrary, everything distinctive about them—that is to say, all distinguishing genetic characteristics. (The one exception is, I suppose, that of being human zygotes rather than those of some other species, since Rawls did not include nonhuman animals in the contract drawn up in his original position.) It is surely plain that equal opportunity—an equal prospect of success in life— for entities that are not in any way distinguishable from one another can be nothing other than equal prospects of success for all zygotes. And since anything that makes for different outcomes for indistinguishable entities is (by the nature of Rawls's conception) morally arbitrary, we can reduce this idea of equal opportunity for equals in the relevant respect to that of simple equality of outcomes.

There is, indeed, an obvious sense in which, from behind a veil of ignorance, everyone has an equal opportunity (that is, an equal probability) of being anything, however the unequal outcomes actually come about in real life. But since these inequalities of outcomes are all, on the "democratic" conception, morally arbitrary, we should plainly be misrepresenting Rawls's whole idea by calling this equality of opportunity. Rawls tried to guard against the interpretation of equal opportunity as equal chances in a lottery by insisting that people in the original position are not disembodied choosers awaiting embodiment but real people (or representatives of real people) denied certain information. He tried to argue that because of this the choice of principles in the original position is not to be construed as a simple maximizing choice under uncertainty. But the consensus of critics has been that the logic of choice in the original position exerts an inexorable pressure for modeling the choice in exactly that way. Hence my suggestion that we would do better to go straight to Rawls's underlying moral intuitions and scrap their formulation in terms of choice in an original position.

One way of putting the essential point is that a "natural lottery" is not somehow made fair by our presenting it in a light in which it might be thought of as a real lottery. An inadvertent reductio is provided by James Fishkin in his *Justice, Equal Opportunity, and the Family*. He imagined "a lottery system at birth that randomly assigned babies to families" and suggested that "equal life chances, in a quite precise sense, would result from the arrangement. For the random assignment of newborn babies to families would serve to equalize life chances from the perspective of newborns before the lottery. Any newborn's chance of reaching any highly valued position would be precisely equal to that of any other newborn infant."[17] Fishkin's only objection to this was the severe impairment of family autonomy that it would entail. But surely there is something very weird about a notion of equal opportunity such that a system of unequal opportunity (e.g., massive differences in life chances depending on one's parentage) could be magically transformed into one of equal opportunity simply by switching babies in their cradles and leaving everything else the same. Suppose that this has in fact been carried out secretly over many years in some country marked by great inequalities of opportunity in the ordinary sense (a rigid caste system if you like). When we now find out about this random switching of babies, do we react by saying something like this? "Those people who were pressing for reforms in the social system to increase equality of opportunity were wasting their time—we now know that opportunity was already perfectly equal all along." I do not think this sounds very plausible.

Fishkin was, in the passage I quoted, assuming equal genetic endowment so that at birth it will be true (in the sense that each faces the same gamble) that each has an identical prospect in life. For each has the same chance of being assigned to any of the environmental conditions available, and these (by hypothesis) will make all the difference to the level of achievement reached. But if that is to count as satisfying (totally, in Fishkin's view) the requirements of equal opportunity, my question is, Why shouldn't we say that, from an original position, where both genetic endowments *and* environments are still to be assigned randomly to, as it were, protozygotes, *any* actual distribution will be compatible with equal opportunity? For, from the original position, every protozygote faces the same gamble in life chances, where life chances depend on the interaction of genetic endowment and environment. We clearly should not; but what that shows is that the underlying notion of equal opportunity on which the question is based is misconceived.

*   *   *

I should conclude this analysis of Rawls by drawing attention to the fact that he actually had two ways of getting from equal opportunity to equality. The primary way, which is the first he put forward and the more watertight, runs as follows: (1) the (liberal) idea of equal opportunity is that all environmental differences that affect occupational achievement should be eliminated; (2) this will entail that all remaining differences are of genetic origin; but (3) if (as is assumed) the case for eliminating environmental differences is that they are "morally arbitrary," all we should be doing is making occupational achievement rest on genetic factors that are (in exactly the same sense) morally arbitrary; therefore (4) since what is morally arbitrary should not affect what people get, differences in occupational achievement should not affect incomes. This is the argument that has been discussed so far. The second, which is by way of being an afterthought in Rawls's sequence of presentation, runs as follows. Point (1) is as before: The ideal is to eliminate all environmental differences that affect occupational differences in achievement. The new premise is (2) that this ideal cannot be realized—or at any rate cannot be realized without unacceptable inroads into personal liberty. The conclusion (3) is that as a second best solution occupational achievement should not affect incomes.

The two lines are not of course incompatible, and it is perfectly reasonable for Rawls to put both forward. But discussions of Rawls often proceed as if he had only the second line of argument,[18] and it is I think worth making clear that Rawls was not in fact saying that if we could only achieve equality of opportunity (in the sense of "liberal equality") all would be well. He was saying that *everything* about the sources of differential occupational achievement is contingent and morally arbitrary.

II

The upshot of the discussion so far would seem to be that equal opportunity is a Holy Grail: It disappears as one approaches it. What I have been saying has been humorously but seriously expressed by the provost of one of the colleges at the University of California, Santa Cruz, Herman J. Blake:

> Blake likes to tell a story about how college teachers blame high
> school teachers and high school teachers blame grade school teachers
> [for the inadequate preparation of minority students]. "Eventually,"
> Blake said, "they realize the problem is in the home. But just about
> the time they come to that realization, you hear a voice from the
> kitchen. It's the grandmother who's yelling back, 'Don't blame me. I
> was against the marriage in the first place.'"[19]

The humane and sensible conclusion drawn from this story of placing the responsibility ever further back in time is that the whole game of buck-passing should be given up. Thus, as far as higher education is concerned (and the same point could be made at each lower level) "the only way to solve this problem . . . is to take on the responsibility ourselves here and now. . . . We've got to take the position that we don't give a damn about their preparation before they come to us and do the best we can. . . . Nothing short of that will ever work."[20] As three British sociologists have put it, more soberly: "While we would not wish to challenge the general truth that he who learns earliest learns best, with its inference, much emphasized in the past decade, that a 'positively discriminatory' preschool programme could reduce educational inequality, we cannot ignore the evident contribution to be had from the reform of post-secondary schooling."[21]

The case for extending access to higher education need not, I think, rest on the dubious metaphysics of equal opportunity. It naturally comes from an alternative notion of justice. In other words, if the admission of minority students with lower test scores or what not is objected to as a violation of equal opportunity, the answer is not to say that it is the fulfillment of equal opportunity at some deeper level: that under some counterfactual circumstances the students admitted would have scored equally highly. Equal opportunity is an important idea with a wide field of valid applications. It should be the normal standard for filling jobs. But it should not be made to carry the whole burden of argument about justice in society.

It is good and right for a certain number (and there is no formula for the number) of members of grossly underrepresented social groups to be admitted and retained so long as they are prepared to do the work required to catch up. This is, I believe, defensible as part of one's conception of what a just society should be like. In arriving at this conception, the empirical considerations raised in the first part of this chapter are relevant, but they do not enter in via a notion of equal opportunity for zygotes or disembodied human essences. I shall argue for this conclusion here.

I want to pull back to Rawls's second conception, that of "liberal equality." As will be recalled, the move from there to equality of outcomes assumed that liberal equality was all right as far as it went but then argued that it did not go far enough. It got rid of some morally arbitrary features that were left untouched by the "system of natural liberty" but still permitted natural endowments equally arbitrary from the moral point of view to play a role.

Let us subject that assumption to scrutiny. How attractive is the ideal in itself? Suppose we imagine away the problems posed by inequalities of natural endowment by stipulating that everyone has the same natural capacities. Does it then become straightforward that the liberal ideal is completely unobjectionable? The more we ponder its implications the more liable we are, I suggest, to doubt it.

Rawls himself drew out the implications clearly enough when he said that in conditions of perfectly equal opportunity "the extent to which natural capacities develop and reach fruition" would have to be equal.[22] In other words, given two children of equal natural endowment, their level of achievement should be equal no matter what else about them differs. There are, obviously, two problematic terms in this statement. The first is "natural endowment." This is simply an X, standing for whatever it is about people that is of genetic origin that affects the level of achievement. (It might, for example, include a genetically determined predisposition for an infant to smile in a winning way that encourages its parents to talk to it more than they otherwise would.)[23] One thing we do know is that IQ tests do not measure it, since we have direct evidence that they are partially affected by environmental factors.

The other problematic concept, upon which the definition of natural endowment is parasitic, is that of an equal level of achievement. Presumably this does not have to mean that the developed abilities should be identical in nature but that they should somehow be equivalent in quality. Since our present context is the distribution of income inasfar as it is determined by occupational earnings, the most reasonable way of defining an equal level of achievement would be as follows: Two people have the same level of achievement if their prospects in the job market are equally good, in other words, if the range of occupations open to them is of equal value and if their chances of success in those occupations are equal.

"Equal achievement" is, it should be observed, no more directly observable than "equal natural endowment." (There is not even any special case like that of identical twins where we are entitled to assume it on the basis of a theory.) It is "whatever it takes to get ahead occupationally." We might think of the highest level of educational attainment somebody reaches as, in a modern society, bearing about the same sort of relation to the unobservable factor of achievement as IQ measured at a tender age does to the unobservable factor of natural endowment. Educational qualifications vouch for more than cognitive skills: They also give indications of adequate socialization into traits such as punctuality, reliability, adaptability, and biddability that are of concern to employers. Hence education is a broad-spectrum preparation for entry into the job market.[24]

It should scarcely need to be pointed out that this whole discussion is specific to the conditions of modern industrial societies—as is Rawls's. Education in such societies functions as a generic resource that can be cashed into a range of occupational positions. As Ernest Gellner stated, "capital, ownership and wealth" have given way as major determinants in the stratification order to "another one, generically designated as access to education," which means "possession or access to the bundle of skills which enable men to perform well in the general conditions of an industrial division of labour."[25]

In the economists' terms we can say that human capital in modern societies is less and less occupationally specific. The standard way into the crafts and even many of the professions used to be long formal apprenticeships or "working one's way up." The result was mastery of a nontransferable skill. Education topped with on-the-job training makes for a different relation to one's occupation. Education is, as Gellner shrewdly observed, what defines people socially in modern societies— far more than (as in earlier societies) their specific occupations, which they may well change several times in their lifetimes: "The employability, dignity, security, and self-respect of individuals, typically, and for the majority of men now hinges on their *education*" (italics in original).[26]

It should be noticed that, as I have defined "equal achievement," it does not entail an equal probability of finishing up with a given income. What it says is that the same range of occupational positions, in a system of stratification whose existence I presuppose, is open. My thought here is this: Let us imagine two people graduating from the same law school in the same year with the same grades and equally warm letters of recommendation from their professors. To the extent that we can ever say that two people are equally well placed in the job market these are. But one may go into a highly paid position in the legal department of a corporation while the other exercises a preference for small-town (maybe home-town) living, leisure, little stress, and a lot of autonomy by hanging up his or her shingle, thereby reaping various nonmonetary rewards at the expense of getting, say, half the income.

It may be that Rawls would want to incorporate this kind of preference for a way of life into the "willingness to make an effort," which is "dependent on happy family and social circumstances,"[27] but if so I think that any such tendency should be resisted. How one trades off money (or more generally occupational success) against other things such as stress, long or inconvenient hours, danger, unpleasantness, and undesired location, given a certain range of opportunities, is a matter of choice. It may indeed be that the choice can itself be explained in terms of past experience (though it may well be that a happy family background has a tendency to lead to putting a higher rather than a lower value on things competitive with income), but that does not make it any less a matter of choice.

I have expanded on the notion of "equal achievement" because I shall want to use it later. For the present purpose, however, the main thing to observe about it is how extremely restrictive it is in the form of society it will permit. Let us, to simplify the analysis, assume that educational attainment, suitably categorized, can be regarded as an adequate surrogate for what I am calling achievement—the "whatever it takes" factor. And let us also abstract from the compilation introduced by natural endowments. Then equal opportunity will entail that, however we slice through a society—by region, class, ethnic group, religious affiliation, or what you will—we shall find exactly the same profile of educational achievement.

It might be asked why we should even talk of distributions. In the absence of genetic differences, surely equal opportunity will entail identical levels of educational attainment. It is, of course, a tautology that if everyone's environment adds exactly the same amount to a postulated equal starting point the outcomes will be equivalent. But we know that identical twins brought up in the same family will to some degree diverge in measured IQ and level of educational attainment, and this kind of divergence might be regarded reasonably as an irreducible minimum. We should therefore allow for random individual variations in educational attainment, but we can then define a society of equal opportunity as one in which once we aggregate across a number of cases these random variations will cancel out, so that all groups, however they are defined, will show the same distribution.

Adding back natural endowment simply involves the stipulation that *all* departures from this pattern of identical attainment profiles must be capable of being explained by appealing to differences in natural endowment between different groups. Since we have no way of getting direct access to the factor of natural endowment, we lose the ability to tell by looking at the outcomes whether opportunities were equal. But we can do two things. First, we can show that, if we take IQ as giving the outer bounds of group differences in natural endowment, differences between groups in educational achievement cannot be explained without invoking environmental differences. (Thus, in the United States, slicing through by religious denomination or country of origin in Europe will produce virtually identical average IQs, and we have no reason to expect any genetic differences; yet there are still systematic educational differences.) Second, we have some general idea of what factors in a child's environment make for more or less educational attainment, and we can say that if equal opportunity is to exist all children must be exposed (within the limits of random variation mentioned earlier) to equally educogenic conditions.

This obviously means that we are talking about an extraordinarily homogeneous society in which there is, essentially, no variation across families or any larger groupings in terms of the value placed on educational attainment or in terms of the extent to which the environment predisposes toward a disposition to learn. As A. H. Halsey and his coauthors wrote: "In their more unguarded and romantic hopes, the British reforming optimists in education have pictured all children as earnest seekers after grammar-school scholarship and all teachers as middle-class Fabians devoted to the peaceful transformation of middle-class privileges into a universal common culture."[28] However, the reality is, as they observe, "that stratification along class, ethnic, status, or cultural lines heavily conditions both what knowledge is regarded as socially valuable and the eagerness and capacity of the children of the different strata to receive it."[29]

Now, a point that must be emphasized here is that we are not at present entertaining what Rawls would call "perfectionist" considerations. We are not here thinking about education as something valuable in itself for the access it provides to the cultural heritage. Unlike Rawls, I have no qualms in saying that a society is better if it is at a higher cultural level; but that judgment is, as perfectionist judgments usually are, devoid of distributive commitments. A society with a common, high culture may be good, but is any other *unjust*? That is our present question.

In this context, education is significant as the thing that opens doors to occupations; as we are conceiving it, the level of educational attainment determines the range of positions in the occupational hierarchy that is accessible. We are assuming that, although different people may trade off in different ways the advantages and disadvantages of different jobs (and in particular money against other things) there is an educational hierarchy such that a higher position on it opens up a more desirable set of positions. This seems broadly correct for modern societies: To put it crudely, somebody with a higher test score generally has the opportunity of doing all the things that somebody with a lower one can do and more.

This makes education unquestionably relevant for fairness, and exclusion (either by formal barriers or financial constraints) from educational opportunities that anyone wishes to take up, and is personally qualified to take up, is indeed unfair. Thus, for example, bursaries to enable children to stay in school who could not otherwise stay because of family poverty are a necessity for fairness. Even short of exclusion, children may be at a disadvantage because of family circumstances in pursuing educational success, and a fair educational system should mitigate these disadvantages, even if doing so is expensive. Material obstacles include such things as the lack of a quiet place in which to study at home, and I think that it is essential to a fair distribution of educational opportunity that there should be (whether in the schools or in public libraries) congenial places open in the evening in which work can be done.

Thus, the removal of impediments to learning is by no means a limited demand. But it still falls far short of the concept of equal opportunity with which we are working, which says that all group variations in wanting to benefit or being able to benefit from education are unfair unless they correspond to group differences in natural endowment. This has the implication that all cultural subgroups in a society must value achievement equally highly and provide an environment equally well calculated to foster it. But this is, of course, such a stringent condition that almost any real cultural differentiation will violate it.

What is the basis for saying that all cultural variation of the kind that results in differential educational attainment is unfair? The answer is presumably the following, given by James Fishkin: "The conditions underlying a competition can be judged unfair if we can predict how people will do in it merely from the knowledge of the strata into which they were born."[30] This notion of fairness implies operationally that "unless a native characteristic withstands [the] justificatory burden of predicting the development of qualifications under equal conditions, it will be considered morally irrelevant to the development of qualifications and, hence, arbitrary. Thus race, sex, ethnic origin, family background, and other such familiar dimensions of discrimination will be considered arbitrary here."[31]

There are, it seems to me, three moves here that are questionable. The first is the assumption that a society as a whole is properly construed as a competition. There are, of course, many competitions within it, but to enroll every boy and girl willy-nilly at the moment of birth in a single big competition with every other is immediately to set up a way of thinking about things that leads straight to a notion of fairness as equal success for those with the same endowments. This way of thinking, then, imposes immediately a very strong assumption that everyone ought to have identical ends and an identical ranking of them. But where does this assumption come from? As far as I can see, it comes in only because it is required by the claim that fairness requires equal chances in a single societywide competition. We still do not have a free-standing claim that differences in values are themselves unfair.

The second questionable claim is that we can attribute all differences in achievement to discrimination. Obviously we could if we liked make that true by the definition of "discrimination," but then we would be adding nothing to the fact of differentiation. For discrimination to be unfair the use of the word must connect with its standard meaning. To discriminate against someone is, roughly speaking, to deny that person some advantage (food, lodging, a job, admission to a university) for which he or she is otherwise qualified (by willingness to pay, ability to do the job, scholastic attainments) on the basis of some improper consideration such as "race, sex, ethnic origin [or] family background." This concept of discrimination gives no warrant to the claim that, say, white Anglo-Saxon Protestant Americans discriminate (as a statistical tendency) against their children by imbuing them with what it takes to pass examinations less fully than do parents of Jewish, Chinese, or Japanese descent.

This brings me to the core of the question, which is whether we must say that every statistically predictable difference in achievement that cannot be accounted for genetically is unfair. Since there is no reason for thinking that group distributions have a genetic base, we can drop the qualification and talk about group differences in achievement *simpliciter*.[32] (This is of course consistent with there being a genetic basis to some of the variation between individuals, including siblings.) The underlying notion is that what can be predicted is "morally arbitrary." So, "I should not be able to enter a hospital ward of healthy newborn babies and, on the basis of class, race, sex, or other arbitrary characteristics, predict the eventual position in society of those children."[33]

An example will, I think, illustrate the point that we should not identify predictable outcomes with outcomes for which people feel no personal responsibility. We can predict, in a society like Britain, the eventual distribution among religious denominations (and none) of children raised by Roman Catholics, Methodists, Baptists, members of the Church of England, and so on. These distributions will be different for each group and will show a tendency for those brought up in one denomination to stay in it. But there is no reason to suppose that people could not recognize these facts and still feel that their adult religious position was their own—was something for which they took personal responsibility.

In the same way, the details of upbringing that make for a greater or lesser thirst for educational attainment and a greater or lesser capacity to give educational institutions what they want are part of the constituents of people's personal identity. They are not necessarily to be repudiated as something that merely "happened to them." Of course one's parentage and all the rest are radically contingent in the sense that there is no purely logical reason why they should not have been other than they were. But in that sense it is radically contingent that the universe exists at all, that there is a planet capable of sustaining life, that human beings evolved on it, and so on. It seems to me that nothing of moral significance follows from this sort of radical contingency of everything. The only possible reply when the issue is pitched at that level is that things might have been different but they were not.

The point I am trying to make is simply that the fundamental attitudes, values, behavioral traits, and so on that make up people's characters would (uncontroversially) have been different had they (i.e., the identical collection of cells) been placed in different conditions, but that does not entail the conclusion that they are not *theirs* in a way that is morally relevant. The issue in fact comes up sharply in contemporary discussion in relation to one of the categories mentioned already, namely, sex. Notoriously, there are systematic differences, re-peated in broad form across all the Western industrial societies, between the occupational levels reached by men and women, and in the occupational directions pursued. (Women, for example, are heavily underrepresented in science and engineering at the undergraduate level.) Some of this is (or certainly has been in the past) due to sex discrimination, formal and informal. But unquestionably a great deal is a result of socialization. (How much if any stems from genetic differences is a question we need not raise because it seems incon-ceivable that it all does.) Is there anything *unfair* about a process that gives rise to a pattern of statistically predictable choices? As George Sher suggested, in an article whose title, "Our Preferences, Ourselves,"[34] indicates its drift, if women identify with their choices, it is hard to see what is unfair about having them. (Again one might, as Sher conceded, say on perfectionist grounds, that it would be better if they had different ones. But that claim is other than one of unfairness.) If, on the other hand, women come to feel that they have been held back or debarred from pursuing ends that they now have through, say, discouragement or inadequate opportunities in the past, then they have a legitimate complaint of unfairness.

These remarks are, I should emphasize, intended to be no more than suggestive. I do not claim that I yet have a general way of sorting out which characteristics should count as "morally arbitrary" and which should be regarded as morally relevant. But I have, I hope, said enough to throw light on the matter with which I began this half of my essay: the claim that if certain minorities (notoriously blacks) are grievously underrepresented in higher education, some of their number, who want to proceed to it and are willing to do the work required to make up, should be admitted and then helped to succeed. The reason for saying that this is a question of fairness is, I think, that there is a poignant discrepancy between the occupational aspirations of many blacks and the educational qualifications that they are able to achieve. We are not talking here about cultural differences but of deprivation with all too apparent historical roots in slavery, oppression, and discrimination. Those who, in spite of all this, still emerge with the will to go on to higher education deserve a chance to.

I believe that those who derive special admissions programs from the notion of equal opportunity as an equal distribution across all groups do their cause a disservice. For they open themselves up to questions from ill-intentioned opponents about whether there has to be a quota for slightly underrepresented white groups, say those of Serbo-Croat origin. The attempt that I have made here to undermine the ideal of equal attainment across groups (at any rate as an ideal of equal opportunity) while allowing a case for special admissions for members of severely disadvantaged groups is, I must confess, less than fully worked out. But it does have the great merit of according with the conviction, which seems to me absolutely right, that the case in favor of special admissions for blacks is not merely on the same continuum as the case in favor of quotas for statistically somewhat underrepresented white groups. Rather, the difference is between some case and no case.

*   *   *

I said in the first section of this chapter that I thought Rawls's argument for equality in the second chapter of *A Theory of Justice* was valid in its own terms. That is, if one accepts the premise that inequalities arising from morally arbitrary differences are unjust, and also agrees that the move from "natural liberty" to "liberal equality" does consist in nothing but eliminating the influence of morally arbitrary factors, then the final move to equal outcomes is very hard to resist. If so much is already on the "morally arbitrary" side of the line, why not everything?

My strategy in this second part of the chapter has not been to question the premise—that in a perfectly just society morally arbitrariness would be eliminated—but to call into doubt the conception of the morally arbitrary that is implicit in the view that is styled by Rawls "liberal equality." If I am right in suggesting that not all differences in attainment that cannot be traced to differences in natural endowment are morally arbitrary, then the final move, drawing natural endowments into the net as well, necessarily falls with it. It takes the form of an extension of the conception of moral arbitrariness already established.

Does this entail, then, that we are driven back to the "system of natural liberty"? Not at all. Rawls presented us with three complete menus.[35] But we can be more discriminating than that and make selections from within these menus. Thus, if I am right, we can draw some kind of distinction among environmentally induced factors, dividing them into those that make people what they are and those that inhibit their ability to pursue their goals in life. And I suggest that the same can be said of natural endowments: Natural strength and dexterity are, we might say, a part of someone's personality in a way in which a club foot or congenital heart disease is not. One is what we are, the other what befalls us (even if it befell us at the time of conception).

This is, I am well aware, little more than hand waving. But even if I knew how to make it more precise, I should not have the space to take the matter any further here. All I want to leave you with is the point that the consequences of rejecting the ideal of liberal equality, as formulated (not particularly idiosyncratically) by Rawls, still remain to be worked out.

NOTES

1. John Rawls, *A Theory of Justice* (Cambridge, Mass.: Belknap Press of Harvard University Press, 1971). "Pareto improvement" occurs when one makes someone else better off without making anyone else worse off [Editor's note].

2. I include in this my own treatment of chain connection in *The Liberal Theory of Justice* (Oxford: Clarendon Press, 1973), pp. 110–111.

3. Rawls, *A Theory of Justice,* p. 60.

4. Ibid., p. 72.

5. Ibid.

6. Ibid.

7. Ibid. Rawls also called it "the liberal interpretation of the two principles" of justice, which I find less perspicuous.

8. Ibid., p. 73.

9. Ibid.

10. See, for example, A. H. Halsey, A. F. Heath, and J. M. Ridge, *Origins and Destinations: Family, Class, and Education in Modern Britain* (Oxford: Clarendon Press, 1980), pp. 201–205.

11. Rawls, *A Theory of Justice,* p. 66.

12. Ibid., p. 73.

13. Ibid., p. 74.

14. Ibid., pp. 73–74.

15. Christopher Jencks et al., *Inequality: A Reassessment of the Effect of Family and Schooling in America* (London: Allen Lane, 1973), p. 73. (First published in the United States in 1972.)

16. Rawls, *A Theory of Justice,* p. 75.

17. James S. Fishkin, *Justice, Equal Opportunity, and the Family* (New Haven, Conn.: Yale University Press, 1983), p. 57.

18. This is true, for example, of Fishkin.

19. "Minorities: Isolation on College Campuses," *Los Angeles Times,* December 11, 1983, pt. 1, p. 29.

20. Ibid. The first ellipses covers the removal of an editorial interpolation in the quotation; the others are in the original article.

21. Halsey et al., *Origins and Destinations,* p. 215.

22. Rawls, *A Theory of Justice,* p. 74.

23. This is an adaptation of Jencks et al., *Inequality,* p. 67.

24. See Christopher Jencks et al., *Who Gets Ahead? The Determinants of Economic Success in America* (New York: Basic Books, 1979).

25. Ernest Gellner, *Nations and Nationalism* (Ithaca, N.Y.: Cornell University Press, 1983), pp. 96–97.

26. Ibid., p. 36.

27. Rawls, *A Theory of Justice,* p. 74.

28. Halsey et al., *Origins and Destinations,* p. 217.

29. Ibid.

30. Fishkin, *Justice,* p. 110.

31. Ibid., p. 33.

32. "Simpliciter" is a term from Scots law and means "of its own nature" or "unqualifiedly."

33. Fishkin, *Justice,* p. 4.

34. *Philosophy and Public Affairs* 12 (1983):34–50.

35. These correspond closely to three models of society distinguished by John Roemer in *A General Theory of Exploitation and Class* (Cambridge, Mass.: Harvard University Press, 1982). "Natural liberty" gets rid of "feudal exploitation," "liberal equality" gets rid of "capitalist exploitation," and "democratic equality" gets rid of "socialist exploitation."

PART 2

A Useful Ideal

3

What Must Be Equal for Opportunity to Be Equal?

CHRISTOPHER JENCKS

Americans never argue about whether equal opportunity is desirable. Egalitarians say it is not enough. Pragmatists say it is unattainable. But no significant group says it would be a bad thing if we had it. Nonetheless, though equal opportunity is compatible with almost everyone's vision of a good society, we disagree about what such a society should be like. As a result, we disagree about the meaning of equal opportunity. Like Aristotle's conception of justice, our conception of equal opportunity requires us to "treat equals equally and unequals unequally." But neither doctrine tells us whom we must treat equally and whom we must treat unequally. Indeed, the enduring popularity of equal opportunity, like that of justice, depends on the fact that we can all answer this question in different ways without realizing how profound our differences really are.

Almost all Americans would agree that opportunity is equal when individuals who are alike in all relevant respects have the same choices available to them. But this definition leaves open both the question of what personal characteristics are "relevant" in specific situations and the question of when choices are "the same." Most Americans today agree that attributes like skin color and ancestry ought to be "irrelevant" and that distinctions based entirely on such characteristics are therefore incompatible with equal opportunity. But there is no such consensus about what characteristics we should consider "relevant." Conservatives usually assume that differences in past performance require us to treat people unequally. Liberals usually think that past disadvantages require us to treat people unequally. As we shall see, many other criteria also appear relevant to some but not others.

The question of when opportunities are "the same" is equally fraught with potential controversy. Conservatives usually argue that two people have the same choices when the objective costs and benefits of each option are the same. If Johnny and Mary can attend the same colleges at the same prices, if their parents are equally prepared to underwrite the costs, and if they can expect to reap the same benefits from attending these colleges, then they confront the same range of choices. Liberals and radicals habitually take account of subjective costs and benefits as well. If Johnny has grown up in a household where studying is a low priority activity, for example, while Mary has grown up in a household where it is a religious obligation, Johnny will usually find the subjective cost of doing schoolwork higher than Mary finds it. All else being equal, Johnny will therefore choose a less academically demanding college than Mary. Liberals and radicals will then say that Johnny had less "opportunity" than Mary to attend a good college. Conservatives usually reject this argument, insisting that Johnny and Mary had the same opportunity to attend a demanding college and that Johnny's decision reflects lack of "motivation," not "opportunity."

Most Americans would also agree that equal opportunity implies a "fair race," in which all participants enjoy an equal start but compete for unequal prizes. If you ask people to develop this analogy, however, you will find that they disagree about when the race starts, what constitutes an "equal" start, and what rules are "fair." Many contemporary liberals believe that the race should begin anew every day and that society should do everything in its power to put all competitors on an equal footing at the start of the day. Most conservatives believe that advantages accumulated early in life can legitimately be carried over into later life. They oppose liberal efforts to wipe the slate clean and let people have "second chances," on the grounds that those who know they will have a second chance make less effort the first time around.

Trying to win general acceptance for any single "correct" definition of equal opportunity is a fool's game, with no greater likelihood of success than trying to win general acceptance for a single definition of justice or liberty. Trying to persuade people that they should stop using the term because they cannot agree on what it means is equally pointless. The most we can hope for is more general recognition that equal opportunity has a number of distinct—indeed, contradictory— meanings. To illustrate this argument I will discuss five common ways of thinking about equal opportunity, each of which draws on a different tradition and each of which has different practical consequences. Experience suggests that few readers will remember all five alternatives for long. Memorable distinctions contrast two, or at most three, ways of looking at a problem. But perhaps the very fact that I need so many categories to capture the full range of popular thinking about this issue will help dramatize my argument that no two people are likely to mean the same thing when they use the term.[1]

To illustrate the different meanings of equal opportunity I will focus primarily on educational opportunity, turning only briefly at the end of the chapter to the problem of equal opportunity in employment. To make the argument concrete, I will confine my attention to a single sixth-grade "language arts" class in a small town, taught by a teacher whom I will call Ms. Higgins. Ms. Higgins believes in equal opportunity. Her problem—and ours—is what her belief in equal opportunity implies about the distribution of the main educational resources at her disposal, namely her time and attention. Ms. Higgins must face this problem no matter how she organizes her class. Assuming her class is typical, it will include several students who can read only the simplest sentences and several who can read as fluently as the average adult. It will also include some students who are eager to learn and others who are almost completely uninterested in either school or reading. If Ms. Higgins asks these diverse pupils to do a lot of individual work, she will never have enough time to deal with all their problems, so she will have to develop some strategy for rationing her time. If she divides the class into small groups with similar reading skills, she will have to decide how to divide her time among these groups. If she teaches the entire class together, she will have to decide which students to call on, how much time to spend on different sorts of questions, and how much of the class to aim at her best readers, how much at her worst readers, and how much at those in between. (In theory, students also learn to write in a language arts class, but I have simplified the discussion by ignoring writing.)

When Ms. Higgins thinks about how to spend her time, she must first decide whether to base her behavior on some theory of justice, which will require her to ask what different students "deserve," or on some variant of utilitarianism, which will emphasize efficiency and require her to ask how much various people will benefit from different uses of her time. If she decides to pursue justice for individuals, she will have to decide between theories that focus on what individuals deserve because of their virtues and theories that focus on what individuals deserve on the basis of their past or current disadvantages. If she opts for a utilitarian calculus of costs and benefits, she will have to decide whether to maximize her students' short-run satisfaction or the long-run satisfaction of society as a whole. If she does not find any of these alternatives satisfactory, she may conclude that equal opportunity simply means devoting equal time and attention to all students. Ms. Higgins's ruminations will therefore leave her with five options, to which I propose to attach the following labels:

1. *Moralistic Justice.* Moralistic justice requires Ms. Higgins to reward virtue and punish vice. In principle, it requires her to equate virtue with effort and hence to reward those who make the most effort. In practice, Ms. Higgins will find it hard to decide who has made the most effort, so she will often end up equating virtue with achievement rather than effort and rewarding those who do the best work, even if they do it relatively effortlessly.

2. *Humane Justice.* Humane justice tells Ms. Higgins that all students are equally deserving in the long run. But since some students have gotten less than their proportionate share of advantages in the past, Ms. Higgins has an obligation to give them more than their proportionate share while they are in her classroom. Because it is hard to know who has been shortchanged in the past, advocates of humane justice often assume that Ms. Higgins should devote most of her time and attention to those who are currently worst off, for whatever reason.

3. *Myopic Utilitarianism.* Myopic utilitarianism tries to maximize students' short-run satisfaction. It encourages Ms. Higgins to ask who wants her time and to distribute her time on the basis of demand. Those who want her time the most get the most.

4. *Enlightened Utilitarianism.* Enlightened utilitarianism tries to maximize the long-run welfare of society as a whole. Like myopic utilitarianism, it tells Ms. Higgins to use her time efficiently, but it tells her to maximize the long-term welfare of the entire citizenry not the short-term welfare of her own students. This means that instead of asking who wants her time right now she must ask who will benefit over the long haul. It also means that she must take account of indirect benefits to others as well as direct benefits to her own students.

5. *Democratic Equality.* Democratic equality requires Ms. Higgins to give everyone equal time and attention, regardless of how well they read, how hard they try, how deprived they have been in the past, what they want, or how much they or others will benefit.

Advocates of all these goals claim that they are compatible with equal opportunity. Equal opportunity can therefore imply either a meritocratic distribution of resources, a compensatory distribution of resources, or an equal distribution of resources. A meritocratic conception of equal opportunity can, in turn, favor either those who try hard or those who achieve a lot, whereas a compensatory conception of equal opportunity can favor either those who have suffered from some sort of handicap in the past or those whose current achievement is below average.

THE MORALISTIC THEORY OF JUSTICE

If Ms. Higgins is a traditionalist, she will probably adopt what I have called a moralistic theory of justice. Moralistic justice tries to reward virtue and punish vice. When students make an effort to do what Ms. Higgins asks of them, moralistic justice encourages her to respond not only with praise but with extra attention. When students make no effort to do what she asks of them, moralistic justice tells her she need not "waste her time" on them. While she might not put it this way, moralistic justice encourages her to think of her classroom as a moral community, held together by an unwritten contract which states that "I'll do my best if you'll do yours." Those who respect the contract reap its benefits. Those who do not respect it are subject to internal exile—or to expulsion if they behave badly enough.

In principle, a moralistic view of the classroom should focus on acts of will. This means that it should define virtue in terms of effort, not achievement. In practice, Ms. Higgins can seldom observe effort directly. All she can usually observe is actual achievement, which depends not only on current effort but on ability and prior knowledge. Because Ms. Higgins cannot judge a student's current effort very accurately, she will encounter all sorts of practical problems if she tries to reward it. If students know that Ms. Higgins tries to reward effort, they will have an incentive to exaggerate the effort required to achieve any given result. To make this deception plausible, they will feign lack of ability, lack of prior knowledge, or both. Even if Ms. Higgins sees through these deceptions and estimates their effort accurately, she is likely to confront problems in persuading her students that her judgments are fair. If two sixth-graders perform equally well, and if Ms. Higgins rewards one more than the other because one supposedly made more effort than the other, the loser is likely to feel that Ms. Higgins is playing favorites. Knowing that adult society usually rewards accomplishment not effort will reinforce the loser's sense of injustice.

A system that encourages dissembling and breeds feelings of injustice is not likely to attract Ms. Higgins, so she is likely to end up rewarding achievement rather than effort. She is also likely to forget that she ought, in principle, to be rewarding effort. Instead, she will convince herself that achievement per se is morally commendable, even when it requires little effort. Since ability and prior knowledge are by definition fixed at any given moment, rewarding achievement should still lead students to maximize their effort. From a moralistic perspective, however, rewarding achievement will lead to a lot of injustice because able pupils who make little effort will get more rewards than inept pupils who make more effort.

The notion that society should reward effort is rooted in our shared experience that more effort usually means more "output" and that more output is usually better for everyone in the long run. But moralistic justice focuses on eliminating only one of the many possible obstacles to increased output, namely our chronic reluctance to make a lot of effort when the payoff is remote or may go mainly to others. Moralistic justice tries to ensure that such efforts will also have some short-term payoff. When lack of effort is the principal obstacle to learning, moralistic justice can play a central role in the classroom. But when most students already want to learn, motivation becomes a secondary problem and rationing technical assistance becomes central. When Ms. Higgins's main task is to ration technical assistance, she is likely to pay more attention to competence, demand, and expected benefits than to effort per se.

In principle, moralistic justice has two kinds of effects. First, it tells students that Ms. Higgins will reward them directly for doing their best. Second, it tries to convince students that society as a whole, and perhaps even their classmates, will respect them more if they do their best and will exclude or punish them if they do not. To make her classroom a community in which effort is the price of citizenship, Ms. Higgins will usually praise and blame in public rather than in private. Each time she interacts with a student she will think not just about the effect of her words and behavior on that student but about their effect on other students as well. As a result, she is likely to end up thinking of her time not as a "private" good that has to be distributed to some students at the expense of others, but as a "public" good that benefits everyone, even when she is nominally talking to only one student. In this chapter, however, I will deal only with the aspect of Ms. Higgins's time and attention that constitutes a divisible private good.

Although moralistic justice is based on ethical arguments, its appeal to Ms. Higgins—or almost anyone else—will depend to a great extent on how well it works. If Ms. Higgins can get children to make an effort simply by *threatening* to withhold her time and attention, she will find this strategy very attractive. If she frequently has to *carry out* her threats, she is likely to look for a different strategy because she is likely to feel that ignoring students who make no effort is counterproductive in the long run. Prudential considerations are also likely to play a major role when she chooses among possible incentives for effort. If, for example, she can get students to do what she wants simply by praising and blaming, or by using grades as an incentive, she is likely to prefer this to using time and attention as incentives because withholding praise or giving low grades seems to do students less harm than withholding attention. Nonetheless, if time is in short supply, as it usually is, moralistic justice clearly provides Ms. Higgins with a rationale for withholding time and attention from some students.

Moralistic justice appears easy to reconcile with equal opportunity. One simply says that all students have an equal opportunity to make an effort and that all who make equal effort get equal treatment. There is the practical difficulty that rewards are seldom really based on effort, but then the world is always afflicted with practical difficulties. There may also be a moral difficulty, however. In the real world, some kinds of students make more effort to do what Ms. Higgins wants than others make. Girls, for example, tend to make more effort than boys, and middle-class children tend to make more effort than working-class children. Under these circumstances we must ask what it means to say that everyone has an equal opportunity to make an effort. I will return to this problem in the next section.

HUMANE THEORIES OF JUSTICE

Instead of deciding what we deserve on the basis of our virtues and vices, "humane" theories of justice focus on what we deserve simply because we are members of the human species. Because we are all equally human, our claims as members of the species are all equal. Such claims, based on the mere fact of being human, are commonly labeled "rights." Since there is no general agreement about the nature of these rights, there are many versions of humane justice. For convenience, I have tried to array these variants of humane justice on a spectrum running from "strong" to "weak."

In its strongest variant, humane justice asserts that all individuals have an equal claim on all of society's resources, regardless of their virtues or vices. Few people subscribe to this version of humane justice, however, and it need not concern us here. What I will here call the "strong" variant of humane justice holds that society can make an adult's claim to its resources conditional on various forms of socially useful behavior, but that society must offer all children an equal chance of meeting whatever requirements it sets. If some students need special help to develop the skills or character traits society values, society must give them whatever help they need. If, for example, some children need unusually good schooling to compensate for an unusually unfavorable home environment, or for unusual physical handicaps, society must make sure they get it.

Advocates of humane justice often describe their policy as distributing resources on the basis of need, but "need" turns out to be an ambiguous term. When we say that Johnny needs a minute of Ms. Higgins's time more than Mary does, we can mean either that Johnny is a worse reader, and therefore needs to improve more, or that Johnny will actually improve more if he gets the time. The first usage is implicit in a phrase like "the 100 neediest cases." The second is implicit in the statement that "adults need to eat more than children." Distributing resources on the basis of "need" can thus imply either humane justice or enlightened utilitarianism, depending on how you interpret need. Given this ambiguity, I will talk about giving extra resources to those with the greatest "disadvantages" rather than the greatest "need."

Advocates of "strong" humane justice usually say that society must do everything in its power to ensure that every child can grow up to live a "normal" life. If we take a "normal" life to be an "average" life, and if we assume that one must have "average" skills and character traits to lead an "average" life, the "normal life" argument clearly implies that society must do what it can to ensure that every child reaches an average level of accomplishment. The only way everyone can reach the average is for none to exceed it, so the "normal life" argument implies—though it almost never explicitly asserts—that all students have a right to more or less equal educational outcomes.

What I will call the "weak" variant of humane justice has less stringent requirements. It holds that all students have an equal lifetime claim on educational resources, broadly construed. Students have a claim to additional educational resources if they are currently disadvantaged because of some deficiency in their previous education but not if they are disadvantaged for noneducational reasons. If a student has had unusually bad schooling prior to entering Ms. Higgins's classroom, for example, she has an obligation to provide the student with extra help. If a student has had unusually incompetent parents, the case is more ambiguous, but in recent decades most advocates of humane justice have seen the home primarily as an "educational" environment and have felt that Ms. Higgins owed children compensatory help if their parents were unable to do as much for them as the typical middle-class parent does. If students are "slow" for genetic reasons, however, advocates of "weak" humane justice are not concerned about their fate.

The moral logic behind the "weak" variant of humane justice seems to be that society is responsible for the educational environment in which children are raised but not for the genes they inherit (or the physical accidents that befall them). This view has always baffled me. I can understand the argument that society is not responsible either for a child's genes or for its upbringing. I have never seen a coherent defense of the proposition that society is responsible for one but not the other.

The most compelling argument for compensating the victims of unfavorable home environments derives from the fact that society allows any adult, no matter how incompetent, to have children. Almost all of us endorse this view because we feel that restricting the right to have children is an unacceptable limitation on adult liberty. One can certainly argue that a collective decision to maximize adults' freedom, regardless of the costs to children, implies a collective obligation to compensate those children on whom this decision imposes significant costs. But this line of argument requires us to compensate children whose parents provide them with the wrong genes as well as children whose parents provide them with the wrong home environment.

A more common but less compelling argument for compensating children who have been raised in unfavorable home environments is that these environments are a byproduct of our collective commitment to capitalism, with its attendant pattern of socioeconomic inequality. Having committed ourselves to an economic system that produces a high level of inequality among adults, we acquire an obligation to neutralize the effects of such inequality on children. We have no comparable commitment to perpetuating genetic inequality among adults, so we have no comparable obligation to neutralize the effects of genetic inequality on children. This argument strikes me as faulty in two respects. First, if it can be said that we have "chosen" capitalism and have thus acquired a special obligation to its victims, it can equally well be said that we have "chosen" not to limit the fertility of the genetically disadvantaged and have thereby acquired an obligation to compensate the victims of this policy as well. Second, although our commitment to capitalism certainly entails special obligations to its identifiable victims, the argument that capitalism victimizes the children of poor parents requires evidence that such children do significantly worse under capitalism than under other economic systems. Unfortunately, poor children perform worse than their classmates in all economic systems on which we have data. Furthermore, the gap between them and their more privileged classmates appears to be as wide under state socialism as under U.S. capitalism.[2] This makes it much harder to argue that by choosing capitalism over state socialism we have made poor children worse off academically, though we may have made them worse off in some other respects. One can, I believe, argue that poor children would be better off under regimes other than either U.S. capitalism or state socialism. But Americans have not consciously rejected these alternatives in the same sense that they have consciously rejected state socialism. Thus, one cannot argue that they have chosen capitalism with full knowledge that they were imposing costs on poor children or that this "choice" implies special obligations to such children.

I suspect, however, that all these arguments are beside the point and that the real reason most people want to limit society's responsibility for the genetically disadvantaged is prudential, not ethical. Most people assume it is harder to offset the effects of genetic than environmental disadvantages. They think the effects of genes must be immutable because genes themselves are immutable. They think the effects of the environment must be mutable because the environment is mutable. But there is no necessary relationship between the mutability of causes and the mutability of their effects. Two examples should suffice to dramatize this point.

First, consider two children who are deaf, one because of an early childhood disease, the other because of a genetic defect. The fact that one child's problem is genetic whereas the other child's problem is environmental tells us nothing about the physical character of the problem or the likelihood that it has a medical remedy. If no remedy is available, both children face the same educational problems. Whether they will develop the skills and character traits required for a "normal" life depends on their other characteristics, not on the initial cause of their deafness. The cost of educating them also depends on these factors, not on the origin of their disorder.

Second, consider an eager but slow-witted girl who has great difficulty mastering reading. Assume her difficulty is genetic in origin and that it manifests itself in a generalized inability to master skills that require her to see analogies or remember large amounts of miscellaneous information for long periods. Compare her to another girl who also has great difficulty reading, because she comes from a disorganized and abusive home, is always angry at her teachers and fellow students, and cannot concentrate on any task long enough to learn much. If we ask which of these children will benefit most from a minute of Ms. Higgins's time, the answer is far from obvious. If we ask experienced teachers, some will say they think it would be easier to teach the "slow" child, whereas others will say that they think it would be easier to teach the "disturbed" child. This would remain true if the "slow" child had been brought up in the wrong way, while the "disturbed" child had an inherited metabolic disorder.

For all these reasons the moral and empirical foundations of "weak" humane justice seem to me very shaky. Nonetheless, the "weak" interpretation of humane justice is far more widely accepted than the "strong" interpretation. In effect, it defines equal educational opportunity as "equal opportunity for the genetically equal and unequal opportunity for the genetically unequal." (It seldom has anything to say one way or the other about physical differences that are not genetic in origin.)

Another weak variant of humane justice, which I will call "moralistic humane justice," requires society to ensure equal educational outcomes only when students make equal effort to do what their schools ask of them. Those who advocate this form of humane justice believe that society must provide all students with equal educational resources, including extra school resources to compensate for deficiencies in their home environments and perhaps even their genes, but they do not believe that society is responsible for an individual's values or character. They therefore reject the notion that society must compensate children for the consequences of having the wrong values, even if these values are a product of the environment in which the child was raised. If a parent fails to provide a child with books or gives the child very limited exposure to unusual words at home, society has an obligation to provide the child with compensatory help at school. But if a parent teaches the child that mastering unusual words is a waste of time, the school has no obligation to alter the child's values.

There does not seem to be any principled reason why we should hold society responsible for giving all children equal educational resources but not for ensuring that they learn to use these resources in ways that will promote their long-term self-interest. The argument for this view is strictly pragmatic. It correctly asserts that the only way to ensure that all children value learning equally is to make child rearing a collective rather than an individual responsibility, as the kibbutz does. This being politically unacceptable, making all children value learning equally is impractical. Equalizing access to educational resources requires less drastic institutional changes and is therefore deemed more practical. But though it is impossible to ensure that all children value learning equally, it is certainly possible to organize schools so that some students whose parents have not taught them to value learning discover its pleasures and benefits. Any theory that exonerates society from all responsibility on this score is morally suspect because it provides an excuse for doing nothing in circumstances where a lot can and should be done. Unfortunately, it is difficult to find a middle ground between holding society completely responsible for children's values and holding children completely responsible for them. Most advocates of humane justice therefore choose to hold society responsible, at least in their public pronouncements and political arguments.

The assumption that society as a whole is responsible for children's values, and hence for their level of effort, inevitably changes the meaning of equal opportunity. Instead of asserting that opportunities are equal when the objective costs and benefits of various choices are equal, this stance requires us to take account of all the factors that influence an individual's choices, including subjective costs and benefits. If Johnny's parents do not praise him for reading as often as Mary's parents praise her, Johnny does not get the same subjective benefits from reading. Other things being equal, Johnny will therefore make less effort to read. Most advocates of humane justice feel that under these circumstances Johnny has less "opportunity" to master reading than Mary has, even if he has the same books on his shelves at home and the same teacher at school.

This is not, of course, the way we use the term "opportunity" in everyday language. If Johnny and Mary have the same access to books and are taught in the same way, we ordinarily say that they have the same opportunity to learn. If Mary's parents encourage her to take advantage of this opportunity, while Johnny's do not, we say that Mary has more "incentive" or "motivation" to learn, not that she has more "opportunity" to do so. But if society as a whole is responsible for an individual's preferences and values, the boundary between the individual and the larger society no longer has the moral significance that Europeans and Americans have traditionally assigned it. Indeed, the boundary almost disappears. Under these circumstances the notion that individuals are the proper units for moral accounting is bound to break down. The distinction between objective and subjective costs and benefits also becomes irrelevant, making it natural to assume that equal opportunity requires equal *overall* rewards for different choices, not just equal *objective* rewards. This conception of equal opportunity attracts advocates of humane justice precisely because it implies collective responsibility for individual choices without making this controversial assumption explicit.

At least since the 1960s, the notion that society as a whole is responsible for children's choices has been widely accepted. If Ms. Higgins accepts this notion, she herself must take some responsibility for her pupils' choices. She can no longer ignore pupils just because they make no effort. If they would benefit from her attention, they have a right to it whether they appear to want it or not. When they make no effort, Ms. Higgins must try to "motivate" them.

Humane Justice and Socioeconomic Inequality

The way in which contemporary liberals and radicals discuss socioeconomic differences in achievement provides a useful indication of the relative popularity of the three variants of humane justice previously discussed. Contemporary liberals and radicals usually define equal opportunity as requiring that children from different socioeconomic backgrounds have the same probability of learning to read competently, attending good colleges, getting good jobs, and enjoying a good life. If these probabilities vary, opportunity is unequal. This is almost always a matter of definition. No evidence regarding the reasons for the difference is ordinarily required.

Most contemporary liberals and radicals also assume that children from different socioeconomic backgrounds are genetically indistinguishable. This implies that socioeconomic differences in achievement are entirely attributable to the environments in which different children are raised. This assumption persists despite the fact that there are powerful logical and empirical arguments against it. We know, for example, that genes have some influence on academic achievement, though the magnitude of the effect is a matter of continuing controversy.[3] We also know that academic achievement has some effect on adults' socioeconomic position, independent of everything else we have been able to measure.[4] Logic therefore suggests that a child's genes must have some influence on its adult socioeconomic position. If that is so, adults in different socioeconomic positions must differ genetically and so must their children. The only real questions are how large these differences are and how much of the achievement gap between children from different backgrounds is explicable in genetic terms. Adoption studies support this view. An adopted child's test scores are more closely related to the educational attainment of its natural mother than to that of its adoptive mother, for example.[5]

Nonetheless, few liberals or radicals will even entertain the possibility that genes contribute to achievement differences between socioeconomic groups. The explanation seems obvious. Though some people believe that society should do everything in its power to help the genetically disadvantaged, far more people believe that it should do everything in its power to help the environmentally disadvantaged. Thus even if you believe in your heart that poor children labor under genetic as well as environmental handicaps, you are likely to think it expedient to deemphasize this possibility when you are campaigning for programs to help such children. If most people were committed to the "strong" variant of humane justice, liberals and radicals would not feel compelled to deny the possibility that genes contribute to socioeconomic differences in achievement.

Some advocates of humane justice ·also deny that children from different socioeconomic backgrounds differ in the amount of effort they make to master cognitive skills. Those who take this position typically

insist that working-class children enter school eager to learn and that
they are then "turned off" by large classes, authoritarian teachers, low
expectations, and a curriculum that assumes knowledge or experience
they do not have. There is certainly some truth in all this. Indeed, if
we were to measure "effort" simply by looking at the number of minutes
children spent doing schoolwork, we might not find much difference
between middle-class and working-class children in the early grades.
But "effort" also includes the games children choose to play (Scrabble
versus basketball), the things they think about at breakfast (childish
puns versus fast cars), and a multitude of other activities that contribute
in subtle ways to cognitive development. If we define effort in this
comprehensive way, the claim that middle-class children value cognitive
skills more than working-class children do is almost surely correct,
though I know no hard evidence supporting it. Although some advocates
of humane justice reject this conclusion, most seem to accept it,
presumably because the political cost of conceding the point is relatively
small. This suggests that moralistic humane justice has few advocates.

Although most advocates of humane justice believe that society
should ensure that children from different socioeconomic backgrounds
are equally motivated to master cognitive skills and succeed in school,
few have had anything concrete to say about how we might achieve
this elusive goal. If working-class parents value cognitive skills less
than middle-class parents do, the only way to eliminate class differences
in achievement is for schools to reward working-class children more
than middle-class children who learn the same amount. Only in this
way could we make the subjective value of learning equal for working-
class and middle-class children. Some postrevolutionary societies have
tried to achieve something like this by making bourgeois origins an
explicit obstacle to advancement, but such policies hardly conform to
American notions of equal opportunity and they have all sorts of other
unattractive consequences.

The argument that society is responsible for children's values also
creates what students of insurance call a "moral hazard" for children.
If children are not responsible for the consequences of their own
choices, they have no incentive to make choices that are disagreeable
in the short run but beneficial in the long run. If, for example, society
were to compensate working-class children for not having been raised
in households that encouraged them to read, such children would have
no incentive to read unless they enjoyed it. They would therefore read
even less than they now do. The same problem arises when an
organization is fully insured against the consequences of its employees'
carelessness or stupidity. Carelessness and stupidity tend to become
endemic in such organizations, which is why insurance companies

almost always insist that organizations bear part of the risk in such situations.

Such practical difficulties do not call into question the fundamental moral premise of humane justice: that educational resources should go disproportionately to the disadvantaged, however they may be defined. The practical difficulties do, however, suggest that if equal opportunity means that children raised in different families must have equal probabilities of success, we can never fully achieve it. Because most of us think of "rights" as goals that can be achieved, we must either reject the argument that equal opportunity is a right, substituting the notion that it is an ideal, or reject the conventional "humane" definition of equal opportunity.

If advocates of humane justice concede that equal outcomes are unattainable, they must face another difficulty. If all students—or at least all students of similar "native ability"—can achieve the same level of reading competence, Ms. Higgins's obligation is clear: She must do whatever is necessary to achieve this end. But if this end cannot be attained, what should she do? Presumably she should still give more time to her worst readers, since they deserve her help more than other children do. But how much more time do they deserve?

The most extreme deprivation-based argument requires Ms. Higgins to devote all her time and attention to the worst reader in her class. If the worst reader moves ahead of the next worst, she shifts her attention to the next worst. She keeps doing this until everyone reads equally well. Nobody takes this extreme position, presumably because nobody thinks that the worst reader would catch up even if he or she had a monopoly on Ms. Higgins's time. But many believe that Ms. Higgins should devote almost all her time and attention to children with serious reading problems. If these children improve faster than the rest, everyone will eventually read about equally well. But if they improve slower than the rest, they will have a permanent monopoly on Ms. Higgins's time and attention, and the rest of the class will suffer.

Instead of urging Ms. Higgins to devote herself exclusively to her worst readers, some advocates of humane justice therefore believe she should try to minimize inequality in reading skills. The practical implications of this doctrine depend both on how she defines inequality and on how much different students benefit from her time. Assuming reading scores have been transformed so that all one-point increments are equally "valuable" in some larger social sense, inequality depends on the mean and dispersion of the transformed scores. Raising the mean lowers inequality unless the dispersion widens even faster. Narrowing the dispersion also lowers inequality unless the mean falls even faster. The best strategy for lowering inequality therefore depends on how Ms. Higgins's time and attention affect each student's skills. Ms. Higgins might end up spending all her time with her worst readers, but she might also spend some time with all but her very best readers. Indeed, if she were to think of inequality not just in terms of her own classroom but in terms of the larger society, she might even spend some time with her very best readers. Of course, if humane justice is only one of her goals and maximizing social welfare is another, she will have an even greater interest in raising the mean and will probably distribute her time and attention even more equally.

Moralistic Versus Humane Justice

No society or individual ever fully resolves the conflict between moralistic and humane justice. Every parent, for example, confronts the conflict every day. The moralistic theory of justice tells us that we should reward our children when they behave well and punish them when they behave badly. The humane theory of justice tells us that we owe all our children the same amount of love, attention, and assistance simply because they are our children. The two theories are only compatible if our children are all equally virtuous, which they seldom are.

In practice, the conflict is even deeper than this formulation implies. Parents who believe in humane justice usually assume that if one of their children behaves particularly badly that child must have grown up in a particularly unfavorable environment. They therefore tend to blame themselves for their children's sins and feel that when a child behaves badly they should try to "make it up" to the child with additional time, money, or whatever else they think will help. If one of their children gets in trouble with the law, for example, they often neglect their other children's interests to raise bail, pay for lawyers or therapists, or make clear to the offending child that they still love him. (It usually seems to be a "him.") Even when they attribute a child's bad behavior to genes, hormones, illness, or other physical factors over which they had no control, they tend to see the child as a victim rather than a villain. Instead of rewarding virtue they therefore end up rewarding vice.

The moralistic theory of justice assumes that children are responsible for their own behavior. This does not mean denying the importance of the environment. Moralists use rewards and punishments to create an environment they hope will promote virtue and discourage vice. But if their efforts fail, they blame the child, not themselves.

Parental rewards and punishments work fairly well when children are young because parents control most of the incentives that affect a young child's behavior. As children get older, parents lose their monopoly over rewards and punishments, which increasingly come from within the child's head or from outside the family. As a result, larger and larger parental rewards and punishments yield smaller and smaller changes in children's behavior. At some point most parents stop trying to improve their children's behavior and try to accept their children as they are. This means abandoning moralistic justice and trying to practice humane justice instead.

The same logic applies at a societal level. If a society can take concerted action to reward virtue and punish vice, it can usually enforce a high degree of conformity to its norms, whatever these may be. Moralistic justice has great appeal in such societies because it works. Such societies seldom have to carry out their threats. In societies like our own, which have great difficulty taking concerted action against those who violate their norms, violations are far more common. Paradoxically, as the likelihood that violations will be punished declines, the absolute amount of misery that society inflicts on those who violate its rules may well increase. When punishment is certain, violations are usually rare, so punishment is also rare. When punishment is less certain, violations become common, and punishment, though less likely in any individual case, may well be more common in the society as a whole. This paradoxical development often leads compassionate observers to discover reasons for rejecting moralistic justice. They are likely to argue that moralistic justice has "failed," without asking what would happen if we abandoned it altogether. They are also likely to argue that those who reject society's rules are simply reacting to the fact that society rejects them. Humane justice has considerable appeal in such societies, especially to the virtuous, who assume that everyone else is as "naturally" virtuous as they are, and explain vice as an irrational byproduct of oppression rather than a rational response to incentives.

The tension between moralistic and humane justice is related to the old problem of free will versus determinism. The moralistic theory of justice assumes that children have free will. Parents should provide appropriate incentives for children to make the right choices, but if a child then makes a wrong choice, the child rather than the parent is expected to suffer for the mistake. The humane theory of justice assumes that the environment in which a child finds itself determines its choices. As a result, those who create the environment are ultimately responsible for the child's choices and should absorb the costs of foolish choices.

Both theories of justice are compatible with the "fair race" theory of equal opportunity, but they assign Ms. Higgins different roles in this race. Moralistic justice is a system for awarding prizes. It tells Ms.

Higgins to act as a judge, giving different students what they deserve on the basis of their past academic performance. Humane justice focuses on preparing runners for the next race. It tells Ms. Higgins to act as a coach, whose job is to ensure that all runners get "enough" training.

Every moment in our lives is both an ending and a beginning. When we think of the moment as an ending, we apply the standards of moralistic justice. When we think of it as a beginning, we apply the standards of humane justice. When we recognize that the moment is both, we find ourselves in a quandary. Suppose, for example, that Ms. Higgins asks her pupils to write a book report. Moralistic justice will lead Ms. Higgins to spend more time reading and commenting on papers she thinks took the students a lot of time and no time on the papers of students who spent no time themselves. Humane justice requires her to spend more time on the worst papers, even if the authors spent very little time on them, because the authors of these papers need the most help if they are to write adequate papers in the future.

MYOPIC UTILITARIANISM

What I have called "myopic utilitarianism" focuses on maximizing pupils' short-term satisfaction. If Ms. Higgins pursues this goal, she will try to satisfy demands on her time in the order of their intensity. Those who want her time the most intensely will get more than their proportionate share; those who want Ms. Higgins to leave them alone will get left alone. I will call this a demand-based strategy.

To maximize student satisfaction Ms. Higgins needs some device for measuring the relative intensity of different students' desire for her time and attention. If students had to pay for her time, if they all had equal amounts of money to spend, and if they could also spend their money on baseball tickets, dolls, and candy bars, Ms. Higgins might sell her time to the highest bidders. But since none of these conditions holds, she is likely to estimate the intensity of students' desire for her time from their classroom behavior. If they ask a lot of questions, she will give them a lot of answers. If they hold up their hands when she asks a question, she will call on them. If they are too shy or too ignorant to want her attention, she will let them be.

Myopic utilitarianism has something in common with moralistic justice: Both provide Ms. Higgins with a rationale for ignoring students who show no interest in learning. But moralistic justice tells Ms. Higgins to favor those who have made the most effort in the past, whereas myopic utilitarianism tells her to favor those who show the most interest now. Though these two groups usually overlap, they are seldom identical. Some students seek a teacher's attention in class but do very little work. Some do their work conscientiously but are too shy to seek attention in class. The two policies also differ in another crucial respect. Myopic utilitarianism provides no incentives for virtue and no punishments for vice. If Ms. Higgins is a moralist, for example, she will probably define looking out the window as a threat to classroom morale and will reprimand those who engage in such behavior. Myopic utilitarianism, with its implicit assumption that students are the best judges of their own needs, provides no rationale for punishing those who look out the window. If some students prefer looking out the window, that is their privilege—and ultimately, of course, their problem.

The most serious difficulty with trying to maximize student satisfaction is that what students want (and hence what they will choose, if given the chance) often differs from what will benefit them in the long run. The fact that some children do not want to improve their reading skills, for example, does not mean these children will not benefit from such skills when they reach adulthood. Thus though ignoring apathetic pupils seems both natural and just in the short run, it will often do these pupils irreparable damage in the long run. A strategy with this predictable result seems seriously flawed. (Popular discussions of this conflict often contrast what people "want" with what they "need," but because need can also be a synonym for "disadvantages," I will not use this terminology.)

Despite these objections, Ms. Higgins has at least three reasons for distributing her time and attention on the basis of student demand. First, she is likely to enjoy working with children who want her attention more than with those who do not. Second, ignoring apathetic students often helps keep the peace in the classroom. If Ms. Higgins puts pressure on those who want to be left alone, they may respond by misbehaving. If she leaves them alone, they may leave her alone too. Third, since there is never enough time in the day, Ms. Higgins will always see advantages in any policy that reduces the total number of things she feels she ought to do.

Although Ms. Higgins has self-interested reasons for espousing myopic utilitarianism, outsiders have equally good reasons for rejecting it. If Ms. Higgins accepts her pupils' values as fixed and ignores those who show no interest in learning, illiteracy will be more common than if she tries to alter their values. Those who are not in the front lines of the struggle against youthful ignorance and indolence will therefore urge Ms. Higgins to concentrate on her students' long-run interests rather than on their short-term preferences.

ENLIGHTENED UTILITARIANISM

Enlightened utilitarianism requires Ms. Higgins to distribute her time and attention so as to achieve the greatest good for the greatest number over the long run. I have described this policy as requiring Ms. Higgins to ask who will benefit most from her time, but this phrasing is potentially misleading. If adults were always fully compensated for whatever good they did others, and if adults also had to compensate others fully for any harm they did, a policy that maximized the long-term welfare of Ms. Higgins's students would also maximize the welfare of society as a whole. But Ms. Higgins cannot count on this happening. Many people who contribute either directly or indirectly to the happiness of others are not themselves happy in consequence. If Ms. Higgins thinks one of her students could become a widely read writer, for example, she can easily argue that this would promote the welfare of society as a whole, but she may have great difficulty convincing herself that it would benefit the student in question, who might be happier— and might also be a more responsible parent and a better citizen—if he or she ended up selling real estate. Thus, when I say that Ms. Higgins must ask which students will benefit most from her time, the reader should understand this query as requiring her to consider indirect benefits to society as a whole along with direct benefits to students in her class.

The first requirement of enlightened utilitarianism is a clear definition of the ultimate "output" Ms. Higgins is trying to maximize. Most research on the relative efficiency of different teaching strategies assumes that the only output of any importance is performance on a standardized test and that every one-point gain on such a test counts as much as every other. This implies that Ms. Higgins should try to maximize her pupils' mean reading score. But if Ms. Higgins sees her classroom as part of a larger social enterprise, she will think of her "output" not in terms of reading scores per se but in terms of what reading skills can do both for her pupils and for others. This may well lead her to value raising some pupils' scores more than raising other pupils' scores by an equal number of points.

If she is concerned with her pupils' eventual health and happiness, for example, she may conclude that helping her worst readers is more important than helping her best readers. She will not, it is true, be able to find detailed data on the health and happiness of adults who read at various levels of proficiency. But she will find that moving from the bottom to the middle of the socioeconomic distribution does more for an individual's health and happiness than moving from the middle to the top. So in the absence of more direct evidence she is likely to think that helping her worst readers will increase the mean level of health and happiness more than helping her best readers.[6] If her pupils must read at a specified level in order to be promoted to the seventh grade, this will presumably reinforce her commitment to helping her worst readers.

Ms. Higgins may, however, care more about the progress of the species than about the fate of individual pupils. In that case she is likely to worry more about whether her pupils will pursue careers that "make a difference" to others than about whether they will be happy themselves. If Ms. Higgins thinks about her "output" in these terms, she is likely to put more weight on helping her best readers than if she cares only about her own pupils' welfare.

Yet even if Ms. Higgins figures out how helping each of her students will influence long-term social welfare as she defines it, this will not suffice to tell her how she should spend her time. She must also figure out how much it will cost her to improve different students' skills. Two points are crucial here.

1. It takes more time to raise some students' scores than others'. Putting the point slightly differently, some students benefit more from a minute of Ms. Higgins's time than others do. Ms. Higgins is likely to believe, for example, that a minute of her time is more valuable to those who want it than to those who do not. She may also believe that the value of her time depends on a student's current skills. She may believe, for example, that her best readers learn as much when she gives them interesting books and leaves them alone as when she spends a lot of time with them. Alternatively, she may believe that if she spends a few extra minutes a week with her best readers she can get them to try much more difficult books than they otherwise would, dramatically improving their reading skills. At the other end of the scale, she may believe either that one-on-one attention helps her worst readers a lot or that it has no detectable effect.

2. Time spent with some students is more tiring than time spent with others. The way Ms. Higgins allocates her attention will therefore affect her overall capacity to pay attention. If working with indifferent or incompetent readers is more exhausting than working with eager or skillful readers, for example, focusing on the indifferent or the incompetent will force her to take more unofficial "rest breaks," during which she is not really teaching anyone. Indeed, it may drive her out of teaching entirely.

Taken together, these considerations mean that almost any imaginable distribution of Ms. Higgins's time and attention may turn out to be efficient. We cannot predict the most efficient distribution on a priori grounds. We need empirical data both on the way additional attention influences different students and on the way paying attention to different students influences Ms. Higgins. Furthermore, since efficiency depends partly on maximizing Ms. Higgins's overall capacity to pay attention, what is efficient for Ms. Higgins will not necessarily be efficient for other teachers.

It is also worth noting that even if Ms. Higgins is committed to myopic utilitarianism, humane justice, or moralistic justice, she is likely to claim that these goals are compatible with enlightened utilitarianism. If she is committed to keeping her students happy, for example, she is likely to argue that those who want her attention the most also benefit the most from it. If she is committed to helping her worst readers, she is likely to argue that they benefit most from her help. And if she is committed to rewarding virtue and punishing vice, she is likely to argue that this is the best way to maximize everyone's achievement. This suggests that enlightened utilitarianism has a powerful hold on the American imagination and that everyone feels obliged to claim that their behavior is consistent with it no matter what their primary goal may be. A moment's thought should, however, convince the reader that in practice enlightened utilitarianism will often conflict with myopic utilitarianism, humane justice, and moralistic justice. Students do not pursue their long-run interests in any consistent way, so myopic and enlightened utilitarianism often conflict. Some poor readers benefit very little from extra attention so humane justice and enlightened utilitarianism also conflict in many instances. And although indolence is an important obstacle to learning, withholding time and attention is not always the best way of motivating the indolent, so moralistic justice is often at odds with enlightened utilitarianism.

Despite these conflicts, enlightened utilitarianism is easy to reconcile with equal opportunity. If Ms. Higgins believes that her time is worth more to some pupils than to others, she will find it completely natural to assert that equal opportunity means giving equal attention to those who will benefit equally and unequal attention to those who will benefit unequally. At first glance this argument may strike some readers as tendentious. But we use precisely this argument to justify dramatic variations in college quality. As long as the best colleges take the students who will benefit most from attending them, we tell ourselves that the ideal of equal opportunity is not violated. From this perspective efficiency and equal opportunity are synonymous.

At least in America, the most powerful objection to enlightened utilitarianism is not that it sometimes conflicts with moralistic or humane justice but that it requires Ms. Higgins to know things that neither she nor anyone else knows. She seldom knows her ultimate social goals, and she never knows with any confidence how her social goals relate to individual reading scores or how her own activities affect individual reading scores. Uncertainty about these matters can have several consequences:

1. Although Ms. Higgins may not know the mathematical relationship between social efficiency and reading scores, or between reading scores and the way she spends her time, she is likely to have a keen appreciation of how different ways of spending her time affect her overall energy level and job satisfaction. She may therefore conclude that the most efficient distribution of her time is the one that leaves her with the most time to distribute. If she likes working with gifted students, for example, she may conclude that this is efficient. If she likes working with slow but eager learners, she may conclude that this is efficient.

2. Because she does not know what will maximize social welfare in the long run, she may try to minimize the likely cost to society of her mistakes. Under plausible assumptions this will lead her to devote equal time and attention to everyone. Alternatively, she may give up on efficiency and follow the dictates of justice or democratic equality.

DEMOCRATIC EQUALITY

Given all the uncertainties associated with the pursuit of justice and efficiency, Ms. Higgins may be tempted to look for another approach. One obvious possibility is to equate her time and attention with "opportunity" and conclude that a commitment to "equal" opportunity means giving all children equal time and attention. I refer to this as "democratic" equality not because democracy has traditionally required it but because Americans habitually invoke the fact that they live in a democracy to justify it. We will say, for example, that our Constitution guarantees everyone "equal protection of the laws" and that this implies equal treatment. The idea of treating everyone in the same way, regardless of extenuating circumstances, certainly has a democratic ring to it.

Yet neither the U.S. Constitution nor democratic tradition requires public agencies to treat everyone in exactly the same way. School boards, for example, have never interpreted democratic tradition as requiring them to spend equal sums on all pupils. They have set up programs of varying cost, especially at the secondary level, and have assumed that if they made these programs available on the basis of virtue, past or current disadvantages, demand, or expected benefits, this was compatible with both equal opportunity and the equal protection clause of the Constitution. Public hospitals, parks, libraries, housing projects, and social service agencies also draw distinctions among potential beneficiaries using these same criteria.

Nonetheless, the fact that public agencies often consider virtue, disadvantages, demand, and expected benefits when allocating public resources does not necessarily mean that Ms. Higgins should do so. The principles we use to distribute things vary with the nature of the things we are distributing. We try to distribute medical care on the basis of expected benefits, parks and libraries on the basis of demand, public housing on the basis of disadvantages, and government jobs on the basis of virtue. If the relative weight of these four distributional principles depends on what we are distributing, none can claim to be universal, and in some cases all may be irrelevant. Ms. Higgins must therefore ask whether any of the four principles really applies to her classroom. The arguments for ignoring all four principles would presumably go something like this.

VIRTUE. Virtue must be rewarded and vice punished in some way, but Ms. Higgins need not use her time and attention for this purpose. If judicious use of praise, blame, and grades ensures that most students do their best, Ms. Higgins can make her time equally available to everyone if she wishes.

DISADVANTAGES. Ms. Higgins cannot possibly rectify all the injustices that occur outside her classroom, and trying to do so may create a strong feeling of injustice within her classroom. Her pupils are likely to see her classroom as a self-contained universe, which should be just in its own right. Thus, they are likely to be deeply offended if Ms. Higgins favors some students over others on grounds not directly related to the students' classroom behavior. If Ms. Higgins respects her students' view of the classroom, she will find it impossible to favor the disadvantaged in many cases.

DEMAND. Although some children clearly want more attention than others, the arguments for taking such preferences into account are almost all practical, not normative. If Ms. Higgins is an idealist, she is likely to reject such arguments.

BENEFITS. Although Ms. Higgins will probably agree that in principle she should try to take account of potential benefits when distributing her time, she may well feel that in practice she has no way of knowing who benefits most from her time.

When there is no compelling argument for favoring one group over another, a commitment to equal opportunity implies that the "default option" is equal treatment for all. A commitment to equal opportunity thus requires people to give reasons for treating one another unequally. If Ms. Higgins favors some children over others and cannot give reasons for her behavior, she cannot claim to be providing equal opportunity.

One could take this argument a step further, insisting that if a society is committed to equal opportunity it must be able to justify unequal treatment in terms that almost all its citizens find persuasive. Since there is no general agreement about when Ms. Higgins can legitimately treat children unequally, demanding general acceptance of her reasons for distributing her time and attention unequally would mean requiring her to distribute them equally. In practice, however, outsiders seldom inquire closely into these matters, so she is free to follow any practice she likes as long as she herself finds her reasons persuasive.

CONCLUSIONS

If equal opportunity can mean distributing opportunity either equally or unequally, if it is compatible with inequalities that favor either the initially advantaged or the initially disadvantaged, and if the relative weight of these principles can vary from one situation to the next, it is small wonder that most Americans support the idea. A skeptic might wonder, however, whether an idea that can embrace so much means anything at all.

I think the ideal does mean something, but its meanings are almost all negative. It does not tell Ms. Higgins what to do, but it does tell her that she must avoid certain things. To begin with, as I have already noted, it tells her that if she devotes more time to one child than to another she must be able to justify her behavior. Not only that, but she must be able to justify it in terms of universally applicable principles that bear directly on the learning process. She cannot favor children because their parents are her friends, because they remind her of her daughter, or because they share her passion for bird watching. This ideal can never be fully realized. Ms. Higgins is not a computer, and she cannot see children simply as members of pedagogically relevant categories. Nor would we want her to do so. The ideal of equal opportunity does, however, assert that such "favoritism" must be kept to a minimum. Likewise, Ms. Higgins must ignore "irrelevant" social characteristics, such as race, sex, and family background, in allocating her time. If "irrelevant" characteristics of this sort turn out to be correlated with "relevant" characteristics like past effort, motivation, or actual competence, she must consult her attorney.

These same conclusions apply with equal force in noneducational contexts. When a firm proclaims itself "an equal opportunity employer," for example, its nominal message is that it does not discriminate against ethnic minorities or women. But the real message is that the firm has adopted a set of formal procedures for deciding what characteristics it will consider "relevant" and what characteristics it will consider "irrelevant" in making employment decisions. These procedures may or may not ensure that ethnic minorities or women get their "fair share" of the jobs, depending on how you construe fairness. But they certainly make it harder for the firm to fill positions on the basis of criteria that are completely unrelated to job performance, such as friendship, kinship, or walking in the door just as someone else is quitting.

Although a commitment to equal opportunity does rule out certain justifications for unequal treatment, it does not tell us which justifications are acceptable or when they are acceptable. Virtue, disadvantages, demand, or expected benefits may justify treating people unequally, but then again they may not. This conclusion also holds in employment as well as education.

Many conservatives insist, for example, that when a firm commits itself to equal opportunity in its employment policies it is simply committing itself to hiring and promoting those who will perform best in a given job. This stance leaves room for argument about whether the firm should emphasize applicants' probable performance immediately after being hired (myopic utilitarianism) or whether it should focus on their potential contribution to the firm over the long run (enlightened utilitarianism). But it leaves no doubt that the firm should pursue a policy that is "efficient" and either reject justice as irrelevant or insist that in the marketplace justice is synonymous with efficiency.

Liberals have repeatedly challenged this utilitarian view of equal opportunity. One such challenge is based on moralistic justice and asserts that firms have obligations to workers who have served them well in the past. Most workers feel that this is the case, and labor unions therefore insist that firms should reward workers who have performed conscientiously in the past with job security and promotions. Note that the emphasis is usually on past effort, not on outstanding past performance.

Those with a strong commitment to humane justice have also challenged employment policies that focus exclusively on efficiency. They usually argue that everyone has a right to acquire the habits and skills they need to perform well in a good job. If groups with equal "native ability," such as blacks and whites, currently have different probabilities of acquiring these habits and skills, that is society's fault, and society is responsible for remedying the situation. If schools cannot solve the problem, employers must try to do so. The "weak" variant of this theory requires employers to offer special training opportunities for blacks to compensate them for deficiencies in their schooling or upbringing. The "strong" variant requires employers to offer blacks jobs even if they do poorly in the training programs on the grounds that poor performance is evidence that the training program was inadequate. Readers will note that the problem of "moral hazard," which I discussed in connection with holding adults responsible for children's behavior, recurs when we hold whites responsible for blacks' behavior.

The one option that is not usually available to an equal opportunity employer is "democratic equality." When a firm has more applicants than jobs, it cannot treat all the applicants equally. It must hire some and not others. If the firm were really unable to see any compelling reason for hiring one applicant rather than another, it could, of course, give all applicants an equal probability of getting a job by using a lottery. But in practice firms almost always believe that some applicants are more promising than others, so lotteries are rare.

Because the ideal of equal opportunity forbids behavior we want to minimize while blurring disagreement about what we want to maximize, it will undoubtedly continue to command broad support. It is an ideal consistent with almost every vision of a good society. For liberal lawyers intent on expanding the domain of rights, equal opportunity implies that citizens have a right to lots of things they want but cannot afford, ranging from better schools to wheelchair ramps in public places. For progressive social reformers who want to minimize misery, equal opportunity implies that we need new social programs to help those who labor under one or another kind of disadvantage. For conservative economists who want to maximize economic output, equal opportunity implies that resources should go to those who will benefit most from them. For reactionary entrepreneurs, equal opportunity implies that the prizes for unusual success should not be tampered with in a misguided effort to achieve equal results. For politicians of all persuasions equal opportunity is therefore a universal solvent, compatible with the dreams of almost every voter in a conflict-ridden constituency. This makes equal opportunity one of the few ideals a politician can safely invoke on all occasions.

Without common ideals of this sort, societies disintegrate. With them, conflict becomes a bit more muted. But the constant reiteration of such rhetoric also numbs the senses and rots the mind. This may be a price we have to pay for gluing together a complex society, but if so there is something to be said for smaller, more politically homogeneous societies where the terms of discourse may not have to be quite so elastic.

ACKNOWLEDGMENTS

This paper was originally prepared for a conference on "Equal Opportunity: A Legitimate Ideal or a Cruel Hoax?" sponsored by the Center for the Study of Values at the University of Delaware on May 15–16, 1985. I am indebted to the Center for Urban Affairs and Policy

Research at Northwestern University and the Institute for Advanced Study for support while working on this paper and to Jane Mansbridge and Michael Olneck for critical comments on an earlier draft.

NOTES

1. Because my emphasis is on popular understandings of equal opportunity, I have not tried to tie my discussion to scholarly papers on the subject. Readers familiar with this literature will, however, find that it echoes many of the themes I discuss.

2. Richard Dobson, for example, calculated the correlation between father's education and secondary school grades in Syzran, a middle-sized city in the Soviet Union, and obtained a value of 0.32 (see "Class and Merit in the United States and the Soviet Union: A Comparative Study of the Determinants of Educational Expectations," presented at the 1979 meetings of the American Sociological Association). William Sewell and Robert Hauser reported a similar correlation among Wisconsin high school students (*Education, Occupation, and Earnings: Achievement in the Early Career,* New York: Academic Press, 1975).

3. My colleagues and I summarized this evidence in *Inequality* (New York: Basic Books, 1972). Subsequent work suggests that genes may have slightly more effect on test scores than was found in the *Inequality* data, but the differences are minor.

4. See, for example, James Crouse, "The Effects of Test Scores," in Christopher Jencks et al., *Who Gets Ahead?* (New York: Basic Books, 1979).

5. See Sandra Scarr and Richard Weinberg, "The Influence of 'Family Background' on Intellectual Attainment," *American Sociological Review* 43 (October 1978):674–692, and Barbara S. Burks, "The Relative Influence of Nature and Nurture upon Mental Development," *Yearbook of the National Society for the Study of Education* 27 (1928):219–316.

6. On happiness, see Norman Bradburn, *The Structure of Psychological Well-Being* (Chicago: Aldine, 1969). On health, see U.S. Bureau of the Census, *Social Indicators III* (Washington, D.C.: Government Printing Office, 1980), p. 90.

4

Race, Class, Power,
and
Equal Opportunity

JENNIFER L. HOCHSCHILD

Why are American race relations so tense? Why is racial inequality so hard to eradicate? What would equal opportunity for blacks look like; how can the United States provide it? This chapter seeks new answers to these old questions by starting with the seemingly paradoxical claim that race policy concentrates too much on race. Racial tensions and discrimination are entangled with inequalities of economic class and political power in ways that make them much harder to ameliorate than "simple" racial prejudice would be. Our purportedly most powerful tool for prying apart these entangled inequalities is the norm and historical practice of equal opportunity. It has had impressive, if not total, success in dealing with simple racial discrimination and has helped to loosen the links among race, poverty, and powerlessness for some blacks. Nevertheless, this chapter will contend, it can contribute surprisingly little to solving the current and future problems of race in the United States.

RACE, CLASS, AND POWER IN AMERICAN LIFE

Race

Racial prejudice is declining.[1] Most whites believe and profess to be glad that blacks are no longer second-class citizens. Larger and larger majorities of whites are convinced that racial prejudice by other whites is declining, reject discrimination based purely on race, and deny that they themselves are prejudiced.[2] They also perceive that our society is becoming more integrated.[3] Overall, whites are increasingly optimistic about the general situation of blacks;[4] by now, twice as many whites attribute the continuing disadvantaged state of blacks to personal faults as to discrimination,[5] and only 6 percent of whites see "the civil rights of minority groups" as one of the three most important issues facing the nation today.[6]

Blacks generally disagree. A majority are not optimistic about long-term changes in the situation of blacks.[7] They perceive much more lingering prejudice than whites do,[8] as well as much less reduction in discrimination.[9] Blacks are more than twice as likely to attribute blacks' disadvantaged state to discrimination as to personal faults.[10] Fully four-fifths are "dissatisfied" with "the way things are going in the U.S. at this time" (compared with half as many whites), and over one-third see "the civil rights of minority groups" as a critical issue for the nation today.[11]

We have, then, two very different views of U.S. race relations. Most whites want to believe that prejudice and discrimination, and their economic and political consequences, are declining and even disappearing. Blacks therefore can now be held largely responsible for their glaringly persistent problems. Many blacks, however, contend that the "civil rights revolution" merely provided a formal shell of equal opportunity, leaving most blacks where they have always been (except that whites no longer perceive a problem).[12] Neither belief is correct by itself. Pure racial discrimination has dramatically decreased, but its legacy of physical separation, psychological dysfunction, and behavioral discrimination persists.

Consider prejudice first. Although most whites now reject any expression of prejudice, some do not. In 1978, one-third of whites agreed that "blacks want to live off the handout" and that "blacks are more violent than whites"; in 1985, one-fourth agreed that "blacks have less ambition than most other people."[13] Three-fifths would oppose a friend's or relative's marriage to a black, and four-fifths would oppose their own child dating a black.[14]

And the willingness to express racial prejudice may be only the tip of the iceberg. Some psychologists argue that although "old fashioned racism" has become socially and emotionally unacceptable to most whites, "modern [or symbolic] racism" persists. Although most whites no longer express distaste for blacks, they continue to "resist . . . change in the racial status quo," now because of "moral feelings that blacks violate such traditional American values as individualism and self-reliance, the work ethic, obedience and discipline."[15] Psychologists find both experimental and survey evidence of modern racism. For example, whites who score high on a modern racism scale (as well as high scorers on an old-fashioned racism scale) misperceive the physical distance between themselves and a black experimenter across the room but make few mistakes when the experimenter is white. In another study, subjects evaluated the records of job candidates who were identical except for race; those scoring high on the modern racism scale rated black candidates either more negatively or more positively than they rated equivalent whites.[16]

More controversial are claims that the responses of whites on race-related survey questions express thinly disguised racism rather than what the respondents themselves claim to be arguing. From this perspective, modern racism is indicated by findings that whites' attitudes toward busing, "law and order," and black mayoral candidates are more strongly related to "pure" racial prejudice and political conservatism than to respondents' political party identification or to the effect of busing or crime on their own lives.[17] Finally, even whites who enthusiastically or resignedly accept the principles of integration express great reluctance about policies designed to implement it.[18]

More important, however, than expressed racial attitudes is whether whites act in ways that treat people of different races differently. If they do not, racial prejudice is a personal, psychological problem more than a political one; if they do, then consciousness of racial prejudice may be immaterial from the perspective of the black person being harmed.

Differential treatment by race is declining but has not disappeared. Consider wages first. Slightly more than half of the apparent racial disparity in incomes stems from differences in age or sex (which have no connotations of racism) or from differences in experience, education, seniority, labor market participation rates, family structure, hours worked, or background (all of which may or may not have connotations of racism, depending on how one explains the differences). The rest of the apparent racial disparity in incomes—10 to 20 percent—is explained by nothing measured except difference in race. Thus, to cite only one representative datum, even if the races were identical in their education, work experience, hours worked per year, occupation, and region of residence, black men would still have earned 88 percent of white men's earnings and black women only 64 percent of white men's earnings in 1979.[19]

Wage discrimination has declined overall, especially for certain categories of workers. If we hold labor force characteristics and hours worked constant, black men earned about 81 percent of white men's earnings in 1959 (compared to 88 percent in 1979), and black women earned about 53 percent (compared to 64 percent twenty years later).[20] Full-time working women and well-educated young men have reached parity with their white counterparts,[21] and young black college graduates married to another earner and living in the North or West now earn more than comparable whites.[22] I will address the implications of these data later; for now it is enough to note that wage discrimination has declined, persists, and varies across the black population.

Employment discrimination shows the same three features—decline, persistence, and variation within the black population. The good news is that blacks now occupy positions that they could not have held three decades ago—television news anchors, elected officials in predominantly white districts, supervisors of white subordinates. Blacks, who hold 9.8 percent of all jobs, hold almost 6 percent of "managerial and professional" jobs, 8.4 percent of "technical, sales, and administrative support" jobs, and 7.1 percent of "precision production, craft, and repair" jobs.[23] They were virtually excluded from all these occupations three decades ago.

The bad news is just as easy to document. The black unemployment rate has remained at least twice that of whites since the 1950s, and the disparity is growing. Black unemployment rises first and falls last as unemployment rates change. This phenomenon seems impervious to changes in the overall condition of the economy, the degree and nature of white unemployment, changes in blacks' residence by region and urbanization, and decreasing racial differences in education.[24] It becomes even more serious when we note that many more blacks than whites have dropped out of the labor force altogether in recent years, thereby making them unavailable even for unemployment as we define it.

Youth unemployment shows more disparity between races and a greater increase in disparity than adult unemployment. Almost two and one-half times as many black teens in the labor market are jobless as comparable whites.[25] The white teen unemployment rate has remained almost steady for twenty-five years, whereas the black rate has almost doubled.[26] Black youths are arguably not unemployed by choice; a recent large demonstration project found that 63 percent of eligible unemployed black teens, but only 22 percent of similar whites, accepted a job at the minimum wage, and black participants kept their jobs longer.[27]

Particularly disturbing is the fact that black teens are increasingly disvalued as employees just as they are becoming increasingly well educated. By 1975, the proportion of black children enrolled in school had caught up to the proportion of white children;[28] the black dropout rate has declined since 1970,[29] and blacks are slowly approaching whites in the amount of education they attain.[30] Many more blacks than whites remain functionally illiterate, but black illiteracy is declining.[31] At the other end of the scale, black achievement scores are steadily gaining on white scores.[32] Black Scholastic Aptitude Test (SAT) scores are rising, whereas white SAT scores are not.[33] Thus teens' most important form of human capital—education—suggests that racial disparities in youth unemployment should be decreasing, not increasing.[34]

Even successful blacks hold lower-status jobs and are perhaps less likely to be promoted than similar whites. "Overall, black occupational advancement in the 1970s is not particularly impressive. . . . Although a higher proportion of blacks could be found among the professional and technical occupations in 1980 than in 1972, they were concentrated in jobs at the lower end of the professional pay scale." In addition, blacks' pay increases were small relative to those of whites; the black/white ratio of earnings for white collar workers actually declined in the 1970s from 91 percent in 1973 to 86 percent in 1980.[35]

Finally, racial discrimination in rewards for improving one's job qualifications is also declining but has not disappeared. For example, in 1959 one additional year of elementary or secondary schooling was worth $.35 per hour for a white man but only $.12 for a black man; by 1979, the respective values were $.46 and $.36. An additional year of labor market experience improved white men's earnings by $.15 an hour in 1959 and $.28 an hour in 1979, but "black men are paid roughly half as much for their labor market experience as white men [and] labor market experience has very little, if any, financial payoff for women."[36]

Jobs and earnings are not the only arenas in which we can measure progress or its absence in U.S. race relations. White men were three to four times more likely than black men, and white women were about twice as likely as black women, to attend college from 1955 to 1969. The 1970s showed clear progress; whites of both genders were only one and one-half to two times as likely to attend college as blacks. Since 1980, the odds against blacks' attending college have again risen, although not to the levels of the bad old days.[37] Wealthier blacks are always more likely to attend college than poorer blacks, and the discrepancy has grown considerably since the late 1970s.[38] Again we see progress, persistent racial gaps, and disparity among blacks.

A final social indicator, residential integration, shows the most glacial rate of progress of all. Despite their expressed preference for integrated neighborhoods,[39] wealthy blacks are less likely to live in suburbia than middle- and low-income whites. More precisely, income differences counted roughly one-seventh as much in 1960 and one-eighth as much in 1970 as race differences (controlling for income) in explaining the racial disparity in suburbanization.[40] This fact is particularly important given evidence that "it is the suburban rather than city blacks who were the recipients of most of the occupational upgrading during the 1970s."[41]

Residential segregation declined a bit more during the 1970s than during the previous decade. The index of dissimilarity (a scale ranging from 0, which would indicate random distribution of blacks and whites in a metropolis, to 100, which would indicate complete racial separation) declined from 76 in 1960 to 73 in 1970 to 66 in 1980 for the 203 metropolitan areas in the United States with more than 4 percent black residents. But residential segregation remains immune to changes in economic status; blacks with family incomes over $50,000 remain just as isolated from equally wealthy whites as blacks with family incomes under $5,000 remain from equally poor whites. In short, money does not buy for blacks one of the perquisites it buys for whites—the freedom to live where one wants.[42]

Thus, by all measures of economic success, blacks do worse than whites. Blacks are better off now compared to whites than they were twenty or thirty years ago, and some blacks are much better off, but white complacence is no more warranted than black despair. Perhaps most disturbing is the finding that blacks are less able than whites to translate some success into further success. In the aggregate, more education does not lead to more and better jobs for teens at the same rate across races; professional jobs do not lead at the same rate to higher-level professional jobs; wealth does not lead at the same rate to the residential perquisites of wealth. In short, blacks have a harder time getting a foothold on the ladder of success than do whites and have a harder time climbing the ladder if they get onto the first rung. Nevertheless some, at least, are somewhere on that ladder—a point that makes the relationship of class to race increasingly salient.

Class

The disadvantages of poverty add to, perhaps even multiply, the disadvantages of race. When the stigma of the "wrong" race accompanies the stigma of poverty, white Americans are especially eager to distance themselves from those (they hope) so different from themselves. Rejection of poor blacks may even drive them to accept middle-class blacks. For example, after presiding for ten years over a school desegregation case, one judge wrote a plan that desegregated outlying regions of a large school district but left the central city ghetto almost untouched. He did so, he explained privately, because he realized that middle-class whites would permit middle-class blacks in their schools but would not put up with ghetto children. His political judgment may have been wrong (although subsequent events suggested that, if anything, he overestimated whites' tolerance), and it may even be constitutionally suspect. But the point here is that he, who knew the circumstances of the case better than anyone, saw the real dividing line falling between well-off and poor blacks rather than between blacks and whites.

Other school desegregation plans have also united the middle class of both races against poor blacks, although seldom with such a clear-eyed understanding of why. In Richmond, California, the desegregation plan called for middle-class and "upper-middle-class children [of both races] . . . to be integrated into . . . the only ghetto school that had a brand new plant, that was being developed as a demonstration school with a specially selected staff, and that already had several federally funded special projects offering academic enrichment and innovation."[43] Similarly, middle-class whites who resist mandatory desegregation—*especially* those who resist mandatory desegregation—are often the first to enroll their children in magnet schools for the gifted and talented.[44] This phenomenon demonstrates, not that whites are not racist as magnet school supporters often insist, but that they are discriminatingly racist. That is, their eager acceptance of middle-class blacks underlines their rejection of poor blacks. Since middle-class whites for four decades have encouraged school district consolidations that bring poor and wealthy whites into the same school (through busing, take note), we can infer that the interaction between race and poverty, not race alone or poverty alone, makes forced busing so abhorrent to them.

The only systematic data I know on the importance of class in whites' racial attitudes come from a 1969 study of 204 white members of a Los Angeles County liberal organization. Ninety-six percent reported a strong dedication to integration, and many joined their organization to work for civil rights. Yet they sharply distinguished between middle-class and poor blacks. Only 15 percent would limit busing into white schools to middle-class blacks. However, 56 percent endorsed only middle-class black entrants into their occupation; 75 percent endorsed integration in their neighborhood only for middle-class black families; 55 percent would rent an apartment to middle-class blacks; and 59 percent would hire only a middle-class black.[45] These social and cultural preferences are neither surprising nor hard to explain, but they do underline the difficulty that poor blacks face in entering a predominantly middle-class white society.

Blacks' behaviors as well as whites' attitudes are affected by the double disadvantage of being black and poor. Puerto Rican, Jewish, Chinese, and black children show both "racial and ethnic differences in the *patterns* of . . . verbal, reasoning, numeric, and spatial abilities" and social class effects on level of ability. But "social class has a particularly profound effect on the performance level of black children, lower-class status depressing performance more for these children than for children from the lower classes of other ethnic groups."[46] School desegregation plans that benefit middle-class black children and many white children sometimes make poor black children worse off than when they started.[47] Poor blacks perform worse on SAT tests than poor children of other ethnicities, and the racial discrepancies among poor children are greater than the comparable discrepancies among wealthier children.[48] Average differences in reading scores between blacks and whites have recently increased for disadvantaged urban and rural children, although they continue to decline for children without special disadvantage.[49]

At least through the 1960s, race and class also combined to increase disparities in school funding and resources. Black schools in Chicago (and elsewhere) received consistently fewer local funds than white schools in neighborhoods of similar economic status.[50] Similarly, schools in poor neighborhoods received fewer funds than schools in wealthier neighborhoods, independent of race. And the disadvantages of race and class cumulated: Low-status black schools received the least funding, less than higher-status black schools and less than equally low-status white schools. Conversely, high- and even medium-status white schools received more funds than white schools of lower status or black schools of equal status. The same phenomenon occurs with resources other than money; low-status schools in Richmond, California, had more probationary (inexperienced) teachers than high-status schools, but low-status black schools had many more such teachers than low-status white schools.[51]

The most serious manifestation of cumulative inequalities is the fact that, even as the black middle class is growing in size and strength, poverty among blacks continues to be wider spread and deeper than poverty among whites. Forty-six percent of black children are poor, and half of poor black children live below 50 percent of the poverty line. By comparison, only 17 percent of white children are poor, of whom 40 percent live below 50 percent of the poverty line.[52] Poor blacks are increasingly isolated among other poor blacks, away from middle-class members of their own or other races, not to speak of middle-class institutions such as good schools, jobs with chances for promotion, and a clean and safe neighborhood.[53]

TABLE 4.1: Family Incomes at Selected Points in the Income Distribution for Recession Years, by Race (1982 dollars)

	1961	1971	1975	1983
Mean income, all families				
whites	$21,773	$28,553	$28,839	$28,979
nonwhites	12,717	19,280	19,917	19,755
ratio, nonwhite/white	.584	.675	.692	.682
95th percentile				
whites	48,387	61,790	62,837	67,262
nonwhites	33,123	46,327	47,756	51,131
ratio, nonwhite/white	.685	.750	.760	.760
60th percentile				
whites	22,135	28,880	29,533	29,347
nonwhites	12,748	19,093	20,391	19,516
ratio, nonwhite/white	.576	.661	.690	.665
20th percentile				
whites	9,955	13,511	13,339	12,492
nonwhites	4,584	7,308	7,361	6,020
ratio, nonwhite/white	.460	.541	.552	.482
Ratio, 20th/95th percentile				
whites	.206	.219	.212	.186
nonwhites	.138	.158	.154	.118
Absolute difference, 95th − 20th percentile				
whites	38,432	48,279	49,498	54,770
nonwhites	28,539	39,019	40,395	45,111

Source: U.S. Bureau of the Census, *Current Population Reports,* Series P-60, No. 146, *Money Income of Households, Families, and Persons in the United States: 1983* (Washington, D.C.: Government Printing Office, 1985), pp. 49–50.

More generally, the poorest fifth of black families have a smaller share of total black income than the poorest fifth of white families have of total white income, and the wealthiest 20 percent of black families earn more of black income than the wealthiest fifth of white families earn of white income.[54] And these intraracial disparities are growing stronger over time. Table 4.1 shows incomes at the ninety-fifth, sixtieth, and twentieth percentiles for blacks and whites in recession years (chosen in order to hold unemployment rates roughly comparable).

Table 4.1 shows first that real incomes have risen for both groups and all income levels since 1961. In addition, nonwhite incomes are on average moving closer to white incomes, as the third row indicates. However, the second, third, and fourth columns show that only the wealthy—of both races—enjoyed rises in real income in the 1970s and early 1980s. Poor nonwhites lost so much income that by 1983 they were considerably worse off than they had been a decade earlier, as the eleventh row shows. No other group lost nearly as high a proportion of its income or as much money in absolute dollars.

More important, middle- and (especially) low-income nonwhites—but not wealthy nonwhites—lost ground compared to comparable whites between 1975 and 1983. Finally and most important the poor lost so much income both relatively and absolutely (and the wealthy gained so much) that they lost ground compared to wealthy members of their own race over these two decades. Consider the bottom four rows. The ratio of incomes of the poor to those of the rich within a race is lower in 1983 than it was in 1961. Similarly, the gap between the highest and the lowest incomes considered here is larger, by well over $16,000 for both racial groups, in 1983 than in 1961. In short, poor blacks increasingly have a lot in common with poor whites and well-off blacks with well-off whites. This is not to say that race does not matter any more—it does—but it is to say that race is less and less the only thing that matters in understanding what W.E.B. DuBois termed "the problem of the color line."

Evidence on mobility within and across generations also shows increasing disparities between rich and poor blacks and therefore the increasing importance of considering class along with race. Up to the 1960s, blacks were almost uniformly poor throughout their adult life. Similarly, the black class structure across generations was one of "perverse openness"; severe social and economic discrimination made children of well-off black parents just as likely to be poor as children of poor black parents. Both forms of immobility changed with the advent of civil rights laws and prosperity, so that black patterns of mobility resemble white patterns more than they used to. Between 1962 and 1973, "the effect [on the job held in 1973] of status [i.e., family background] declines for whites while it increases for blacks, reducing the differential in the process." Furthermore, by 1973 there was arguably a more robust class structure among blacks than among whites in two senses of that term. Blacks who were upwardly mobile during the 1960s were more likely to have well-off parents than were comparably mobile whites or were more likely than comparable whites to come from the ranks of blacks with relatively good jobs in 1962.[55]

A critical question about the relationship between race and class cannot be answered by the aggregate data discussed so far: Does it *feel* different to be a poor black than a poor white, in ways that affect how one acts to shape or take advantage of one's life changes? Is the problem of black poverty like that of white poverty, only worse; or is it really a different problem because poor blacks live in a different culture from poor whites?

We have very little reliable evidence on this question, and what we do have points in different directions. Some argue that most poor blacks hold the same values and aspirations as poor whites and the nonpoor; what they lack is opportunity to achieve their aspirations.[56] In this view, the unquestionably higher rates of birth to unwed young mothers, drug usage, crime, and so on in black ghettos are adaptations to a hostile and threatening environment. Poor whites face a less severe environment so manifest fewer of these reactions; the middle class of both races faces a relatively benign environment so manifests even fewer. Others argue that poor blacks and poor whites share a "culture of poverty" created by their economic circumstances and even by efforts to help them escape poverty.[57] Still others agree that the culture of poverty is qualitatively different from middle-class culture, but claim that the culture helps to create the poverty as well as vice versa.[58] Finally, and most disturbing, we have new arguments that the culture of poor black ghettos not only is different from that of white slums and middle-class neighborhoods but also is profoundly harmful and apparently self-perpetuating. Whether poverty and racism have created the black underclass or simply reinforced an already existing pathology, whether the underclass is growing, even how it should be defined and who constitutes it—these questions remain unanswered at present. What is clear is that some poor blacks live far from traditional American values with enormously self-destructive and socially destructive consequences.[59]

The best recent effort to demonstrate the dimensions of the underclass shows that about 2.6 million people live in underclass census tracts. These are neighborhoods of between 2,500 and 8,000 people that are at least one standard deviation above the national mean on four measures of behavioral deviance: high school dropouts, prime-aged men not in the labor force, welfare recipients, and female-headed households. Almost all underclass tracts are in urban areas, virtually all are in tracts in which at least 20 percent of the residents are poor, and 60 percent of them coincide with tracts in which 40 percent or more of the residents are poor. Underclass tract residents are 58 percent black (and 11 percent Hispanic).[60] These data say nothing about the causes or cures of black poverty, but they do at least show that poor black communities have severe behavioral as well as economic problems.

In the next section, I will deal with the political and philosophical implications of whether black poverty is like white poverty only more so or whether it is a different and much more severe problem. Here I conclude only that the addition of class to the consideration of problems of race enormously complicates both our analytic understanding and our programmatic prescriptions. On the one hand, economic

differentiation and a class structure now exist in the black community—
an indisputable improvement over the almost uniform poverty of the
past. On the other hand, that differentiation means that public policies
designed to help blacks as a group have different effects and sometimes
even negative effects on the most needy group. Our society is in danger
of enabling most blacks to escape their disadvantaged past at the cost
of pushing a few into even worse poverty, degradation, and isolation.
Little wonder that the problem of race in the United States is so
intractable; it is at least as much a problem of class.

Power

Regardless of whether deviance causes poverty or vice versa, and
whether prejudice has really or only apparently declined, the position
of blacks on average is and has always been less desirable than that
of whites. Why don't they do something about that? More precisely,
why don't blacks try to impel individual whites or white society generally
to grant respect, education, and jobs to blacks in the same proportions
and for the same reasons as to whites?

Part of the answer, of course, is that they have and continue to try,
through activities ranging from slave rebellions to civil rights marches
to economic boycotts. Another part of the answer is that some, perhaps
many, blacks simply do not want to join white society on any terms.
But part of the answer is that blacks lack power to impel whites to
do much of anything they do not want to do. Blacks continue to suffer
from discrimination and continue to be disproportionately poor, at least
in part because they continue to be relatively powerless.

Social scientists do not even agree on what power is, never mind
how to measure it or evaluate its legitimacy. Nevertheless, it is clear
that powerholding in the United States, like economic opportunity or
social standing, formally is distributed equally but actually is distributed
unequally by race (among other things).

Citizens' beliefs about the distribution of power provide one type
of evidence for this assertion, since power depends partly on perceptions
of who holds power. On average, blacks feel less politically efficacious
than whites do and see the government as less responsive to their
needs.[61] During the past several decades, black alienation has risen
and black feelings of efficacy have declined at a faster rate than white.[62]
Yet 62 percent of blacks (compared to 44 percent of whites) reported
an increased interest in politics between 1980 and 1984, and "blacks
were more likely than whites to have engaged in a variety of campaign
activities, such as attending a political rally (30 percent of blacks vs.
17 percent of whites), distributing candidates' literature (17 percent

vs. 8 percent), and . . . helping to register voters (30 percent vs. 9 percent)."[63] The combination of these findings suggests that black alienation and inefficacy do not reflect lack of effort or involvement by blacks in the political system. Rather, they result despite proportionally greater involvement—implying that the problem lies more in the government being perceived than in the citizens doing the perceiving.

Survey data also suggest one reason why blacks feel powerless—whites' resistance to (potentially) powerful blacks. The number of whites who profess willingness to support a qualified black presidential candidate has dramatically increased, from 38 percent in 1958 to 77 percent in 1984. However, 16 percent still reject a black candidate out of hand, and history shows that "the 'undecided' vote breaks overwhelmingly for a white [candidate]. . . . Thus the 16 percent 'no' response in 1984 added to the 7 percent 'no opinion' response yields a total of 23 percent . . . that we can assume would automatically oppose a black candidate."[64] That arithmetic means that even if a black candidate could count on the support of virtually all black voters, he or she would have to win over half of the purportedly nonracist 77 percent of white citizens. That is a tall order given the likelihood that some of that group gave the socially desirable rather than the accurate answer to the survey question and given the empirical record of black candidates winning no more than 20 percent of white voters in almost all local elections.[65]

Evaluations of specific political leaders also suggest that whites support black political power less than meets the eye. In 1984, fewer citizens saw Jesse Jackson as "part of the group that runs things in the country" than saw Jerry Falwell, Eleanor Smeal, or Ralph Nader as part of the ruling elite.[66] Whites praised Jackson's personal attributes, but his endorsement of Walter Mondale and Geraldine Ferraro led almost twice as many to reject the Democratic ticket as to embrace it.[67] Although a plurality of New Yorkers who watched the Mondale-Hart-Jackson television debate felt that Jackson had "won," he received only 6 percent of the white vote in New York's Democratic presidential primary.[68]

Political actors, like ordinary citizens, did not take Jackson's presidential aspirations seriously. The media portrayed him as a successful campaigner, powerful personality, and important party figure—but not as a contender for the Democratic nomination.[69] The Democratic party rejected his plea to change party rules for delegate selection, with the consequence that he won 18 percent of the popular vote in the primaries but received only 10 percent of the pledged delegates.[70] Walter Mondale and Gary Hart ignored Jackson during the debates, and Mondale complained after the election that Jackson made "life quite difficult for me."[71]

Of course, Jesse Jackson is not the only black candidate, and whites have plenty of reasons to oppose him besides his race. Whites do campaign and vote for black candidates, as Senator Edward Brooke and Mayors Wilson Goode and Tom Bradley can attest. And black constituents have steadily gained political clout even in majority white voting districts since the passage of the Voting Rights Act. Even in the conservative political climate of the 1980s, conservative southern Republican members of Congress are as anxious as liberal northern Democratic colleagues to distance themselves from the South African government and old-fashioned American racism.[72] Most important, of course, the number of black elected officials has risen fourfold in the past fifteen years. So here too progress is incontrovertible, even astonishing by historical American standards.

But more progress is not assured. The recent rise in black office holders from nonexistent to miniscule (just over 1 percent)[73] may slow if typical racial voting patterns persist. That is, "for blacks themselves to secure and retain office, they must generally rely upon black voters,"[74] and the power of black voters to elect blacks to office depends on their concentration, number, and organizational resources. Each factor is problematic.

First, consider concentration. Redistricting to give blacks a majority of voters in a given district is largely responsible for the recent rise in black elected officials. Simple arithmetic implies a ceiling on that means of increasing black power, although I know of no calculations on how far we now are from that presumed ceiling.[75]

The second factor—increasing the number of black registrants and voters—is being pursued with vigor and success. Through recent efforts, "black political participation is at its highest crest since the great breakthroughs of the 1960's."[76] Yet again arithmetic rears its ugly head. The recent 6.3 percent increase in registration of blacks yields fewer people than the parallel 1.2 percent increase in registration among whites, since whites so greatly outnumber blacks. The upshot of the registration drives of the 1980s is more new white than black voters.[77]

The third route to black electoral success—the use of organizational resources—is the first point at which the role of class enters this discussion. "As black income increases in absolute terms, and as it rises vis-à-vis white income, the chances of black representation [on city councils] are improved. . . . In more affluent black communities, one is more apt to find 'appropriate' black candidates, money, political skill, and the precious commodities of time and effort." In short, "for blacks to succeed in electoral politics, socioeconomic resources are critical."[78] Thus until recently blacks had difficulty in attaining office even in districts in which they had the requisite numbers and concentration because whites disproportionately controlled the resources essential to winning elections. That barrier is rapidly being overcome, as the increase in black mayors and other local officials demonstrates. But black candidates in racially mixed districts still face the problem of relatively few organizational resources in the black community as well as the more obvious racial barriers to election.

Even if it is now largely a matter of time until blacks generally win elections in majority black districts, the links between economic and political inequalities do not dissolve. Blacks are concentrated in districts that are especially likely to be poor. For example, "in every southern state, family incomes in majority black . . . counties are substantially below the median for the state. The incidence of families below the poverty level is almost twice as great in black counties as in the region."[79] An examination of the fifty largest cities in the United States shows that seven of the fifteen cities with the greatest growth in poverty population between 1970 and 1980 (including the four worst off on this measure) had black mayors in 1987. Seven of the fifteen cities with the greatest socioeconomic disparity between the central city and its suburbs (including five of the seven worst off on this measure) have black mayors. Conversely, none of the fifteen cities with the least growth in poverty (in all but three of which poverty declined) have black mayors; only (Los Angeles) of the fifteen cities with the least disparity between city and suburbs enjoys a black mayor.[80] In short, successful black candidates often find themselves in districts that have too few resources to permit them to do much with their new power.

For once, evidence bears out the logic of this argument: Black mayors are at most only partly successful in using their office to increase their own or other blacks' power. The presence of a black mayor has a "small but discernable" impact on the number and importance of black public employees in that city.[81] However, "blacks fare better in some cities than in others regardless of whether they have a black mayor, and the presence of a black mayor is no guarantee of success."[82] One study found that black mayors brought in relatively more federal and state funds than white mayors did, but black city council members were associated with fewer funds. "The effect of black mayors on city spending patterns is small," and the effect of increasing black representation on the city council is nonexistent.[83] Only one (Los Angeles) of the ten cities that gained the most in Community Development Block Grants (CDBG) between 1980 and 1985 had a black mayor; four of the ten that lost the most CDBG funds had black mayors during some or all of the period.[84]

Beyond that of very scarce resources, black mayors and city council members have an additional reason for having so few effects. A black mayor can choose either the strategy of Tom Bradley of Los Angeles, who goes out of his way to avoid the image and actions of a "black mayor,"[85] or that of Harold Washington of Chicago, whose campaign and mayoralty are addressed almost entirely to blacks. Both strategies constrain the mayor's actions if the distribution and use of power are at all zero-sum. With the former strategy, the black leader must not offend or harm his or her white constituency, so the leader cannot do too much for blacks. With the latter strategy, the black leader may do as much as possible for the black constituency, but that may be little given the persisting power and resources of the white opponents.[86] The problems of balancing competing claims and stretching scarce resources are not, of course, unique to black mayors, but they do suggest why expanding black power through the electoral process is not a panacea.

The problem is similar at the national level. Blacks can choose either to stand united against white politicians and voters, in which case their claims will be clear but unsuccessful, or to enter into coalitions with whites, in which case their claims may be victorious but compromised. The choice as presented here is too stark, but even in the best of circumstances a 12 percent minority in a racially divided majoritarian democracy has to face some unpleasant arithmetic.

If electoral politics has seemingly inexorable limits, what about other avenues toward power? Blacks clearly are much better represented in foundations, corporate headquarters and boardrooms, university faculties and administrations, judgeships, and other presumed seats of non-electoral power. In the long run, the implications of those changes for power holding may be as great or greater than the implications for economic position discussed earlier.

But here too the extent of real progress is ambiguous. Blacks in large businesses fear that they are tokens, shunted into nonessential positions and quick to be discarded when the economic and political tides turn.[87] Blacks even fear that the increase in the power of blacks in white society may have the perverse effect of reducing it overall. Many blacks, for example, see racial integration as deliberately or inadvertently reinforcing white power at the expense of blacks. The first and most powerful of such claims came from the book and civil rights organization that popularized the phrase "black power."[88] But they are not unique. Proponents of community control of ghetto schools see centralization in large school districts as simply a transfer of power from black neighborhoods to distant, white-controlled bureaucracies.[89] Black opponents of mandatory school desegregation argue similarly:

Thomas Minter, the black superintendent of schools in Wilmington, Delaware, noted in 1970 that metropolitan-wide desegregation would leave blacks "bereft of education, bereft of an educational identity, [and without] a school board just as they have gained some degree of control over it."[90] (White Wilmington parents led the drive to integrate city and suburban schools in New Castle County just—coincidentally or not—when blacks first won a majority on the city's board of education).

Even some former civil rights leaders have second thoughts about their own earlier integrationist goals. Jesse Jackson claimed that "the same forces that were in power controlling segregation are now in power controlling desegregation. They're using desegregation to the same ends that they used segregation."[91] Derrick Bell and Robert Carter now argue that integration too often defuses the community bases for black power without substituting the chance to attain power in white communities.[92] Most shocking of all to well-meaning whites is James Meredith's recent outburst. The heroic integrator of the University of Mississippi in 1962 now declares that "integration is the biggest con job ever pulled on any group of people. . . . It was a plot by white liberals to gain black political power for themselves and their wild ideas, and for a few black bourgeoisie who were paid to exercise leverage as black spokesmen. I've never heard any other black person say integration did one good thing for them." He calls for ending "white superiority" through "tak[ing] control of our neighborhoods, our businesses, our schools."[93]

How should we evaluate such statements? Do they reflect simply the old guard's resistance to changes they did not lead or a desire to make headlines? The evidence is sparse and impressionistic, but it suggests that these claims have some validity. When school districts are consolidated for desegregation, for example, the school board and administrators of the black district typically lose their positions or are demoted. The Louisville, Kentucky, school board voted itself out of existence when the black city schools merged with the surrounding white suburbs of Jefferson County. When the white district of Ferguson-Florissant, Missouri, merged with the heavily black districts of Berkeley and Kinloch, only one school board member from each of the minority districts retained his post on the new school board, compared to three of the five board members from the large white district. The white superintendent kept his position; the black superintendents were demoted. The two black districts handed over the power to make contracts—"all property, records, books and papers, and . . . funds"—to the new, white-run district office. The consequences for pupil reassignment, facility use, and control in general were predictable.[94]

Aggregate data across school districts are unreliable but suggestive. The National Education Association claimed that between 1967 and 1972 (when desegregation reached its peak in the South), at least 8,000 southern black teachers were "dismissed, . . . demoted, assigned out of field, or unsatisfactorily placed." Between 1963 and 1971, the number of black high school principals dropped by two-thirds in ten southern and border states, even though white principals were being hired.[95]

These facts tell us nothing about why black educators are demoted or not hired when districts desegregate, but they do lend credence to the claim that as black children enter the white world, black adults lose power. It does not require too much paranoia to take the next step—to argue that whites will do what is necessary to keep control and that if they lose on one front they will find a way to win on another.[96]

A second kind of indirect evidence also suggests that black fears about integration are not (only?) paranoia. Black businesses have gained few, and in some cases have lost, customers as a result of desegregation of white stores, restaurants, and services.[97] Many black business people and professionals have gone from being big fishes in a small pond to being small fishes in larger ponds, to the degree that material resources and economic standing in a community translate into political power, desegregation has arguably harmed not only them but also blacks as a group.

Finally and most controversially, some commentators argue that the new class and power disparities within the black population have led black elites to abandon the poor and powerless masses left behind. In this view, the NAACP and Urban League focus too much on affirmative action for corporate executives and elite college applicants; Jesse Jackson focuses too much on the aggrandizement of Jesse Jackson; black mayors focus too much on achieving insider status in the Democratic party. Black elites are even accused of not really trying to eliminate black poverty and deprivation so that they can maintain their positions as outraged victims and recipients of social welfare largesse.[98] This view is deeply contentious in the current political atmosphere, but it boils down to the rather mundane observation that blacks are like whites— where they stand depends heavily on where they sit.

We are left at this point with a few answers and many more questions. Does racial integration actually diminish black power in crucial ways? How can we tell? How important for redistributing resources and changing perceptions are electoral offices compared with less obviously political positions such as school principal or factory foreman? How much does the fact of being a small minority in a majoritarian system actually matter in political bargaining and negotiation? Are blacks' experiences of powerlessness similar to those of powerless whites, only more so, or is blacks' lack of political control a qualitatively different and much more severe handicap?

We lack answers to these questions, and I will address implications of various possible answers in the next section. We do, however, know enough to conclude the cumulative inequalities among race, class, and power significantly worsen the inequalities of each dimension alone. If we accept that conclusion, we can move on to examine its implications for the practice and philosophy of equal opportunity.

CUMULATIVE INEQUALITIES
VERSUS EQUAL OPPORTUNITY

Can the United States lessen cumulative inequalities? Will it choose to do so? The answer to these questions, as to so many others, is "It depends." It depends on everything ranging from who is next elected president, to how well the economy does, to what blacks demand. Here I address only one part of this contingent world: how definitions of equal opportunity interact with understandings of cumulative inequalities.[99]

Let us begin with the simplest case. Prospect-regarding equal opportunity "consists of practices under which the prospects of success are equal for all; . . . nothing about the people affects the result." Examples are lotteries, drawing lots, or flipping coins.[100] A necessary condition for this form of equal opportunity is that everyone be subject to the same rules and have the same chance of being chosen. Some people may not have two entries in the pool to win the trip to Niagara Falls, and others none.

Expanding this definition enough to make it useful here yields the claim that prospect-regarding equal opportunity requires ending de jure segregation and ensuring equal citizenship rights. Blacks must be allowed to enter the same schools and restaurants under the same rules of selection as whites. Blacks must be able to vote and run for office by following the same procedures as whites. In short, "nothing about the people [may] affect" the rules under which they operate in society.

Prospect-regarding equal opportunity, both in its pure form of random selection and in its expanded form of abolishing ascriptive criteria for public actions, is relatively unproblematic. It is philosophically coherent and no longer subject to political debate. Virtually no laws mandating racial discrimination remain on the books, and virtually no community in the United States remains untouched by the civil rights reforms of the 1960s. Isolated exceptions probably exist—hence the "virtually"—

but overall blacks are legally equal to whites in their opportunity to attain social, economic, and political goals.[101]

If the problem of race in the United States is only or predominantly a problem of racial discrimination, then ensuring prospect-regarding equality of opportunity may be sufficient as well as necessary to solve it. That is, if blacks are disproportionately poor and powerless because they have been prohibited from engaging in important public actions, then, one can argue, ending those prohibitions will eventually end blacks' disproportionate disadvantages. That outcome will occur because blacks will now have the same prospects for success as whites, so that chance alone will eventually close the gap between the races. Note that this claim holds only for goods that are distributed by rules that take no account of the qualities of the persons involved in the distribution. There are not many such goods in a complex social system.[102] Nevertheless, the argument that, whatever else it must do, a liberal polity must ensure prospect-regarding equality of opportunity to all citizens is politically powerful and philosophically coherent.

It is the contrasting form of equal opportunity that generates political and philosophical trouble. Means-regarding equal opportunity requires the provision of not only equal rules but also equal "equipment . . . —a box of tools, a set of skills. . . . The purpose and effect of these equal means is . . . legitimately unequal prospects of success."[103] Activities ranging from a poker game to a high school education are examples of means-regarding equal opportunity. Everyone abides by the same rules (a full house beats three of a kind, grades of D or better lead to promotion); everyone is given the same means (seven cards; free and compulsory school attendance). The purpose of the activity is to distinguish winners from losers in ways that people deem fair because the outcome reflects relevant characteristics of the actors.

The provision of means-regarding equal opportunity in a racial context requires more than abolishing de jure segregation and second-class citizenship. It calls for providing equal means, not just identical rules, to blacks and whites. At a minimum, schools must be desegregated and/or improved so that black children have the same academic experience as white children; employers must pay the same wages and grant similar promotions to equally qualified blacks and whites; cities must be redistricted so that electoral arithmetic favors black candidates in some places as much as it favors white candidates in others. At a maximum, resources must be redistributed so that every child faces adulthood (and every young adult faces maturity) with a similarly middle-class background.

As these examples suggest, means-regarding equal opportunity ranges from being philosophically coherent and politically feasible to being philosophically unintelligible and politically unattainable. It all depends on how one defines means and what the polity must do to provide equal means.

We can begin to examine the implications of changing the meaning of means-regarding equal opportunity by returning to its original definition. Contestants are to be given equal "equipment," such as "a box of tools, a set of skills." These pieces of equipment, however, differ importantly from each other. Let us define "a box of tools" more generally as external means and "a set of skills" as internal means. The former are things that society can give to a person without in any immediate sense changing the character or personality of that person. The latter are things that society can give to a person only by changing character or personality.

Modern liberals begin with a focus on external means. Someone— presumably the state in the absence of any other actor—should provide better schools to black students, better job prospects to poor black mothers, better odds of winning an election to black candidates. Conservatives generally reply that the state should not so provide, and arguments ensue about how large the box of tools should be, what it should contain, who should receive it, and who should pay for it in order for equality of opportunity to exist. The U.S. political system is well equipped for such arguments. Pluralist mechanisms for interest group representation, our propensity to engage in distributive politics, our society's relative wealth and generally growing economy, our acceptance of the legitimacy of individual self-interest—all make us comfortable with debates over the relationship between external means and equal opportunity.

The idea of an equal box of tools makes equally good philosophical sense as a way to begin to provide means-regarding equal opportunity. It is perfectly intelligible to argue that poor black children in a society in which possibly hostile whites control most resources have fewer opportunities than comparable white children or than black middle-class children, or than black children in black-controlled communities. It does not require great philosophical subtlety to argue that granting poor and powerless black children a relatively large box of tools will diminish the importance of luck at birth and accentuate the importance of individual traits in determining who will win the race of life.

However, the "box of tools" understanding of means is more problematic than I have described so far. Politically, it may be difficult, even impossible, to promulgate and implement laws that grant as many external means as some think necessary to provide means-regarding equal opportunity. School desegregation is a clear case of a powerful political consensus in the abstract combined with controversy and chaos

in particular circumstances. Virtually everyone agrees that equal education is an essential element of equal opportunity and that segregated
or inferior schooling denies equal education to some. Nevertheless, we
cannot agree on the specifics of "an equal education," nor are many
parents willing to risk what they expect will be high costs to their
children so that others' children may acquire whatever "an equal
education" is.[104] Thus the fact that the political process is well-equipped
to debate how many and what kinds of tools to grant does not guarantee
that it will grant many of them. The severe inequalities of race, class,
and power previously described are precisely the kinds of circumstances
that most Americans are not prepared to eliminate through government
grants of external means.[105]

The concept of granting an equal box of tools to all also begins to
break down philosophically when pushed very far. First, the whole
notion relies on the empirical assumption that race, poverty, and
powerlessness are cumulative, not interactive, inequalities. That is, it
assumes that the powerless black poor are just like the powerless white
poor, only more disadvantaged, and that the poor are like the middle
class, only disadvantaged. If that is the case, it makes sense to seek
to eliminate external disadvantages so that internal differences may
shine through. But if poor blacks differ qualitatively from poor whites
(or if the poor differ qualitatively from the middle class), giving everyone
the same external means has an ambiguous normative status. If some
people are emotionally unable to use or do not know how to use their
tools to run the equal opportunity race, providing equal tools makes
their opportunities more equal only in a purely formal sense. A
philosophically responsible argument must then consider whether that
formal provision of tools suffices or whether recipients should be
retrained to use their tools effectively. And what if some choose not
to use their new tools to play the equal opportunity game? Should we
assume that they are simply opting out and leave them alone (but what
of their children?), or should we assume that they have been so
damaged by racism, poverty, and powerlessness that they are not making
a free choice and therefore must be further provided for? The correct
treatment of these issues is not obvious.

I will return to this crucial ambiguity soon but first consider another
philosophical problem with the box of tools. This problem is conceptually analogous to political debates over how many tools the polity
owes its citizens: When does equal opportunity begin, how long does
each opportunity last, and how does one opportunity relate to the
next? If public education is compulsory and funded by the state, has
society satisfied its responsibility to give entrants to the labor market
an equal box of tools? If not (e.g., because schools vary in ways that

students cannot be blamed for), is redistribution of educational resources necessary or sufficient? If not sufficient (e.g., because first-graders begin school with different experiences of books), is day care from infancy onward necessary, sufficient, or desirable? And so on. These questions address the issue of when equal opportunity begins. A more serious if less commonly recognized issue is when it ends. If one does poorly in first grade, thus entering the slow reading group in second grade, how and when can one ever wipe the slate clean and start over again? And hard as it is to imagine what it means for an individual to stop one opportunity cycle and start another, it is even harder to imagine that process for a society. Must the polity intervene continually or intermittently to stop the game, reallocate the tools, and send winners and losers alike to the same (new) starting line? Both doing so and not doing so seem equally to violate the spirit of equal opportunity.

Others have discussed these problems of the psychological and temporal boundaries on equal opportunity.[106] Here I have space only to note the complex links between this philosophical muddle and the political controversy over race. If philosophers could agree that grants of X amount of external means, for Y years, beginning at age Z, were sufficient to provide means-regarding equal opportunity for all, then the political problems would be greatly diminished. They would not disappear; many people might refuse to pay enough taxes to give X amount of external means (and in any case, politicians might well ignore the philosophers). But given the strength of Americans' belief in equality of opportunity, our traditional generosity to others at least during periods of economic expansion, and the evidence presented earlier that most whites now reject racial discrimination, a normative consensus on where public responsibility for ensuring equal opportunity between the races begins and ends might generate a lot of political support.

Of course, no such consensus exists. Nor is it even possible, since the whole metaphor of "the race of life" is intrinsically indeterminate. Note that the absence of philosophical consensus need not imply political dissensus. On some issues, such as the need for affirmative action policies and an Equal Rights Amendment, politicians and citizens are no more united than are philosophers. But on other issues, the lack of a firm philosophical justification for their view does not keep Americans from rough concurrence. Most citizens apparently agree that society should ensure an equal education to all but not an equally good first job. The race of life starts at age eighteen years in this view, for no particularly good philosophical reason. Nevertheless, the fact that philosophers could not possibly agree on what the box of tools ought to include surely does not make it any easier for political actors to reach a stable agreement.

Despite these difficulties, however, means-regarding equal opportunity defined as providing external means seems simple compared to its alternative—providing an equal set of skills. Such internal means, which change the character or personality of their recipient, could range from teaching all first-graders that reading is fun to ensuring that all adults are equally talented and ambitious. The institutional mechanisms could run from Boy Scout troops to Kurt Vonnegut's Handicapper-General.[107] Most debates over this more extensive form of equal opportunity focus on deciding how much energy and resources the state should devote to equalizing a few critically important skills. But the more serious problems lie less in the range of possible expenditures on state actions than in their type.

Twentieth-century Americans are, in general, much more reluctant to intervene in socialization than in the distribution of goods. Although we strongly believe in the sanctity of private property and minimal government, these norms have long been violated in practice through income and property taxes, Supreme Court decisions restricting the use of private landholdings, and the vast array of laws that redistribute resources from some categories of citizens to others.[108] In contrast, our strong norms of individual rights, privacy, and family autonomy have, if anything, been strengthened over the years with Supreme Court decisions on birth control, abortion, the rights of natural over adoptive parents, due process of law for students and welfare recipients, and so on. If providing means-regarding equal opportunity requires intervening in the family, especially with the care of young children, Americans do not support or practice much public provision of equal opportunity.

This point should not be exaggerated, of course. Most Americans are more willing to pay to change welfare recipients' work habits, ability to read, and motivations than to provide the recipients with an attractive job. Schools teach values clarification and sex education. The Supreme Court based the need to desegregate schools largely on the importance of shaping the "hearts and minds" of both black and white children. And it was more willing to require schools to change views than to redistribute educational resources.[109]

Nevertheless, James Madison largely achieved his goal of shifting the terms of debate from "opinions and passions" to "interests." The U.S. political process is much better suited to debating issues of changing people's resources than of changing their character. There is, for example, no analogue for representing ideological or psychological viewpoints to the single-member geographically based congressional districts that make distributive politics so natural in the United States.

Philosophical difficulties with the idea of providing internal means reinforce political difficulties. Consider from a different angle the political problem of deciding where to stop. If it makes sense to try to change children's ability to read, then why not also seek to change their motivation to learn to read? And if that too makes sense, why not seek to change their desire to become an auto mechanic into a desire to become a college professor? At some point down that road, we stop thinking of children as distinct personalities who deserve to be given the skills to fulfill their goals and start thinking of them merely as distinct bodies whose skills and personalities should be made equal (read, "identical") in order to permit them to differentiate themselves as adults. But if "equal skills and personalities" are defined broadly enough over a long period of childhood, then we reach the conservatives' nightmare—children become undifferentiated vessels into which society pours the right mix of ingredients to produce identical contents.

We have here two philosophical problems (as well as a political disaster and a mixed metaphor). First is a variant on the old problem of free will and determinism. What is part of the child's character, and what is contingent on external conditions and therefore an appropriate subject for intervention? Second is a variant on the problem of "the race of life." When do we declare that all children have an equal enough set of skills so that we may switch from providing equal means to encouraging their remaining differences to distinguish them in accord with the ideal of equal opportunity? As far as I can tell, neither of these problems admits of an answer; both are bottomless swamps to be skirted around rather than plunged into.

I have strayed far from race, class, and power, but not, I think, irrelevantly. These political and philosophical difficulties are all too relevant to the question of what to do about racial inequalities. Consider the implications of finding that poor black children have fundamentally different skills and outlooks from poor white or middle-class children. If that is the case, ensuring equal opportunity to succeed in mainstream society requires the provision of much more than an equal box of tools. It requires both abolishing some of the skills and values that poor black children begin with and adding many more.

The political difficulties of that conclusion are clear. Add to our general reluctance to interfere in families and individual choices whites' unwillingness to commit the resources needed to reshape black ghettos and redirect their residents. Add further blacks' understandable reluctance to permit a majoritarian (i.e., white-dominated) political system to direct that interference, and we have a stalemate. Blacks will mistrust special programs for poor blacks, and whites will probably not give such programs many resources in any case. Broader programs for the poor or for all children either will not address the special problems of poor blacks or will be so watered down as to have little effect on anyone, or both.

The philosophical difficulties of concluding that poor and powerless blacks need extraordinary intervention are even clearer. We cannot determine how many and which differences between poor blacks and everyone else are contingent consequences of living in circumstances of severe isolated poverty and impotence, and how many are deliberately chosen personal distinctions or voluntarily retained cultural heritages. The whole idea of an individual or culture deciding which features to retain or abolish is psychologically miscast; many of a person's or culture's most distinctive characteristics are unconscious and unchosen. In short, the more seriously we take the idea of equalizing the internal means of whites and blacks—especially if some poor and powerless blacks form a psychological and cultural "underclass"—the more our politics and our philosophy fail us.

We have reached, to coin a phrase, an important crossroads. Prospect-regarding equal opportunity, with its strong philosophical foundation and its powerful political support, has been a stunning success as far as it goes. After 350 years, blacks finally have attained the same formal rights and chances as whites. More important, the combination of prospect-regarding equal opportunity and the provision of some external means to some blacks has also met with impressive success. Blacks in a good position to do so—those with some combination of a middle-class background, stable two-earner marriage, good education, gumption, and luck—were able to use the civil rights movement and the expansion of social welfare in the late 1960s to break out of the trap of cumulative inequalities. Thanks to them, the United States now has a thriving black middle class and powerful black politicians.

But equal opportunity is ill-suited to dealing with the remaining problems of race in the United States. Prospect-regarding equal opportunity cannot touch them. The current liberal view is that a sufficient amount of external means—whether through guaranteed jobs, a guaranteed annual income, reshaping electoral districts, changing the delegate selection process for presidential conventions, or some other mechanism—would break the links between race, poverty, and powerlessness. But we seldom redistribute from middle-class whites to poor blacks. And liberals' philosophical base for the box of tools is strong only if one assumes that poor and powerless blacks are just like everyone else except worse off and if one ignores the insoluble problem of where equal provision should end and inequality-generating opportunity begin.

Those problems are not trivial, but they pale beside the political and philosophical problems of means-regarding equal opportunity defined as the equal provision of internal means. This much more sweeping form of equal opportunity—by a curious political history, now associated with conservatives—addresses many more of the problems of cumulative inequalities identified than the first two forms but its implementation is extremely problematic. Americans are much less willing to intervene in family interactions than in the distribution of goods, and our political structures are set up to inhibit rather than to foster such intervention. The philosophical basis for changing characters is, if anything, weaker than the political basis because it plunges one into the swamp of distinguishing inherent or chosen traits from contingent or disvalued traits of persons and cultures. In short, if cumulative inequalities of race, class, and power are associated with deep emotional or cognitive failings of poor and powerless blacks (regardless of the causal relation between personality and circumstance), then the ideology of equal opportunity is no longer much help.

Luckily, equal opportunity is not the only norm driving political change and philosophical argument in a liberal society. For that we should be grateful. If my analysis is correct, an ideal that seemed at first blush the most powerful lever available for prying apart the cumulative inequalities of race, class, and power is not so powerful after all. Perhaps we should seek another tool.

ACKNOWLEDGMENTS

My thanks to the National Academy of Education's Spencer Foundation Fellowship for supporting this research and to C. Anthony Broh, Elizabeth Bussiere, Thomas Cavanagh, Amy Gutmann, Christopher Jencks, Jane Mansbridge, Daniel Monti, David Pavelchek, and Alan Wertheimer for their very helpful comments on various drafts of the chapter.

NOTES

1. To keep complexity manageable, I am ignoring ethnic groups other than blacks and whites. This exclusion is defensible for two reasons: (1) The histories of Asians and Hispanics in the United States are distinctive and deserve separate treatment; and (2) the history of problems between blacks and whites eclipses the problems of integrating successive waves of non-Anglo immigrants. See, for example, Stanley Lieberson, *A Piece of the Pie* (Berkeley: University of California Press, 1981); Christopher Jencks, "Affirmative Action for Blacks," *American Behavioral Scientist* 28, no. 6 (July/August 1985):731–760.

2. By 1984, 73 percent of white respondents agreed that "most white people want to see blacks get a better break . . . or don't care either way" (Joint Center for Political Studies, *News from JCPS*, "JCPS Releases In-Depth Survey of Black Political Attitudes," August 30, 1984, Table 2). In 1978, only 15 percent of whites agreed that "blacks are inferior to white people," down from 31 percent in 1963 (Louis Harris and Associates, *A Study of Attitudes Toward Racial and Religious Minorities and Toward Women* [New York: Louis Harris and Associates, 1978], p. 16). Given a choice among "desegregation, strict segregation, and something in between," the proportion of whites choosing "strict segregation" declined from 25 percent in 1964 to 5 percent in 1978 (Philip E. Converse et al., *American Social Attitudes Data Sourcebook, 1947–1978* [Cambridge, Mass.: Harvard University Press, 1980], p. 611).

3. In 1970, about one-third reported black coworkers and only 6 percent had black supervisors; by 1978, one-half had black coworkers and fully 25 percent reported black employers and supervisors. These work relations are almost universally characterized as "pleasant and easy." In 1964, 82 percent of whites reported all white friends; by 1976, only 50 percent had no black friends. Over 90 percent of whites think "blacks are getting a better break in getting jobs than they did ten years ago," and fewer than one-fifth perceive employment discrimination. Only about one-fourth of whites perceive discrimination against blacks in such things as acquiring jobs, pay, and promotions or treatment by police, teachers, labor unions, homeowners, and other actors (Converse et al., *American Social Attitudes*, p. 75; Harris, *A Study of Attitudes*, pp. 4–5, 18–21, 32. See, more generally, pp. 5–13 and 26–34).

4. Thirty-nine percent of white respondents in 1964, 49 percent in 1968, and 63 percent in 1976 felt that there has been "a lot" of "real change in the position of [blacks] in the past few years" (Converse et al., *American Social Attitudes*, p. 79). And by 1984, 68 percent of whites believed that "compared with five years ago, . . . the situation of black people in this country is better" (only 4 percent thought it was worse) (Thomas Cavanagh, *Inside Black America* [Washington, D.C.: Joint Center for Political Studies, 1986], p. 3).

5. CBS News/*New York Times* Poll, *The Kerner Commission—Ten Years Later* (New York: CBS News/*New York Times* Poll), appendix, p. 9.

6. Of the eleven issues presented to them, white respondents chose only one—relations with South Africa—less often than "civil rights of minority groups" (Cavanagh, *Inside Black America*, p. 7).

7. The proportion of black respondents who think there has been "a lot" of "real change in the position of [blacks]" declined from 60 percent in 1964 to 32 percent in 1976, exactly mirroring the rise in white optimism. Similarly, only 37 percent of blacks thought in 1984 that "the situation of black people" is better than it was five years ago; fully 30 percent thought it was worse (Converse et al., *American Social Attitudes*, p. 79; Cavanagh, *Inside Black America*, p. 3).

8. In 1978, only 37 percent of a national sample of blacks thought there was "real hope" of "ending . . . racial prejudice and discrimination in the U.S. in the long run," a decline from 49 percent optimistic respondents a decade

earlier (CBS/*New York Times* Poll, *The Kerner Commission,* appendix, p. 19). If anything, this question underestimates black pessimism because it sampled only urban residents, thus undersampling well-off blacks who are more pessimistic and who perceive more discrimination than poor blacks. See Robert Reinhold, "Poll Indicates More Tolerance, Less Hope," *New York Times,* March 26, 1978, p. 28. In 1984, fewer than one-fourth of blacks thought whites want to see blacks "get a better break"; 40 percent thought whites "want to keep blacks down" (Cavanagh, *Inside Black America,* p. 3).

9. Two-thirds report white coworkers, up from 59 percent in 1970. And 40 percent of blacks report that half of their friends are white, up from 23 percent in 1964. So blacks do perceive some decline in racial separatism. But fewer blacks than whites report "pleasant and easy" work relations—about three-fourths—and over one-half attribute low status jobs or unemployment to discrimination. Blacks' concern about job discrimination increased from 1968 to 1978, while whites' concern declined. Up to 75 percent of blacks have felt discriminated against in at least one important area of their lives, such as housing, treatment by policy, and a variety of employment issues (Harris, *A Study of Attitudes,* pp. 2–5, 18–21; Converse et al., *American Social Attitudes,* p. 75). Seventy-two percent of blacks, compared with 31 percent of whites, think President Reagan is prejudiced (Cavanagh, *Inside Black America,* p. 33).

10. CBS News/*New York Times* Poll, *The Kerner Commission,* appendix, p. 9.

11. Cavanagh, *Inside Black America,* pp. 3–7.

12. For a forceful, though flawed, version of this argument see Alphonso Pinkney, *The Myth of Black Progress* (Cambridge: Cambridge University Press, 1984).

13. Harris, *A Study of Attitudes,* p. 16; Harris Survey, "Poll Results Contradict Claims that Prejudice Is Increasing," February 18, 1985, p. 3.

14. Harris, *A Study of Attitudes,* pp. 3, 14–16. White endorsement of the wishy-washy "something in between" desegregation and strict segregation increased between 1964 and 1978 from 48 to 61 percent. Forty percent of white respondents still agree that "most blacks ask for more than they are ready for" (Converse et al., *American Social Attitudes,* p. 61). Further evidence on continuing, although diminished, racial prejudice is in Tom Smith and Glenn Dempsey, "The Polls: Ethnic Social Distance and Prejudice," *Public Opinion Quarterly* 47, no. 4 (winter 1983):584–600.

15. Donald Kinder, "The Continuing American Dilemma," *Journal of Social Issues* 42, no. 2 (summer 1986):151–172. See also the article by Paul Sniderman and Philip Tetlock, and Kinder's response, in the same issue.

16. For a summary of these and other experiments, see John McConahay, "Modern Racism, Ambivalence, and the Modern Racism Scale," in John Dovidio and Sam Gaertner, eds., *Prejudice, Discrimination, and Racism* (New York: Academic Press, 1986), pp. 91–125.

17. John B. McConahay and J. C. Hough, Jr., "Symbolic Racism," *Journal of Social Issues* 32, no. 2 (1976):23–45; David O. Sears, Carl P. Hensler, and Leslie K. Speer, "Whites, Opposition to 'Busing': Self-Interest or Symbolic

Politics?" *American Political Science Review* 73, no. 2 (June 1979):369–384; Douglas S. Gatlin, Michael Giles, and Everett F. Cataldo, "Policy Support Within A Target Group: The Case of School Desegregation," *American Political Science Review* 72, no. 3 (September 1979):985–995; Michael Giles, Douglas S. Gatlin, and Everett F. Cataldo, "The Impact of Busing on White Flight," *Social Science Quarterly* 55 (1974):493–501; David Sears et al., "Self-Interest vs. Symbolic Politics in Policy Attitudes and Presidential Voting," *American Political Science Review* 74, no. 3 (September 1980):670–684.

18. Howard Schuman, Charlotte Steeh, and Lawrence Bobo, *Racial Attitudes in America* (Cambridge, Mass.: Harvard University Press, 1985), pp. 73–104.

19. Reynolds Farley, *Blacks and Whites: Narrowing the Gap* (Cambridge, Mass.: Harvard University Press, 1984), figures 3–5.

20. Ibid.

21. Black women working full time now earn a median income of $9,300, compared to white full-time working women's earnings of $10,400. The gap between black and white male workers is over $4,000 (Farley, *Blacks and Whites*). On the effects of college education on narrowing the racial wage gap, see James Smith and Finis Welch, "Black-White Male Wage Ratios, 1960–1970," *American Economic Review* 67 (June 1977):323–338.

22. Bernard E. Anderson, "Economic Patterns in Black America," in National Urban League, *The State of Black America* (New York: National Urban League, 1982), p. 29; and U.S. Bureau of the Census, Current Population Reports, *The Social and Economic Status of the Black Population*, Special Studies P-23, no. 80 (Washington, D.C.: Government Printing Office, 1979), pp. 42, 199.

23. U.S. Bureau of the Census, *Statistical Abstract of the United States, 1987* (Washington, D.C.: Government Printing Office, 1987), pp. 385–386.

24. Michael Reich, *Racial Inequality* (Princeton, N.J.: Princeton University Press, 1981), p. 34; U.S. Bureau of the Census, *America's Black Population: 1970 to 1982*, PIO/POP-83-1 (Washington, D.C.: Government Printing Office, 1983), p. 9.

In addition, blacks are unemployed for longer periods of time and are less likely to be working full time when they do hold jobs, compared to whites (William O'Hare, "Unemployment: A Look Behind the Numbers," *Focus* [newsletter of Joint Center for Political Studies, Washington, D.C.] 11, no. 10 [October 1983]:5).

25. Black teenage unemployment has hovered around 40 percent during the 1980s, compared to 15 to 20 percent for white teens.

26. In 1960, 14 percent of white and 24 percent of black teens were unemployed *(Economic Report of the President, 1983* [Washington, D.C.: Government Printing Office, 1983], p. 201).

27. The project ran from 1978 to 1980 and involved 7,100 teenagers (George Farkas et al., *Impacts from the Youth Incentive Entitlement Pilot Projects: Participation, Work, and Schooling over the Full Program Period* [New York: Manpower Development Research Corporation, 1982]). The most elaborate study of black youth unemployment provides evidence both in support of and against this claim of young blacks' willingness to work. See Richard Freeman

and Harry Holzer, eds., *The Black Youth Unemployment Crisis* (Chicago: University of Chicago Press, 1986).

28. Eighty-six percent of both races were enrolled in elementary and secondary school (U.S. Bureau of the Census, *The Social and Economic Status,* p. 88).

29. Richard Whalen, "The Transition from High School," in National Center for Education Statistics, *The Condition of Education, 1985* (Washington, D.C.: Government Printing Office, n.d.):201–237.

30. Robert Hauser, "Notes on the Distribution of Schooling in the Black Population, 1940–1980" (Madison, Wis.: Center for Demography and Ecology, University of Wisconsin, 1986). Despite the title, the data in this paper go up to 1985.

31. National Assessment of Educational Progress, *Literacy* (Princeton, N.J.: Educational Testing Service, n.d. [c. 1986]).

32. National Assessment of Educational Progress, *The Reading Report Card* (Princeton, N.J.: Educational Testing Service, n.d. [c. 1985]); Lyle Jones, "Trends in School Achievement of Black Children" (Chapel Hill, N.C.: University of North Carolina, Institute for Research in Social Science, 1987).

33. Dave M. O'Neill and Peter Sepielli, *Education in the United States: 1940–1983* (U.S. Bureau of the Census, Special Demographic Analysis, CDS-85-1, Washington, D.C.: Government Printing Office, 1985), Table A-4, p. 51. See also Jones, ibid.

34. Furthermore the wages of black male youth have fallen compared to those of white youth since 1968. For discussions of this problem (including the absence of clear explanations for it), see William Darity and Samuel Myers, "Black Economic Progress" (Madison, Wis.: Institute for Research on Poverty, Discussion Paper no. 613-80); Richard McGahey and John Jeffries, *Minorities and the Labor Market* (Washington, D.C.: Joint Center for Political Studies, 1985), pp. 11–18; and Freeman and Holzer, eds., *Black Youth Unemployment.*

35. Diane N. Westcott, "Blacks in the 1970s: Did They Scale the Job Ladder?" *Monthly Labor Review* 105, no. 6 (June 1982):29–38.

36. Farley, *Blacks and Whites,* pp. 67–72. See also Linda Datcher, "Effects of Community and Family Background on Achievement," *Review of Economics and Statistics* 64, no. 1 (February 1982), especially pp. 39–40.

37. Reynolds Farley, Memorandum to Education Panel, Committee on the Status of Black Americans, National Academy of Sciences, April 1, 1987.

38. Robert Hauser, "College Entry among Black High School Graduates" (Madison, Wis.: University of Madison, Center for Demography and Ecology, Working Paper 87-19, 1987), Figure 8.

39. In a 1982 survey of blacks, 60 percent of respondents with an opinion would prefer to live in a neighborhood that is half black, half white (James A. Davis and Tom W. Smith, *General Social Surveys, 1972–1983: Cumulative Codebook* [Chicago: University of Chicago, National Opinion Research Center, 1983], p. 117).

40. Albert Hermalin and Reynolds Farley, "The Potential for Residential Integration in Cities and Suburbs: Implications for the Busing Controversy," *American Sociological Review* 38 (October 1973):595–610.

41. Westcott, "Blacks in the 1970s," p. 33.

42. Reynolds Farley and Robert Wilger, "Recent Changes in the Residential Segregation of Blacks from Whites" (Ann Arbor: University of Michigan, Population Studies Center, May 1987), Tables C and F. Controls for education show the same result as in earlier decades; college-educated blacks are as residentially isolated from similar whites as grade-school educated blacks are from analogous whites. Farley and Wilger go on to show that residential segregation results from whites' preferences to live with other whites; "blacks do not make great efforts to isolate themselves from whites" (pp. 11–13). Blacks are also much more segregated from whites than are other ethnic groups, even groups such as Asians and Hispanics who are recent immigrants with significant language barriers (pp. 13–14).

43. Lillian B. Rubin, *Busing and Backlash* (Berkeley: University of California Press, 1972), pp. 45–49.

44. See, for example, Janet Schofield, *Black and White in School* (New York: Praeger, 1982), pp. 182–211.

45. Their reasons vary from fears about dangers to whites from aggression to concern that poor blacks would not be comfortable in a white middle-class environment. Just to confuse the picture, however, note that the forms of integration that are the least economically oriented—busing in public schools and quotas in colleges—are the most troublesome for these white liberals. No data are reported on respondents' views about poor whites (Judith Caditz, *White Liberals in Transition* [Holliswood, N.Y.: Spectrum Publications, 1976], pp. 56–81.

46. Sue Berryman, "Integrating the Sciences," *New Perspectives* 17, no. 1 (winter 1985):20.

47. Robert Crain et al., *Making Desegregation Work* (Cambridge, Mass.: Ballinger, 1982), pp. 144–147. Conversely, middle-class whites may actually thrive in otherwise poor black schools because the white students suddenly enjoy relatively high status and extra attention. See George Noblit and Thomas Collins, "Cui Bono? White Students in a Desegregating High School," *Urban Review* 13, no. 4 (winter 1981):205–216; Margaret Orr and Francis Ianni, "The Impact of Culture Contact and Desegregation on Whites of an Urban High School," *Urban Review* 13, no. 4 (winter 1981):243–260.

48. Leonard Ramist and Solomon Arbeiter, *Profiles, College Bound Seniors, 1985* (New York: College Entrance Examination Board, 1986), pp. 37, 47, 57, 76.

49. Jones, "Trends in School Achievement."

50. White schools also received more of the other resources we normally associate with better schools, such as more experienced teachers, smaller class sizes, and substitute teachers when regular teachers are absent. We cannot, of course, assume that more resources necessarily translate into better education or more learning, but ceteris paribus, more money is better than less (Harold M. Baron, "Race and Status in School Spending: Chicago 1961–1966," *Journal of Human Resources* 6, no. 1 (winter 1981):3–24). Chicago was not unique, nor was this problem limited to the 1960s. See, for example, Bill Olds, *Are*

Minority Pupils Shortchanged? (Hartford, Conn.: Civil Liberties Union, 1982); Lydia Chavez, "Two Bronx Schools: Study in Inequality," *New York Times,* July 2, 1987, pp. A1ff.

51. Twenty-four percent of teachers in high-status white schools, 43 percent of teachers in low-status white schools, and 63 percent of teachers in low-status black schools were probationary (Rubin, *Busing and Backlash,* p. 45).

52. U.S. Bureau of the Census, *Characteristics of the Population Below the Poverty Level: 1983,* Series P-60, no. 147 (Washington, D.C.: Government Printing Office, 1984), pp. 5, 25, 26.

53. See, for example, Richard Nathan and Paul Dommel, Statement to U.S. Senate Committee on Governmental Affairs, "Needed—A Federal Safety Net for Communities," June 25, 1987: Appendix A; and William Wilson, "The Ghetto Underclass and the Social Transformation of the American City," lecture, Annual Meeting of the American Association for the Advancement of Science, Chicago, February 15, 1987.

54. U.S. Bureau of the Census, *Money Incomes of Households, Families, and Persons in the United States, 1983,* P-60, no. 146 (Washington, D.C.: Government Printing Office, 1985), pp. 49–50.

55. The idea of "perverse openness" comes from Otis Dudley Duncan, "Inheritance of Poverty or Inheritance of Race?" in Daniel P. Moynihan, ed., *On Understanding Poverty* (New York: Basic Books, 1969):85–110. On mobility of blacks and whites during the 1960s, see David Feathermand and Robert Hauser, *Opportunity and Change* (New York: Academic Press, 1978), esp. chapter 6; Michael Hout, "Status, Autonomy, and Training in Occupational Mobility," *American Journal of Sociology* 89, no. 6 (1984):1379–1409; and Michael Hout, "Occupational Mobility of Black Men, 1962 to 1973," *American Sociological Review* 49 (June 1984):308–322. The quotation is from Hout, "Status," p. 1395.

56. See Leonard Goodwin, *Do the Poor Want to Work?* (Washington, D.C.: Brookings Institution, 1972); Leonard Goodwin, *Causes and Cures of Welfare* (Lexington, Mass.: Lexington Books, 1983); Lee Rainwater, *Behind Ghetto Walls* (New York: Aldine, 1970); Martha Hill et al., *Motivation and Economic Mobility* (Ann Arbor, Mich.: Institute for Social Research, 1985).

57. See Oscar Lewis, *Five Families* (New York: Basic Books, 1959); Oscar Lewis, *La Vida* (New York: Irvington, 1983); Ken Auletta, *The Underclass* (New York: Random House, Vintage, 1983); Charles Murray, *Losing Ground* (New York: Basic Books, 1984).

58. See Edward Banfield, *The Heavenly City Revisited* (Boston: Little, Brown, 1974); Susan Sheehan, *A Welfare Mother* (New York: New American Library, 1977).

59. See, for example, the mixed results on whether an underclass exists and is growing in Farley, *Blacks and Whites,* pp. 172–192. For an interesting discussion of the political sensitivity of this issue, see William J. Wilson, "Cycles of Deprivation and the Underclass Debate" *Social Services Review,* 59, no. 4 (December 1985):541–559. For examples of this type of claim, see Leon Dash, "At Risk—Chronicles of Teen-Age Pregnancy," *Washington Post,*

six-part series, January 26–31, 1986; *Chicago Tribune, The American Millstone* (Chicago: Contemporary Books, 1986).

60. Erol Ricketts and Isabel Sawhill, "Defining and Measuring the Underclass," paper presented at the annual meeting of the American Economic Association, New Orleans, December 28, 1986.

61. Warren E. Miller, Arthur H. Miller, and Edward J. Schneider, *American National Election Studies Data Sourcebook, 1952–1978* (Cambridge, Mass.: Harvard University Press, 1980), pp. 274–279.

62. Ibid. See also the Harris Survey, "Feelings of Alienation Drop from Last Year's High," May 10, 1984.

63. Cavanagh, *Inside Black America,* p. 11. Similarly, controlling for class, blacks are more likely to vote than whites and more likely to engage in campaign and cooperative political activities (Sidney Verba and Norman Nie, *Participation in America* [New York: Harper and Row, 1972], pp. 149–173).

64. Cavanagh, ibid., p. 64.

65. Huey Perry, "The Social and Economic Impact of Black Politics in New Orleans, Louisiana," in Dianne Pinderhughes and Linda Williams, eds., *Race and Class in the New Urban Politics* (Chatham, N.J.: Chatham House, forthcoming).

66. Harris Survey, "Anti-Establishment Sentiment Helps Hart's Candidacy," April 5, 1984.

67. Forty-five percent or more whites saw Jackson as "a strong leader," "knowledgeable," "hard-working," "exciting," "compassionate," and able to "get things done." Nevertheless, 19 percent of southern whites said his endorsement of Mondale and Ferraro would make them less likely to vote Democratic, compared to only 8 percent who said it would make them more likely to support the Democrats (Cavanagh, *Inside Black America,* pp. 33, 61).

68. Thomas Cavanagh and Lorn Foster, *Jesse Jackson's Campaign* (Washington, D.C.: Joint Center for Political Studies, 1984), pp. 10, 24.

69. C. Anthony Broh, *A Horse of A Different Color* (Washington, D.C.: Joint Center for Political Studies, 1987).

70. Gary Hart complained about the same rules (they were, in fact, set up to benefit the frontrunner, and they did so), but he was not harmed as badly as Jackson. (William Crotty, "The Presidential Nominating Process and Minority Candidates: The Lessons of the Jackson Campaign," paper presented at conference on "The 1984 Presidential Election and the Future of Black Politics," Joint Center for Political Studies, Washington, D.C., April 30, 1984).

71. Ibid., p. 1.

72. Francis Clines, "A Fledgling Protest Movement Gathers Steam," *New York Times,* August 5, 1985, p. B4.

73. Joint Center for Political Studies, *Black Elected Officials* (New York: UNIPUB, 1985); Spencer Rich, "Blacks, Despite Gains, Hold Few Elective Posts," *Washington Post,* June 9, 1985, p. A5.

74. Cavanagh, *Inside Black America,* p. 50. For evidence supporting this point, see Thomas Cavanagh and Denise Stockton, *Black Elected Officials and Their Constituencies* (Washington, D.C.: Joint Center for Political Studies, 1983), pp. 16–20 and citations therein.

75. For evidence on the importance of electoral districting, see Cavanagh and Stockton, *Black Elected Officials,* pp. 20–21 and citations therein; and Albert Karnig, "Black Resources and City Council Representation," *Journal of Politics* 41, no. 1 (February 1979):134–149.

76. The rate of black registration increased from 60 to 66.3 percent between 1980 and 1984, compared to a white increase from 68.4 to 69.6 percent (Cavanagh, *Inside Black America,* pp. 11, 12).

77. Another way of making the same point, albeit inadvertently, is from Cavanagh, *Inside Black America,* p. 11: "The black portion of the net total increase in registration between 1980 and 1984 was 21.4 percent." That figure is "remarkable," as he points out, because it is "double the black [pro]portion of the total voting age population"; it also, however, represents only one-fifth of the new voters, a figure that matters more in a majoritarian electoral system.

78. Albert Karnig, "Black Representation on City Councils," *Urban Affairs Quarterly* 12, no. 2 (December 1976):233.

79. Charles Bullock III, "The Election of Blacks in the South: Preconditions and Consequences," *American Journal of Political Science* 19, no. 4 (November 1975):735–737. For other discussions of the relative lack of power of black elected officials, see Albert Karnig and Susan Welch, *Black Representation and Urban Policy* (Chicago: University of Chicago Press, 1980), pp. 150–153; and Adolf Reed, Dynamics of Urban Racial Transition and Afro-American Politics," paper presented at symposium on "Minorities in the United States," City University of New York, June 20, 1984, and citations therein.

80. Derived from Nathan and Dommel, "Needed—A Federal Safety Net," Tables A3 and 3.

81. Peter Eisinger, "Black Employment in Municipal Jobs: The Impact of Black Political Power," *American Political Science Review* 76, no. 2 (June 1982):380–392. See also Thomas Dye and James Renick, "Political Power and City Jobs: Determinants of Minority Employment," *Social Science Quarterly* 62, no. 3 (September 1981):480–481.

82. Kenneth Mladenka, "Comments on Eisinger: Black Employment in Municipal Jobs," *American Political Science Review* 76, no. 3 (September 1982):645–647.

83. Karnig and Welch, *Black Representation and Urban Policy,* pp. 124–128, 131, 137, 138; more generally, see ch. 6.

84. Derived from Nathan and Dommel, "Needed—A New Safety Net," Table 4. My calculations from their data exclude cities in Puerto Rico.

85. Raphael Sonenshein, "Bradley's People: Biracial Coalition Politics in Los Angeles," paper presented at the annual meeting of the American Political Science Association, New Orleans, September 1985.

86. For example, see Clarence Stone, "Race, Power, and Political Change," in Janet Boles, ed., *The Egalitarian City* (New York: Praeger, 1986), pp. 200–223.

87. Jonathan Hicks, "Black Professionals Refashion Their Careers," *New York Times,* November 29, 1985, pp. 1, D2; Claudia Deutsch, "The Ax Falls on Equal Opportunity," *New York Times,* January 4, 1987, sec. 3, pp. 1, 27; George Davis

and Glegg Watson, *Black Life in Corporate America* (New York: Doubleday, 1985).

88. Stokely Carmichael and Charles Hamilton, *Black Power* (New York: Vintage Books, 1967); Clayborne Carson, *In Struggle: SNCC and the Black Awakening of the 1960s* (Cambridge, Mass.: Harvard University Press, 1981).

89. Marilyn Gittell, "Community Control of Schools," in Marilyn Gittell and Alan Hevesi, eds., *The Politics of Urban Education* (New York: Praeger, 1969), pp. 363–377; Robert Maynard, "Black Nationalism and Community Schools," in Henry Levin, ed., *Community Control of Schools* (Washington, D.C.: Brookings Institution, 1979), pp. 100–111.

90. Quoted in Raymond Wolters, *The Burden of Brown* (Knoxville: University of Tennessee Press, 1984), p. 206.

91. American Enterprise Institute, *A Conversation with the Reverend Jesse Jackson* (Washington, D.C.: American Enterprise Institute, 1978), p. 5.

92. See the chapters by Bell and Carter ("Reassessment of *Brown* vs. *Board*") in Derrick Bell, *Shades of Brown* (New York: Teachers College Press, 1980).

93. "Meredith: Integration Is a 'Con Job,'" *Washington Post,* February 23, 1985, pp. G1, G7.

94. Board of Education, Ferguson-Florissant School District, Report to the Court, October 15, 1977, pp. 1–8; Daniel Monti, "Administrative Discrimination in the Implementation of Desegregation Policies," *Educational Evaluation and Policy Analysis* 1, no. 4 (1979).

95. John Smith and Bette Smith, "Desegregation in the South and the Demise of the Black Educator," *Journal of Social and Behavioral Sciences* 20, no. 1 (winter 1974):33–40; Everett Abney, "A Comparison of the Status of Florida's Black Public School Principals, 1964–65/1975–76," *Journal of Negro Education* 49, no. 4 (winter 1980):398–406.

96. Charles Lawrence, "'One More River to Cross'—Recognizing the Real Injury in *Brown*," and Carter, "Reassessment of *Brown* vs. *Board*," both in Bell, ed., *Shades of Brown.*

97. Reginald Stuart, "Businesses Owned by Blacks Still Fighting an Uphill Battle," *New York Times,* July 26, 1981, pp. 1, 20.

98. Adolph Reed, *The Jackson Phenomenon* (New Haven, Conn.: Yale University Press, 1986); William J. Wilson, "The Declining Significance of Race: Myth or Reality?" in Joseph Washington, ed., *The Declining Significance of Race? A Dialogue Among Black and White Social Scientists* (privately published, copyright, Joseph Washington, 1979), pp. 16–17.

99. My thanks to Alan Wertheimer for starting my thinking along these lines.

100. Douglas Rae et al., *Equalities* (Cambridge, Mass.: Harvard University Press, 1981), p. 66.

101. Robert Fullinwider has argued, in response to this claim, that blacks do not yet enjoy prospect-regarding equal opportunity—therefore the need to mandate desegregation and affirmative action programs. I see those programs as moving beyond prospect-regarding to substantive or means-regarding equal opportunity, but that is another discussion.

102. Edwin Dorn, in *Rules and Racial Equality* (New Haven, Conn.: Yale University Press, 1979, pp. 112–121) argued that it is mathematically impossible for blacks as a group to reach parity with whites as a group by simply ensuring equal opportunity to individual blacks. He is probably right for most socially desired goods but perhaps not for goods distributed by prospect-regarding rules.

103. Rae et al., *Equalities,* pp. 65, 66.

104. See Jennifer L. Hochschild, *The New American Dilemma* (New Haven, Conn.: Yale University Press, 1984), and Jennifer L. Hochschild, "Approaching Racial Equality Through Indirection," *Yale Law and Policy Review* 4, no. 2 (spring/summer 1986):307–330.

105. For a defense of this claim, see Jennifer Hochschild, "Race, Class, Power, and the Welfare State," in Amy Gutmann, ed., *Democracy and the Welfare State* (Princeton, N.J.: Princeton University Press, forthcoming 1987).

106. A good, nontechnical discussion of why the metaphor of the "race of life" is "a mess" is Garry Wills, *Nixon Agonistes* (Boston, Mass.: Houghton-Mifflin, 1970), pp. 235–240.

107. Kurt Vonnegut, "Harrison Bergeron," in *Welcome to the Monkey House* (New York: Delacorte Press, 1950), pp. 1–13.

108. Jennifer Nedelsky, "American Constitutionalism and the Paradox of Private Property" (Toronto: University of Toronto, Faculty of Law, unpublished paper, 1986); Thomas Grey, "The Disintegration of Property," in J. Roland Pennock and John W. Chapman, eds., *Nomos XXII: Property* (New York: New York University Press, 1980), pp. 69–85; Benjamin Page, *Who Gets What from Government?* (Berkeley: University of California Press, 1983); Walter Blum and Harry Kelven, *The Uneasy Case for Progressive Taxation* (Chicago: University of Chicago Press, 1963).

109. Compare *Brown* v. *Board of Education of Topeka* (347 U.S. 483, Sup. Ct., May 17, 1954) with *San Antonio Independent School District* v. *Rodriguez* (411 U.S. 1, Sup. Ct., March 21, 1973).

5

Qualifications, Fairness, and Desert

GEORGE SHER

The view that persons should be hired or admitted to educational institutions on the basis of their qualifications can be defended in at least three ways. It can be argued, first, that selection by merit is the most efficient way of filling positions; second, that a history of such selection is a de facto promise to those who have responded by developing their skills; and, third, that best-qualified applicants have independent claims of fairness or desert. Of these modes of argument, the first is consequentialist and so is vulnerable to countervailing consequentialist considerations, whereas the second provides no reason to condemn a long-standing and well-publicized nonmeritarian system. For these (and other) reasons, I believe the root meritarian impulse is best captured by the third argument. Yet, surprisingly, this argument has rarely been developed in detail. Here I want to rectify that omission. Although I believe the argument is best developed in terms of desert, I will begin by trying to show that selection by merit is at least not unfair. After that, I will mount a more positive defense of the desert of the best qualified.

Parts of this chapter are drawn from George Sher, *Desert* (Princeton, N.J.: Princeton University Press) and are reprinted with permission. © 1987 Princeton University Press.

I

The issue of unfairness was raised in an influential discussion by John Schaar. Responding to the claim that "nothing could be fairer or more generous [than arranging] social conditions [so] that each individual can go as high as his natural abilities will permit,"[1] Schaar asked:

> What is so generous about telling a man he can go as far as his talents will take him when his talents are meager? Imagine a footrace of one mile in which ten men compete, with the rules being the same for all. Three of the competitors are forty years old, five are overweight, one has weak ankles, and the tenth is Roger Bannister. What sense does it make to say that all ten have an equal opportunity to win the race? The outcome is predetermined by nature, and nine of the competitors will call it a mockery when they are told that all have the same opportunity to win.[2]

I think we can dismiss Schaar's charge of ungenerosity; for this would only be an issue if it were already established that the best qualified have no prior claim to be chosen. But the worry that selection by merit is unfair is a different story; for if well grounded, it would arguably imply that best-qualified candidates do not have serious claims to be chosen. Hence, the charge of unfairness does threaten the desert of the best qualified.

Why should selection by merit be thought unfair? Although much of what Schaar says is couched in different terms, his footrace analogy is clearly meant to highlight the inequality of those who compete for desirable positions.[3] Whether his race is taken to represent the tests that determine who qualifies for positions or the earlier preparations through which persons develop their skills, its outcome is influenced by differences in ability that are arguably no greater than those that separate persons who seek desirable jobs or educational opportunities. For this reason, the race illustrates the fact that even if the untalented are nominally eligible to "win" the desirable positions, they have no real chance to do so. Given their comparative lack of ability, their defeat is preordained. And this does imply that selection by merit is unfair if fairness in competition requires that each competitor have an equal chance to win.

Let us examine the claim that a contest is not fair unless each competitor has an equal chance. Can we construe this requirement in a way that both explains why Schaar's footrace seems objectionable and yields intuitively acceptable judgments about other contests? To begin, we may provisionally equate a person's chance of winning with the probability that he will win. That done, we must interpret probability in turn. And here we find several familiar possibilities.

1. We might say, first, that one's probability of winning is one's relative frequency of victory against the same opponents in the hypothetical long run. On this reading, each competitor has an equal chance if each would win equally often in an indefinitely lengthy sequence of contests. This interpretation raises obvious questions about which of the competitors' current circumstances would be held constant in those further contests. However, a more urgent problem concerns the effects of small differences in ability on long-run performance. In some types of competition, even such small differences can have an extremely consistent effect on the outcome. For example, when Edwin Moses was in his prime, he won over a hundred consecutive hurdle races against world-class competition. On the relative-frequency interpretation of the equal-probability-of-victory requirement, these races were all unfair. Yet clearly Moses's small but decisive edge did not render the contests unfair in any normatively significant sense.

2. Instead of construing probabilities as relative frequencies of events, we might understand them as logical relations between sentences describing events and sentences describing the evidence for those events. On this interpretation, each competitor has an equal chance of winning if no prediction of any competitor's winning is better supported by antecedently available evidence than any other.[4] Like its predecessor, this suggestion nicely explains why Schaar's race is objectionable; as presented, the antecedent evidence does imply that nine of his ten racers will lose. Yet if a competitor's chances are relative to evidence, then even the weakest competitor will have as good a chance as any other if no one has antecedent reason to suspect his limitations. Thus, under different epistemic conditions, even Schaar's race could be fair. Because this proposal relativizes probabilities of victory (and thus fairness) to knowledge, it fails to capture the intuition that a contest's fairness should depend entirely on the competitors' situation itself.

3. There is, of course, a related suggestion that does capture this intuition. Instead of equating a competitor's chance of winning with his probability of winning relative to what he or anyone else knows, we may equate it with the probability of his winning relative to all possible evidence. By thus eliminating all reference to actual knowledge, we avoid the implication that a contest's fairness turns on an irrelevant contingency. But in so doing, we open ourselves to yet another objection. For if determinism is true, then prior to any contest the relevant laws and descriptions of antecedent conditions are potentially conclusive evidence as to how that contest will turn out. Before the contest, they

will deductively imply a true prediction of the outcome. Hence, if we assume determinism, our third proposal implies that there is an antecedent probability of one that the eventual winner will win and a probability of zero that anyone else will win. This yields the absurd consequence that determinism renders all contests unfair.

Thus, we cannot equate competitive fairness with any plausible interpretation of the requirement that it be equally probable that each competitor will win. But we still might equate competitive fairness with equality of chances if we understood equal chances in some other way. In particular, since in Schaar's race nine of ten competitors will lose no matter what they do, we might contrast that contest with a race in which no competitor has a monopoly of control over the outcome. On this account, a contest will be fair if each competitor is equally able to win by doing certain things within his power. Although Schaar does not argue for this suggestion, we can easily see its appeal; for if a losing competitor could have won then he has no one to blame for losing but himself.

Yet, appealing though it may be, this view is no more plausible than those we have rejected. To see why not, consider a footrace more even than Schaar's. Suppose the runners are the same age, equally fit, and equally good athletes. If there is any contest over which each competitor has an equal degree of control, it is this one. Yet even here, a competitor's success or failure depends not only on what *he* does but also on the performances of his rivals. Since each competitor would prevent the others from outperforming him if he could, and since some competitors must lose nonetheless, there is still an asymmetry in the competitors' degree of control. Assuming that each competitor has done his absolute best, the statement "X could have won by doing something within his power" will be false of the losers but (trivially) true of the winner. Hence, this proposal again implies that no contests are fair.

In the preceding paragraphs, I have taken as a reductio the implication that all competition is unfair. But some elements of Schaar's discussion suggest that he did want to contrast competition in general with other methods of allocating opportunities. For example, he wrote that

> the doctrine of equal opportunity is the product of a competitive and fragmented society, a divided society, a society in which individualism, in Tocqueville's sense of the word, is the reigning ethical principle. It is a precise symbolic expression of the liberal-bourgeois model of society, for it extends the market-place mentality to all the spheres of life. It views the whole of human relations as a contest in which each man competes with his fellows for scarce goods, a contest in which

there is never enough for everyone and where one man's gain is usually another's loss.[5]

In this and similar passages, Schaar can be taken as saying that all competition for positions shares some basic defect that his footrace merely exaggerates. In part, his complaint appears to be that in addressing only the question of how the relatively few desirable opportunities are to be distributed, a competitive system leaves intact, and thus tacitly condones, the larger situation in which desirable positions are scarce. But lamentable though it may be, the fact that some jobs and opportunities are more desirable than others seems deeply entrenched and likely to remain so for the foreseeable future. The problem may be mitigated, but is unlikely to be eliminated, by the adjusting of reward schedules. Thus, the more interesting question is whether competition itself is an improper—and, in particular, an unfair—way of allocating the more desirable positions.

Is there any reason to regard competition as less fair than other methods of allocation? Clearly no account that defines fairness in terms of equal probabilities of acquiring positions will support this conclusion. Although some such definitions were found to imply that all competition is unfair (or that all competition depends for its fairness on irrelevant considerations), these imply precisely the same about allocation on such alternative bases as need, effort, and lot. Moreover, if applicants for scarce jobs and opportunities lack control over competitive searches and entrance exams, then a fortiori they lack control over outcomes determined in these other ways. Whatever our method of selection, the fact remains that each disappointed job- or opportunity-seeker would have produced a different outcome if he could. It is true that lotteries, unlike competitive contests, give nobody control over the outcomes. However, as I have argued elsewhere, the requirement that nobody exercise control is only appropriate if all those seeking a good have equal claims and if their claims are better than those of all others.[6] But our current question is precisely whether best-qualified applicants do have stronger claims than others. Hence, this notion of fairness cannot be invoked to resolve the issue.

Thus far, I have argued that even if competitors for jobs and opportunities do differ greatly both in native ability and in developed skill, it follows neither that selection by merit is less fair than other forms of competition nor that competition itself is less fair than other methods of allocating desirable jobs and opportunities. But even if my arguments are convincing, they may seem to miss a crucial point. Whatever the exact difficulty, there is surely something objectionable about Schaar's race. Thus, mustn't all similarly mismatched contests be similarly objectionable?

In fact, they need not be; for whether the difficulty can be generalized will depend on what we find objectionable. Since the charge of unfairness cannot be sustained, the next most likely reason for our negative reaction to Schaar's race seems to be that it pointlessly humiliates the less able competitors. But if this is the worry, then the difficulty will not carry over to selection by merit. For, first, under that system, neither the applicants for positions nor the public at large need know of any embarrassingly large margin of defeat. And, second, unlike Schaar's race, allocation by merit is far from pointless. Where there are more applicants than openings, we plainly need some procedure for allocating desirable positions; and, as already noted, allocation by merit brings obvious gains in productivity and efficiency.

Thus, even if the desert of the best qualified provided no serious reason to choose them, selection by qualification would not be wrong. But, having come this far, I want to go further. For, as I will now argue, the fact that one is best qualified, and thus deserves a position, is a serious reason to choose him.

II

Not all desert-claims are normatively significant. For example, when we say that an insightful person deserves our attention, we do not imply either that those who ignore him act wrongly or that our failure to heed his advice (as opposed to the harm resulting from that failure) makes the world a worse place. Thus, to show that best-qualified applicants ought to be chosen, we cannot merely note that it is customary to say that they deserve to be chosen. In addition, we must show why such desert-claims have real normative force.

The issue is complicated by the fact that qualifications do not correlate neatly with effort. If they did, we might appeal to the past efforts of the best qualified to account for their desert. This would leave questions about why a person's efforts in the past should provide reason for him to receive anything special in the future; but I believe such questions can sometimes be answered. Yet asking them here is pointless; for often the best-qualified applicant is not the one who has worked the hardest but simply the most natively gifted. For this reason, no satisfactory justification is apt to emerge from James Rachels's suggestion that "when we think of the most skillful as the most deserving, it may be because we think of them as having worked the hardest."[7] For, as Rachels goes on to note, "sometimes that assumption is not true."[8]

There is a more promising line of argument. To appreciate it, we may first note that there are close internal connections between jobs and the skills and abilities they require, and between education and the ability to learn. No job can be done unless a worker has the requisite skill or ability, so the primary purpose of seeking someone to do a job will only be accomplished if one hires a suitably skilled applicant. Moreover, that purpose will best be accomplished if one hires the most skilled applicant. Similarly, the primary purpose of admitting persons to educational institutions will best be accomplished by admitting those who are most able to learn. In other contexts, such internal connections between goods and traits have been taken to provide strong reasons for allocating the goods to those possessing the traits. For example, Bernard Williams wrote that "[l]eaving aside preventive medicine, the proper ground of distribution of medical care is ill health: this is a necessary truth."[9] More generally, Michael Walzer suggested that "for all our personal and collective resources, there are distributive reasons that are somehow *right,* that are naturally part of our ideas about the things themselves."[10] But without further argument, such suggestions are incomplete; for they do not tell us why an internal connection between a good and a trait—in our case, between an opportunity to perform a task and a person's superior ability to do so—is a significant reason for awarding him the good.

In one sense, the answer in the current context is clear. As we just saw, the primary purpose of hiring or admitting—to select someone who will work or learn—is apt to be best accomplished if one selects the most able applicant. Since showing that an action will best accomplish a purpose is a way of justifying the action to anyone who has the purpose, this does provide a kind of justification of selection by qualification. Yet if we left things here, our justification would at best explain why selecting best-qualified applicants is rational from the hiring officer's perspective. It would not answer the quite different question of why such selection is owed to the best-qualified applicants themselves. Hence, it would fail to capture the desert-claim's real import.

To do that, we must look beyond the act of selecting by merit and consider the attitude toward persons which that act expresses. When we hire by merit, we abstract from all facts about the applicants except their ability to perform well at the relevant tasks. By thus concentrating on their ability to perform, we treat them as agents whose purposeful acts are capable of making a difference in the world. Moreover, by concentrating on abilities that are internally connected to jobs and opportunities that exist to serve independent purposes, we affirm the applicants' involvement in the wider life of the community. For both reasons, selecting by merit is a way of taking seriously the potential agency of both the successful and the unsuccessful applicants. Conversely, when an applicant is selected on some other basis, there is a recognizable if elusive sense in which he and his rivals are not taken seriously. And this suggests that we may justify selection by merit by arguing that persons ought to be taken seriously in the relevant sense.

I believe, in fact, that some such argument does underlie the claim that best-qualified applicants deserve jobs and educational opportunities. It is worth emphasizing that the argument is not an appeal to consequences. Although it does invoke the internal connections between jobs and qualifications, it does so not to establish the inefficiency but rather to show the wrongness of departures from merit criteria. Yet just because of this, the argument raises many further questions. Do the aims of employment and education require selecting the most able person or only a competent one? Whatever these aims require, how is the situation affected by the intimate connections between opportunities and rewards—between desirable jobs and education and the money and prestige that these allow people to acquire? And, most important, what is the force of the claim that departures from merit criteria "do not take applicants seriously"? To what principle, value, or other normative consideration does this claim appeal?

III

The first question—whether the aims of employment and education really require the selection of best-qualified persons—gets its bite from the facts that jobs done adequately are still done and material learned adequately is still learned. Given these facts, it may be held that the aims of employment or education are satisfied whenever the chosen applicant's ability exceeds the appropriate threshold. It is granted on all sides that we should not hire persons who cannot do the work, or provide education for persons who cannot learn. However, beyond this, appeals to the prerequisites of performance may seem to prove little.

But this objection presupposes a very limited—I think an unacceptably limited—vision of the aims of employment and education. It presupposes that the point of employing someone is merely to ensure that the job is adequately done and that the point of educating is merely that academic subjects be mastered in some fashion. However, in general, purposive activity aims not merely at achieving satisfactory results but at achieving the best results that prevailing conditions allow. A weekend gardener may be resigned to his small plot, his poor soil, and his lack of time to pull weeds; and he may therefore be happy to produce tomatoes above a certain number and quality. Nevertheless, his aim is still to grow as many and as good tomatoes as his resources permit. Similarly, an employer may be willing to settle for work whose quality exceeds a certain threshold, but he nevertheless aims at obtaining the best work available for the price. Still more obviously, there is no theoretical limit to the breadth and depth of understanding that education aims to instill. Given these considerations, the aims of education and employment are considerably more comprehensive than the objection allows. To satisfy them fully, we must indeed choose best-qualified members of applicant pools.

The second objection looks more serious. Thus far, I have spoken as though, when someone is hired or admitted to an educational institution, he acquires only the chance to work or learn. But this is clearly oversimplified. Many coveted jobs bring high salaries and prestige, and many sought-after forms of education lead predictably to similar rewards. Where such connections hold, opportunities to work or learn are also opportunities to acquire wealth and prestige. Moreover, whatever we say about prestige, being best qualified to work or learn is clearly not internally related to earning a high wage. Thus, the proper grounds for allocating opportunities to work or learn need not coincide with the proper grounds for allocating opportunities to acquire the associated rewards. But if not, then it may indeed seem acceptable to allocate jobs or education on some basis other than qualifications. As Thomas Nagel put the point,

> where the allocation of one benefit on relevant grounds carries with it
> the allocation of other, more significant benefits to which those
> grounds are irrelevant, the departure from those grounds need not be
> a serious offense against justice. . . . [Although] it may be acceptable
> to depart from the "relevant" grounds for undramatic reasons of social
> utility, that would not justify more flagrant and undiluted examples of
> unfairness.[11]

To this, we need only add that if Nagel was right, departures from merit criteria may also be defensible on other grounds—for example, that they promote equality (either among individuals or groups), that they meet pressing individual needs, or that they reward past efforts.

This objection to selection by merit is often accompanied by the claim that highly paid workers do not deserve (all) their wages. For this reason, the objection may be taken to assert that deviations from merit criteria are justified because the prevailing reward structure is indefensible. But this interpretation is neither charitable nor necessary. It is not charitable because even if there is no reason for anyone to earn the high wage that attaches to a job, it does not follow that there is no reason for anyone to have the job to which the wage attaches. If merit is a good reason for someone to have a job, it does not cease to be a good reason merely because the job pays an indefensible wage. And the interpretation is unnecessary because the question of how to allocate what in fact are dual opportunities would arise even if the prevailing reward structure were completely defensible. Given these facts, the strongest version of Nagel's objection is not the bad argument just discussed. Rather, it is that when the proper reasons for allocating opportunities to work or learn do not coincide with the proper reasons for allocating the associated opportunities to earn high salaries, the latter reasons ought to dominate.

To insist that this argument can never succeed would be unrealistic. Any kind of moral pluralist must believe—and I do believe—that there are goals so urgent and needs so pressing that they simply override the reasons for hiring or admitting by merit. But it is one thing to concede that this may occur and quite another to agree that it generally does. To establish the latter, one would have to go on to show why the favored nonmeritarian reasons for allocating opportunities to acquire wealth and prestige are generally dominant over the meritarian reasons for allocating opportunities to work or learn.

Can the nonmeritarian reasons be shown to dominate? To establish this, one might argue either that these reasons are themselves weightier than meritarian reasons or that the opportunities to which the non-meritarian reasons are linked—opportunities to acquire wealth and prestige—take priority over opportunities to work or learn. Nagel suggested an appeal of the first sort when he wrote that "the presumption [in favor of hiring and admitting by merit] may not be very strong to begin with."[12] But Nagel's only basis for regarding this presumption as weak is his implication that wealth and prestige are "more significant" benefits than opportunities to work or learn. This is inadequate because the strength of a reason for allocating a benefit in a certain way need not be proportional to the significance of that benefit itself. And when we turn from the strength of the competing reasons to the relation between the linked opportunities, we find that this if anything favors hiring and admitting by merit. For since one cannot acquire the salary and prestige associated with a good job without actually doing the job—since the salary and prestige attach to the job rather than vice versa—it is the opportunity to do the job that is naturally prior. Thus, if the priority of one of two linked opportunities can imply that the criterion for allocating that opportunity should also have priority, it is the merit criterion that ought to dominate.

IV

But what, in the end, does the case for using this criterion come to? We saw that superior qualifications are internally connected to the aims of education and employment and that inattention to such connections seems to involve some sort of failure to take applicants seriously. But what, exactly, does this mean? What sort of failure is involved, and why is it normatively significant?

To answer these final questions, we must pursue the contrast between the attitudes that underlie merit and nonmerit criteria. I suggested earlier that when someone is hired or admitted because he is best qualified, he is treated as a full participant in the relevant productive and creative arrangements. But suppose that someone is selected for reasons other than his qualifications. In that case, his decisive feature may be entirely unrelated to his ability to advance any independent purposes. This occurs when someone is hired because he needs the job so badly or because he is the nephew of the company president. Alternatively, his decisive feature may indeed suit him to advance some independent purpose but only in a way that is unconnected (or is merely incidentally connected) to his actions. This occurs when a weak student is admitted to a competitive institution in the hope that his parents will donate a wing to the library and when members of minority groups are hired to decrease the "underrepresentation" of those groups or to break down stereotypes. In neither type of case is either the chosen candidate or his better-qualified rival treated as an individual whose actions themselves will matter. Instead, all parties are treated as mere bearers of needs or claims, as passive links in causal chains, or as interchangeable specimens of larger groups or classes.

This contrast makes the core argument for selection by merit easier to grasp. Properly understood, our obligation to select among applicants on the basis of qualification must follow from our more general obligation to treat all persons as rational agents. Because we most readily associate practical reason with deliberation and choice, that general obligation is most often taken to require that we not coerce others' decisions. But practical reason encompasses not only decisions but also the acts and intended effects to which they lead; and it ranges over both acts intended to serve the agent's own interests and acts with other aims. Given all this, any requirement that we treat persons as rational agents must demand respect not only for their ability to advance their own ends, but also for their ability to advance other ends. Yet, as we just saw, when we select among applicants for reasons other than their ability to perform the tasks that define the positions they seek, we treat them as passive recipients of largesse or links in causal chains rather than as active contributors to anyone's ends. By thus disengaging their practical wills from the aims that have generated the positions, we violate the requirement as explicated. For this reason, there must indeed be a strong presumption in favor of awarding opportunities on the basis of the ability to perform the relevant tasks. Even where the tasks are mechanical and repetitive, selecting in this way affirms the applicants' status as choosers and doers, whereas selecting on other grounds as clearly does not.[13]

This, surely, is an important (nonconsequentialist) reason for choosing only best-qualified applicants. But is it also the main basis for holding that best-qualified applicants deserve to be chosen? On the surface, this may seem doubtful; for while treatment as an agent is owed equally to all applicants, only best-qualified applicants deserve to be chosen. Hence, the proffered reason may seem to have the wrong form to justify the desert-claim. But this objection is confused. What needs to be established is not that only the best-qualified applicant is owed treatment as a rational agent but rather that he and only he is owed the contested position. To establish this, I have argued that only selection by qualification accords all the applicants the respect they are owed as rational agents and that under such selection the best-qualified applicant, and he alone is owed the position. On this account, what the best-qualified applicant alone is owed just is what he alone deserves. Hence, the proffered reason does have the right form to justify the desert-claim.

Indeed, by accepting the account, we bring out an important continuity between the desert of the best qualified and other, superficially dissimilar forms of desert. As we have seen, desert for merit ties what persons deserve to their current traits rather than what they have done in the past. For this reason, it may seem to have little in common with such backward-looking claims as that persons deserve to succeed because of their past hard work or that they deserve to be punished for their past misdeeds. But given what has been said, these forms of desert are indeed connected. Even when a person's desert is grounded in a present trait and not a past action, that trait is (and is important because it is) an ability to perform certain future actions. And this suggests that the concepts of desert and agency are themselves linked at some suitably deep level.

Because an adequate discussion of the linkage would raise a variety of complications, I cannot attempt it here.[14] Rather, I shall end by exploiting the unanalyzed connection to explain why certain departures from merit criteria seem far less objectionable than others. Consider, first, a case in which such a departure is justified by appealing to some other form of desert, such as that which accrues to hard workers.

Even an ardent meritarian is not apt to be overly disturbed if a somewhat less-qualified applicant is hired because he has worked much harder than his rivals. Moreover, given the preceding, we can see that this intuition is sound. If departures from merit criteria are generally wrong because they fail to respect the applicants' prospective agency, then their wrongness is at least mitigated when the countervailing factor is precisely what the applicants have already done.

A second reason for bypassing best-qualified applicants is more complex. In recent years, the practice of hiring and admitting by merit has been challenged on the grounds that special preference is owed to persons who either were themselves victimized by previous discrimination or were harmed by its effects on other members of groups to which they belong. It is indeed largely this challenge that has motivated many discussions of selection by merit. Thus, any justification of such selection must be examined with an eye to preferential treatment. What does our account imply about this?

That depends on the rationale for extending the preference. If the point is merely to promote desirable consequences such as the presence of more blacks and women in high-paying positions or the existence of exemplars to encourage others, then our strictures against treating persons merely as links in causal chains will surely apply. But a different rationale for preferential treatment is also possible. Applicants sometimes are best qualified because others were prevented by past discrimination, or by its effects, from developing their skills. Had there been no wrongdoing, a different applicant would have been better qualified. I have argued elsewhere that in such cases we should, if possible, extend just enough preference to the less-well-qualified applicant to restore him to the competitive position that he would have occupied in the absence of wrongdoing.[15] I shall not repeat that argument here. However, what is worth noting is that if the argument is otherwise satisfactory, it is far less vulnerable than other defenses of preferential treatment to the charge that it gives insufficient weight to the desert of the best qualified. For unlike those defenses, but like our justification of the desert of the best qualified, this rationale for preferential treatment does accord all applicants the status of agents. It does so not by appealing either to their actual past actions or to their potential future ones but rather by focusing on the actions that each applicant would have been able to perform in a more just world. Although these actions are merely possible, and thus cannot create actual desert,[16] any argument that turns on them does share with desert-claims a vision of the parties as agents. Thus, if the usual wrongness of deviating from merit criteria is due to a failure to acknowledge this, that wrongness is here again at least mitigated.

ACKNOWLEDGMENTS

I am indebted to Alan Wertheimer for his helpful comments on this chapter.

NOTES

1. John Schaar, "Equality of Opportunity, and Beyond," in J. Roland Pennock and John W. Chapman, eds., *Equality: Nomos IX* (New York: Atherton Press, 1967), p. 233.

2. Ibid.

3. My reason for attributing to Schaar the charge that equal opportunity is unfair is not that this is the main thrust of his position—it is not—but only to exploit a formulation that many have found compelling.

4. A more complete account would of course specify to whom the relevant evidence is available and why it is just those persons' epistemic states that matter. But we need not pursue these complications here.

5. Schaar, "Equality of Opportunity," p. 237.

6. George Sher, "What Makes a Lottery Fair?" *Nous* 14 (1980):203–216.

7. James Rachels, "What People Deserve," in John Arthur and William H. Shaw, eds., *Justice and Economic Distribution* (Englewood Cliffs, N.J.: Prentice-Hall, 1978), p. 156.

8. Ibid., p. 156.

9. Bernard Williams, "The Idea of Equality," in *Problems of the Self* (Cambridge, England: Cambridge University Press, 1973), p. 240.

10. Michael Walzer, "The Idea of Equality," *Dissent,* fall 1973, p. 403. This idea is developed further in Walzer's *Spheres of Justice* (New York: Basic Books, 1983). In the latter work, Walzer observed that he regarded the proper reasons for having goods to be determined by the social meanings that constitute the goods, whereas for Williams, "relevance seems to connect to essential rather than to social meanings" (*Spheres of Justice,* p. 9). But whoever is right about this, I cannot see that either philosopher has taken the crucial next step and asked exactly what is wrong with any particular irrelevant distributive procedure.

11. Thomas Nagel, "Equal Treatment and Compensatory Discrimination," *Philosophy and Public Affairs* 2, no. 4 (summer 1973):359.

12. Ibid., p. 359.

13. Because this argument grounds the desert of the best qualified in an obligation to respect the applicants' status as agents, it may seem to fail for cases in which qualifications are "passive." For example, for a job as receptionist, the qualifications are apt to include being attractive (or at least presentable). But as long as one's attractiveness is important because it increases one's ability to interact smoothly with others, it does contribute to the efficacy of one's actions. On the other hand, if the receptionist will do nothing, or virtually nothing, but sit and look attractive, we may concede that the resulting desert-claim either lacks serious force or must be justified in some other way. For

further discussion of such qualifications, see Alan Wertheimer, "Jobs, Qualifications, and Preferences," *Ethics* 94, no. 1 (October 1983):99–112.

14. For detailed discussion, see chapter 9 of my book *Desert* (Princeton, N.J.: Princeton University Press, 1987).

15. See my "Justifying Reverse Discrimination in Employment," *Philosophy and Public Affairs* 4, no. 2 (winter 1975):159–170; and also my "Preferential Hiring," in Tom Regan, ed., *Just Business: New Introductory Essays in Business Ethics* (New York: Random House, 1984), pp. 32–59.

16. For pertinent discussion, see my "Ancient Wrongs and Modern Rights," *Philosophy and Public Affairs,* 10, no. 1 (winter 1981):3–17.

PART 3

Equal Opportunity in the Democratic Process

6

The Equal Opportunity to Exercise Power

JANE MANSBRIDGE

I will argue in this paper that we cannot make sense of the democratic norm of the equal opportunity to exercise power without distinguishing between the exercise of power in situations of common interest and its exercise in situations of conflicting interest.

I will begin by defining what I mean by equal opportunity and by power, distinguishing, in the definition of power, between what I will call "coercive power" and "influence." I will then argue that the democratic norms appropriate to situations of conflicting interest forbid unequal coercive power. Those norms therefore forbid, except possibly in two conditions that I will specify, the competition for unequal coercive power under conditions of fair equal opportunity. However, democratic norms do not forbid unequal influence in situations of common interest. What many writers mean by the equal opportunity to exercise power therefore turns out on inspection to mean the equal opportunity to exercise unequal influence in situations of common interest.

ON EQUAL OPPORTUNITY MORE GENERALLY

I understand the "opportunity" in "equal opportunity" as simply liberty. Thomas Hobbes defined liberty as the "absence of external impediments."[1] His underlying metaphor is one of individual atoms, like individual rocks or stones, hurtling off frictionless into outer space, propelled by their desires for power after power that ceaseth only in death.[2] Retaining the Hobbesian metaphor, I see *legal* equal opportunity, the eighteenth-century career open to talents, as removing legal barriers to this individual motion. What John Rawls called "fair" equal opportunity removes other (social) barriers, leaving, in its purest form, only ability and effort to determine how far one will go in one's desired direction, and how fast.[3]

Although it is a conceptual improvement to distinguish legal equal opportunity from fair equal opportunity, neither Rawls nor Bernard Williams, who originated the distinction, gave us a clear conception of what fair equal opportunity might mean. Take the most usual case of scarce goods. Williams described equal opportunity as a way of distributing a good fairly when the supply of the good is limited compared to the demand.[4] The metaphor, appropriate to Hobbes, who reduced all human activity to motion, is one of a race. The race is unfair, Williams suggested, "if the unsuccessful sections [of society] are under a disadvantage which could be removed by further reform or social action."[5] This formulation, however, seems to require removing every disadvantage that could possibly be removed by reform or social action. Removing every disadvantage might require genetic engineering or concentrating social resources on the deeply handicapped. Language that directs us only to the *possibility* of removing disadvantages does not, I believe, capture the complexity of our inchoate conceptions of fair equal opportunity. I will argue that as we try to distinguish among disadvantages in a world of limited resources, we should consider, along with the costs of removing each disadvantage, the corollary normative principle of its origin.

Williams's own discussion suggests that a disadvantage society itself has caused is particularly suspect. To argue against mere legal equal opportunity, Williams told the story of a hereditary warrior class that replaced direct succession with legal equal opportunity in competition but preserved its ascendency "because the rest of the populace is so under-nourished by reason of poverty that their physical strength is inferior" and they cannot compete successfully.[6] In such a case, Williams contended, "the supposed equality of opportunity is quite empty—indeed, one may say that it does not really exist."[7] Williams believed that equal opportunity is empty in this example because the barrier to successful competition is a state that social reform *can* alter. I would say that his story derives much of its force from the socially generated nature of that barrier. We feel that this competition between the nourished and undernourished is not fair in part because we suspect that the nourished in some, perhaps indirect, way *caused* the under-nourishment of their competitors.

John Rawls came to a similar conclusion, without a rationale based on causality, in arguing that a race meets the criterion of fair equal opportunity when it measures nothing more than innate, or "natural," ability and effort. Fair equal opportunity, he wrote, would eliminate "the influence of social contingencies," allowing "the distribution of wealth and income to be determined by the natural distribution of abilities and talents."[8]

Fair equal opportunity is a far more murky concept than legal equal opportunity. The criterion of social origin (or Rawls's distinction between the "natural" and the socially caused), though helpful conceptually, does not give clear practical guidance. Human action affects the natural order so deeply that we often find it hard to exonerate society fully from even the most seemingly natural accidental tragedies. Nor do considerations of social origin fully explain the complexities of our intuitive understandings of fair equal opportunity. If an individual or group could compete with an equal likelihood of reward after a relatively inexpensive operation for a "natural" defect, we might well believe that the ideal of fair equal opportunity required us collectively to provide that operation for those who could not otherwise afford it. This example would support Bernard Williams's criterion of the simple possibility of removing a disadvantage. On the other hand, we might require the operation on humanitarian grounds alone, wholly divorced from the ideal of fair equal opportunity. When we move from "legal" to "fair" equal opportunity, other normative criteria, each with an independent status, begin to infiltrate the borders of the concept.

The idea that agents should provide some redress for harm they have caused has this kind of independent status as a norm in its own right.[9] But considerations of origin may actually be embodied in the concept of equal opportunity itself. If, as I urge, we think of equal opportunity as another form of equal liberty, then Helvetius, by way of Isaiah Berlin, suggested precisely when society ought to try to remove barriers to individual motion. Helvetius concluded that "it is not lack of freedom not to fly like an eagle or swim like a whale." Berlin expanded upon the point:

> If I am prevented by others from doing what I could otherwise do, I am to that degree unfree. . . . Coercion is not, however, a term that covers every form of inability. If I say that I am unable to jump more than ten feet in the air, or cannot read because I am blind, or cannot understand the darker pages of Hegel, it would be eccentric to say that I am to that degree enslaved or coerced. Coercion implies the deliberate interference of other human beings within the area in which I could otherwise act. You lack political liberty or freedom

only if you are prevented from attaining a goal by human beings. Mere incapacity to attain a goal is not lack of political freedom.[10]

For our purposes, we must remove Berlin's requirement of "deliberate" interference and allow unconscious or automatic interferences by human beings to constitute coercion.[11] Then, applied to equal opportunity as liberty, this insight allows us to conclude that fair equal opportunity ideally requires the removal of any interference or barrier that human agents have put there. Regarded collectively, fair equal opportunity requires "society" to remove any barriers that "society" has put there, even if the specific agent that produced the interference is not the same as the agent mandated to remove it.

The costs of even attempting to remove all socially generated barriers to competition—as opposed to the costs of removing legal barriers—are unacceptable. Since "society" includes the family and differences in resources between families, removing all the barriers that society has erected would mean, as many have realized, doing away with the family.[12] The costs would also include, beyond the destruction of the family, the costs and opportunity costs of genuinely compensatory programs for the physically and mentally handicapped, which in a world of limited resources would be bound to result in de facto handicaps for the able. In its full application, then, the criterion of social causation has no practical advantage over the criterion of possible removal. However, the criterion of social causation does suggest a coherent partial response. We may conclude that as the pattern of society's involvement in the creation of any barrier becomes clearer, fair equal opportunity demands that we hold society more and more responsible for removing that barrier from the race. The more society can be shown to be responsible for the barrier, the higher the costs we should be willing to pay to remove it.

EQUAL POWER

If we assume that even a perfectly just society would want both to reward those it honors and to provide some incentives to motivate and allocate people efficiently,[13] we must conclude that even a just society would generate some inequalities in reward. Money, prestige, and power constitute the usual trilogy of social rewards. But these three rewards are not perfectly interchangeable. To use Michael Walzer's term, each has its natural "sphere."[14]

Of the three, power involves, by its nature, the most coercion. Prestige involves the least coercion. Money falls in between. Although the sole function of money is to affect others (e.g., to persuade them to sell blintzes or work in a factory), background conditions that provided for everyone's minimal needs would reduce money to, in most cases, an inducement rather than an instrument of coercion. Power, on the other hand, which I will define as involving threats of either sanction or force, always involves coercion, the deprivation of liberty. If we put a high value on liberty, we may want either to ban coercive power altogether or at the least to try to block attempts to gain more than equal power.[15]

Liberalism is founded on the ideal of equal power. In the *Second Treatise,* for example, John Locke began his description of the state of nature by saying that in this state all men can order their actions as they think fit, "without asking leave, or depending upon the Will of any other Man."[16] When he called the state of nature a state of "equality," Locke meant a state of equal power, in which "all the Power and Jurisdiction is reciprocal, no one having more than another . . . without Subordination or Subjection."[17] Although age, virtue, or birth may entitle a man to more than equal respect in the state of nature, all this "consists with the Equality, which all Men are in, in respect of Jurisdiction or Dominion one over another, which was the Equality I [earlier] spoke of, as proper to the Business in hand, being that equal Right that every Man hath, to his Natural Freedom, without being subjected to the Will or Authority of any other Man."[18] This passage suggests that Locke equated equal power with equal liberty. His right to natural freedom implies not the right to have *no* power exercised over one, but the right to equal power, "no one having more than another."

Establishing equal liberty, and therefore equal power, has priority in Locke's and other liberals' thinking over ideal arrangements for any other good, including money. The liberty right is the primordial entitlement.[19] Within the liberal tradition, arguments for equal money derive primarily from the argument for equal power. Inequalities in the ownership of money are condemned when they make it possible for one person, or group of people, to buy and sell another.[20] The major evil in inequality of money lies in its potential for domination.[21]

To understand what this liberal ideal of equal power might mean, we need to define power itself. For simplicity, I will limit myself in this chapter to discussing only political power, not social or economic power. I will define all power in Jack Nagel's terms as "an actual or potential causal relation between the preferences of an actor regarding an outcome and the outcome itself"[22] but will consider only the subcategory of political power, or outcomes that involve both (1) other actors ("social power," broadly speaking), and (2) the political arena ("political power" being a subcategory of social power).[23]

Our democratic norms regarding political power work differently depending on whether we have in mind situations where the interests of the parties conflict or situations in which their interests coincide. In most cases, the power exercised when interests conflict is what I will call "coercive power." My "coercive power" includes both what Peter Bachrach and Morton Baratz called "power" (causing B to act through a threat of sanction) and what they called "force" (causing B's new situation without B's acquiescence).[24] Getting B to leave the room by threatening to shoot her, simply picking her up and carrying her out of the room, and leaving her where she is but taking down the walls and building the room elsewhere are all examples of what I will call "coercive power."

When interests coincide, however, in most cases the kind of power exercised is what I will call "influence." My "influence" involves actual or potential rational persuasion. Pointing out to B that the room is on fire or saying "Leave the room at once" in a way that (either through one's tone of voice or one's formal position) implies the capacity for rational persuasion[25] all constitute examples of "influence."[26]

I argue elsewhere that when interests conflict, democratic theory mandates that we make decisions by distributing coercive power equally— one citizen/one vote—to ensure that in the democratic process each citizen's interests are protected equally. We consider the tug of war of majority rule a "fair fight" and allow the majority legitimately to coerce the minority, so long as no individual amasses greater power resources than any other. Thus, in what I have called the theory of "adversary" democracy, unequal coercive power is illegitimate.[27]

To the extent that a situation approaches one of common interest, however, unequal power (influence) becomes legitimate. When interests do not conflict, the unequal power (influence) of one does not harm the interests of another.

If unequal influence (actual or potential rational persuasion in the interest of the other) is legitimate, it follows that the equal opportunity to gain unequal influence is legitimate as well. If unequal coercive power is illegitimate, it follows that the equal opportunity to gain unequal coercive power will be illegitimate as well. However, I will suggest two instances—one where desire, and therefore effort, varies among individuals, and the other where both ability and effort vary— in which unequal coercive power may be legitimate.

EQUAL OPPORTUNITY AS A MEASURE OF EFFORT:
THE CASE OF COERCIVE POWER

Assuming conflicting interests, adversary democracy mandates equal coercive power in decisionmaking. Theorists in this tradition, however, are divided as to whether the democratic ideal requires that citizens actually exercise equal power in decisions or merely have the equal opportunity to exercise power.[28] With the exception of Peter Bachrach and Robert Dahl, few have tried explicitly to argue for the ideal of equal power against that of the equal opportunity to exercise power, or vice versa.[29]

Some of the confusion surrounding this subject derives from ambiguities in the concept of power itself. Some theorists who argue for equal power may use the word "power" not to mean power *relations* (i.e., the exercise of power in a relationship, A over B) but rather to mean power *resources* (the possession of the bases for the exercise of power, as in the phrase "A has [owns, possesses] more power than B"). If one defines "power" as power resources, there is no difference in meaning between saying that A and B have equal power (possess the bases for equal power, which they may or may not use) and saying that A and B have the equal opportunity to exercise power. Similarly, Nagel's definition of power as "an actual or potential" causal relation helps blur the distinction between the equal opportunity to exercise power (potential power) and the equal exercise of power (actual power) by making the opportunity to exercise power simply a form of power itself.

Yet the possibilities for defining the problem away through a broadly encompassing definition of power should not obscure the practical difference between actual and potential power or between the possession and exercise of power resources. Adversary democratic theory mandates equality in one of these, and the question is which.

A relatively weak argument for equal opportunity is that it constitutes a realistic substitute for the unattainable ideal of ensuring the actual exercise of equal power. In Robert Dahl's words, "it might be argued . . . that if inequalities in direct influence are inevitable, at least we should insure that there is equal opportunity to gain influence."[30] The problem with this argument is that, as Dahl himself later pointed out, the "fair" equal opportunity to exercise power may be no easier to attain than the equal exercise of power.[31]

A stronger argument for equal opportunity is that citizens never want actually to exercise power on every decision that affects them; they want only to be able to exercise power when the decision might otherwise go against them. Brian Barry put the matter nicely when he argued that most of us do not want power at all; we want the outcomes that power might bring about, and if we can get those outcomes without exercising power, so much the better.[32]

In a more general form, this argument for equal opportunity, which I will expand upon here, assumes that whenever *desires* for a given good vary, egalitarians should promote not equal possession of that good, but only the equal opportunity to possess it. This usage differs from the more usual use of "equal opportunity" to describe situations in which *abilities* vary in competition for a desired but scarce good. Equal opportunity thus applies in two situations—when we want to reward only desire (which may be measured by effort) and when we want to reward both effort and ability. Compare the equal opportunity to cast a vote with the equal opportunity to gain entrance to a university. Every adult citizen is entitled to an equal vote but not to a place at a university. Voting power is "abundant," unrestricted; places at a university are scarce. Voting power is also ascribed; places at a university are earned. For the abundant, ascribed vote, equal opportunity requires only the measurement of effort; for the university, equal opportunity requires two criteria: effort and ability.

In cases like voting, in which we use equal opportunity to distribute relatively abundant goods when not everyone who might want a good actually desires it, we may place a slight impediment in the way of fulfilling a desire and use the effort individuals exert to overcome this impediment as a measure of the intensity of their desires. This procedure allows effort (either as a good in itself or as a measure of unequal intensity of desire or unequal need) to generate legitimately unequal results. In our norms regarding democracy, unequal coercive power can be legitimate when it derives from unequal effort because that effort is assumed to measure intensity of desire or need. If we allow intensity into the equation, we effectively modify the democratic goal of the equal protection of interests to read, "the equally intense protection of equally compelling interests."[33]

A common example of this use of equal opportunity in the nonpolitical realm is the open trough. A pig can eat as much as it wants from the trough, depending only on its hunger and deterred only by the effort it takes to pick the food up in its mouth, chew, and swallow it. This is the case of pure abundance. In conditions of slightly greater scarcity, we adopt mechanisms like the handle on the public paper towel dispenser, levered so that it takes several turns to produce a sheet of paper long enough to dry one's hands properly. There is a supply of paper toweling in the dispenser large enough so that if anyone needed a greater quantity or wanted it with sufficient intensity, he or she could turn the handle many times to produce the appropriate amount. For conditions of even greater scarcity in which we want to measure intensity, we invent queues, giving out the relatively scarce goods to those who are willing to stand in line the longest.[34]

All these methods of distribution depend for their fairness on the assumption that the costs and benefits of the distributing act are the same for everyone. The paper towel dispenser distributes less than is fair to the arthritic, and more than is fair to a child fascinated by the act of turning the crank. The queue distributes less than is fair to people with no free time and more than is fair to those who find it romantic to sleep on the sidewalk the night before. In these unfair cases, the distribution mechanism does not accurately measure effort (and therefore intensity or need) because some individuals incur special costs or receive special sidepayments from the distributing act itself. When the distribution system is set up implicitly to measure effort, any difference in ability that makes the costs of producing the outcomes vary between individuals subverts the system.

To return to the political realm, some voters, because of their positions in society, are more likely than others to get benefits out of the voting act itself, quite apart from how intensely they feel about the political policy their vote is designed to affect. Citizens in small districts with a stable population often have the chance of seeing a neighbor at the polls, an encounter that turns the occasion into a minor social event and makes the benefits of the act of voting greater than for the voters in an anonymous city district. It is also likely that middle-class citizens derive more intrinsic satisfaction from the voting act than do working-class voters because the act tends to reinforce the middle-class voters' greater sense that they have influence and because their vote plays a more important social role in their lives (as evidenced in their being more likely to talk with others about politics).[35] If the costs and benefits of the act of voting vary in this way across individuals, it is easy to see how the costs and benefits of more difficult acts, like working for or giving money to a campaign, might vary even more dramatically.

In the theory of adversary democracy, inequalities in the costs and benefits of a participatory act are irrelevant if they vary randomly across individuals. They are irrelevant even if the inequalities vary selectively, advantaging some groups and disadvantaging others, so long as the groups that have an advantage in the participatory act do not have interests that conflict with those of the disadvantaged groups. The adversary goal of the equal protection of interests leads us to be concerned about inequalities of power only when those inequalities correlate with conflicting interests.[36] We do not worry if redheads have more power than blonds until redheads and blonds develop conflicting interests.

In the case of class, the inequalities of power that evolve from the legally equal opportunity to exercise power do, in fact, correlate with conflicting interests. Poor people, for example, are not only less likely to vote than the rich; they are less likely to contact a representative (by phone, by letter, or in person) and much less likely to get up a petition or participate in an electoral campaign.[37] Nor will they appear frequently in the ranks of the heavy campaign contributors to whom legislators listen carefully. Because the conflict of interest between rich and poor is major and pervasive, the discrepancies between classes in the costs and benefits of the acts that influence legislation violate most obviously the norms of adversary democratic theory.

In an adversary context, voting and giving money to a campaign—indeed, even some forms of contacting, petitioning, and campaigning—are acts of coercive power. They are instances of the preferences of one group causing other people to do what they would otherwise not have done through threatening sanctions or changing the situation against the others' interests. Adversary democracy generates legitimate decisions by pitting citizen power against citizen power in a fair fight. The fight can be fair either in the simple model when each citizen exerts equal power in the struggle or in the expanded "equal opportunity" model that I have presented here, when all differences in exertion spring only from differences in effort and not from any differences in ability or in the costs and benefits of the participatory act itself.

EQUAL OPPORTUNITY AS A MEASURE OF MERIT: THE CASE OF COERCIVE POWER

The more usual use of equal opportunity is as a method of allocating goods by merit when the goods are scarce relative to the demand. Unequal power in a hierarchy is a perfect example of such a good. Indeed, Bernard Williams chose unequal power ("command") to illustrate his point that equal opportunity is a means of allocating scarce goods, of which some are limited by their very nature: "Some desired goods, like positions of prestige, management, etc., are *by their very nature* limited: whenever there are some people who are in command or prestigious positions, there are necessarily others who are not" (emphasis in original).[38] The usual concept of fair equal opportunity distributes these limited goods through a race that measures, if possible, only ability and effort.

However, because unequal coercive power is not a legitimate goal in adversary democratic theory, it is not legitimate to make positions of coercive power the reward in a race. In simple adversary theory, although political representatives can and should assemble in their own persons the aggregate power of the individuals they represent, they should have, as individuals, no more power resources than each citizen. The simple theory allows no legitimate place to a race for unequal individual power resources.

We can remain within the simple theory and allow only the prestige of collecting in one's person the aggregated wills of others to serve as a reward for which one competes under the conditions of fair equal opportunity. Or we can moderate the theory to reflect reality a little better by allowing representatives a legitimate sidepayment of individual power. That is, part of their pay for fulfilling the job of representative is to exercise as individuals, not just as representatives, more coercive power than other citizens. As soon as we make this realistic modification, we can conceive not only of prestige but of power as a prize in a race to be won under conditions of equal opportunity. Yet because expanding the simple model in this second way allows more long-standing inequalities than expanding it to incorporate intensity, the equal opportunity to acquire positions of unequal coercive power will always remain suspect in a fundamentally adversary, or liberal, system.

EQUAL OPPORTUNITY AS A MEASURE OF MERIT: THE CASE OF INFLUENCE

The case is quite different for situations of common interest and the exercise of influence. The goal of equal protection of interests does not require distributing equally the bases for influence. If A has great influence over B, and that influence is (as stipulated) in B's interest, B's interests by definition do not suffer. One may desire to exercise influence over others both for the prestige it brings and for the gratifying feel of affecting the world, but the people who are influenced do not suffer from this exercise, except insofar as the comparison of relative prestige and effect on the world makes them feel diminished as persons.[39]

Because unequal influence does not interfere with the equal protection of interests, it is a legitimate democratic goal in a competition governed by the rules of fair equal opportunity. Accordingly, many writers in the liberal tradition assume a context of common interest and, consequently, the exercise of influence rather than coercive power, when they discuss the equal opportunity to exercise power. I will examine here the writings of Michael Walzer and John Rawls.

Early in *Spheres of Justice,* explaining that most of his book is "simply an exposition" of the meaning of this and a similar passage from Pascal, Michael Walzer quoted Marx on what we may think of as the equal opportunity to exercise influence: "Let us assume man to be man, and his relation to the world to be a human one. Then love can only be exchanged for love, trust for trust, etc. . . . if you wish to influence other people, you must be a person who really has a stimulating and encouraging effect upon others."[40] Walzer commented on this passage:

The first claim of . . . Marx is that personal qualities and social goods have their own spheres of operation, where they work their effects freely, spontaneously, and legitimately. There are ready or natural conversions that follow from, and are intuitively plausible because of, the social meaning of particular goods. [No ruler can] rightly claim to influence my actions: if a ruler wants to do that, he must be persuasive, helpful, encouraging, and so on.[41]

In an earlier work on the same subject, Walzer concluded that although it is "hard to see how a man can merit the things that money can buy . . . it is easy to list cases where merit (of one sort or another) is clearly the right distributive criteria [sic]." The very first case he listed is the case of influence: "Six people speak at a meeting, advocating different policies, seeking to influence the decision of the assembled group."[42] Walzer here advocated, as many of us would, the distribution of influence on the basis of merit—merit meaning, presumably, the combination of effort and ability measured by fair equal opportunity.[43]

Walzer's choice of the word "influence" tips us off to his implicit context of common interests, in which inequalities of influence do not impede the equal protection of interests. It would be absurd, Walzer argued, to insist that citizens have "literally the same amount of influence." Rather, we should insist that all the citizens "at least have a chance" to exercise influence.[44] To put Walzer's point another way, influence itself, a good scarce almost by its nature, can be allocated through fair equal opportunity—not here the equal opportunity of effort alone, but the equal opportunity of effort and ability.

Walzer rejected the adversary ideal of equal coercive power because he rejected the larger rationale of adversary democracy. Although he recognized that present democratic norms mandate giving each citizen equal coercive power in the form of a vote, he believed that the vote and other potential ways of ensuring equal coercive power (like push-button referenda) are and should be insignificant parts of the democratic process.[45] Because he wanted politics to be, and therefore sees it as, a matter of persuasion rather than coercive power, Walzer envisioned political inequality only as a matter of inequality of influence.[46] Rejecting coercive power entirely, he had no difficulty subscribing to the criterion of equal opportunity for distributing influence.

John Rawls also looked at political power primarily in the context not of a democracy based on conflicting interests but rather of a democracy in which each citizen's "first interest" is in just legislation.[47] When Rawls assumed a context of common interest, he could forgo trying to make coercive power equal, and can formulate the problem of distribution, in the political realm as in the economic, as one of guaranteeing fair equal opportunity in the race for unequal reward.

Rawls discussed the race for unequal influence in his somewhat obscure sections on the "worth" or "value" of liberty. Here he distinguished between "equal liberty," which includes "the principle of (equal) participation"[48] and which his theory of justice makes lexically prior to all other values, and the equal "worth" or the equal "value" of that liberty, which is the equal ability "to take advantage of one's rights and opportunities." "The worth of liberty," he wrote, "is not the same for everyone. Some have greater authority and wealth, and therefore greater means to achieve their aims."[49] How is this inequality of influence to be justified? Through fair equal opportunity.[50]

As soon as Rawls turned to the worth of political liberty, he wrote,

> [The Constitution] must underwrite a fair opportunity to take part in and to influence the political process. The distinction here is analogous to that made before [in the section on fair equal opportunity]: ideally, those similarly endowed and motivated should have roughly the same chance of attaining positions of political authority irrespective of their economic and social class.[51]

In short, inequalities of political influence (inequalities in the worth of political liberty) should be allocated by a race determined only by ability and effort. Rawls is less sensitive to the difficulties of achieving fair equal opportunity in the political than economic realm. He assumed that fair equal opportunity in the political realm requires, beyond freedom of speech, thought, conscience, and assembly, only that all should have the means to be informed about political issues and should be in a position to assess how proposals and policies affect both their own well-being and the public good.[52] This means keeping property and wealth widely distributed, providing government monies on a regular basis to encourage free public discussion, and subsidizing funding for political campaigns while preventing major private campaign contributions.[53] He concluded that if the steps he proposed are taken, the small number of persons who devote much of their time to politics "will most likely be drawn more or less equally from all sectors of society."[54]

The first problem with Rawls's conclusion is factual. Rawls explicitly disclaimed expertise in political sociology,[55] and did not know when he wrote these words that even when monetary contributions are equal, as in the vote, the rich participate in politics more than do the poor.[56] Although Rawls's measures would go a long way toward equalizing the worth of political liberty, the costs and benefits, particularly of the difficult participatory acts, would still vary greatly by the social class of each participant. As a consequence, the small number of persons who devoted time to politics would continue to be drawn from the middle and professional classes. This pattern would be particularly strong in Rawls's just society, where the upper economic and social sections of society would owe their positions, as much as possible, to ability and effort alone. Because political skills are not very different from administrative and other generally valued skills, the political fraction would undoubtedly be drawn mainly from the highly skilled groups in society—that is, the upper economic and social sectors in society. Rawls did not say that *citizens* would "have roughly the same chance of attaining political authority irrespective of their economic and social class," but only that those "similarly endowed and educated" would have roughly the same chance. Far from having the same chance "irrespective of class," those similarly endowed would tend to come from the already highly endowed classes.

The second problem with Rawls's conclusion is analytic. His goal, he said, is to draw the active participants in politics "more or less equally from all sectors of society." Yet in a context of common interests there is no need to protect citizen interests equally, as his passing comment on unequal voting suggests.[57] There might well be a need to include in the process of deliberation representatives with different experiences and different points of view, but in order to protect everyone's interests it is not necessary to draw these actors equally from all sectors of society.

It is conceivable that Rawls's commitment to drawing the group with more political influence more or less equally from all sectors of society might derive from a concern for protecting interests equally in those parts of any democracy in which conflicting interests prevail. However, to protect their constituents' interests representatives need not be drawn from the same sectors of society as those constituents.

I suspect that this commitment of Rawls to drawing the influentials more or less equally from all sectors derives, rather, from a concern with the self-respect of each citizen, who would find the salient facets of his or her self mirrored only in such an equally drawn sample.[58] To meet this requirement for self-respect, those with more influence would have to be drawn not just equally from the groups with competing interests, as in the argument from equal coercive power, but equally from all groups with identifying characteristics salient to their members' conceptions of themselves. It is hard, however, to see how influentials could be drawn for this purpose through the mechanism of a race, for any race would systematically leave behind those with some salient characteristics, like their lower likelihood of winning races of that sort.

If Rawls wants the influentials to mirror the rest of society, he must abandon the mechanism of a fair equal opportunity that measures ability as well as effort.

REJECTING EQUAL OPPORTUNITY

In his classic, *The Rise of the Meritocracy,* Michael Young pointed out that if we could approach fair equal opportunity, removing from the path of individual advancement the most obviously socially generated barriers, then "for the first time in human history, the inferior man [would have] no ready buttress for his self-regard."[59] In the imperfect world of unfair equal opportunity, we use the patent unfairnesses of the process to shield our self-respect against harsh judgments regarding our place in the resulting hierarchies. The presence of myriad small unfairnesses and several major ones prevents the successful from feeling too self-satisfied about their positions and the unsuccessful from feeling too much self-blame. The problem with equal opportunity is that to the very degree that it is fair, it allows everyone in the society to believe that the inequalities that result have been earned.[60] Truly fair equal opportunity would undermine equality of respect, and unequal influence resulting from fair equal opportunity would be particularly insidious if political equality is, as Rawls suggested, the centerpiece of a society's commitment to underlying equal respect.

With these considerations, we move from equal opportunity to equal result. To the degree that shoring up each individual's self-respect is a central value, and to the degree that any "earned" inequality undermines the self-respect of those who lose in the race, any earned deviation from equal result must count as a cost. Restricting competition to protect the psyches of the losers, on the other hand, has its own costs, in the world of politics as elsewhere.

WHEN IS THE EQUAL OPPORTUNITY
TO EXERCISE POWER LEGITIMATE?

In this chapter I have argued for three different conceptions of the equal opportunity to exercise power. These conceptions are not necessarily incompatible, but they have different meanings and implications.

The first is the equal opportunity to exercise coercive power, when access to that power is unrestricted and, in a sense, "abundant." Fair equal opportunity means in this context that inequalities in the exercise of power should derive only from differences in individual effort. Differences in effort would in turn derive from differences in intensity of feeling, or need, regarding the political issues on which power was being exercised. Inequalities of this kind can be legitimate if one makes an exception, in adversary theory, to accommodate intensity.

The second conception is the equal opportunity to exercise coercive power when access to that power is by its very nature limited. In this case, only a few hold positions of command in which they have the resources either to threaten sanctions or change others' situations without their acquiescence. Fair equal opportunity means in this context that differences in the exercise of power, used as a reward, should derive only from differences in both effort and ability. Inequalities of this kind can be legitimate if one makes an exception, in adversary theory, to accommodate using power as a reward, but there are important drawbacks to such a use.

The third conception is the equal opportunity to exercise influence in situations of common interest. Fair equal opportunity means in this context that differences in the exercise of influence should derive from differences in both effort and ability. The resulting inequality, however, would not threaten the goal of the equal protection of citizen interests. Inequalities of this kind are legitimate in adversary theory because they fall outside the sphere of conflicting interests. Promoting each citizen's equal self-respect may require restricting even this kind of inequality, but with important normative and other costs.

ACKNOWLEDGMENT

I am grateful to George Sher for insightful comments on an earlier draft of this paper. For time to work on this article, I am grateful to the Institute for Advanced Study in Princeton. The work was supported by funds from the National Endowment for the Humanities.

NOTES

1. Hobbes (1651/1950), ch. 14, p. 106.

2. Hobbes, ch. 2, p. 9; ch. 10, p. 69; ch. 11, p. 79. For an insightful exegesis of this extended metaphor, see Spragens (1973).

3. Rawls (1971), p. 73. Rawls's own phrases are "equality of fair opportunity" (e.g., pp. 65, 87) and "fair equality of opportunity" (e.g., pp. 73, 83, 299, 300).

4. Williams (1962), p. 124–125. See also below, p. 17. Williams actually put forth three conditions. One is that the goods be limited, another that they be "desired by large numbers of people in the society," and the third that they be "goods which people may be said to earn or achieve." Later I will argue that in some cases of equal opportunity goods need not be limited, so long as they are differently desired. Nor is it necessary for large numbers to desire the good, so long as the demand is sufficiently greater than the supply to

outweigh the organizing costs of a competition. Nor, finally, need the good itself be intrinsically something one must earn or achieve. One might decide for many reasons to allocate an indifferent good (e.g., a box of chocolates or money itself) through a competition. In short, Williams's three criteria for equal opportunity do not apply in all cases.

5. Ibid., p. 127.

6. Williams, p. 126.

7. Ibid.

8. Rawls, p. 74. Because Rawls considered the natural distribution of abilities and talents undeserved, he turned from fair equal opportunity to a combination of fair equal opportunity and the difference principle to produce justice. He made fair equal opportunity lexically prior to the difference principle but primarily, as I read him, for the practical reason that this procedural rule with appropriate background conditions will in fact in the long run produce outcomes approximating those required by the difference principle and will work more smoothly, with less civic dissension than more administrative ways of enforcing the difference principle. For more on Rawls's ideal of fair equal opportunity, see Brian Barry in Chapter 2.

9. Pace Goodin (1985).

10. Berlin (1958/1969), p. 122.

11. On reflection, Berlin might not want to insist that interference be deliberate in order to constitute coercion. But we need not go into this issue here.

12. Talcott Parsons (1953), for example, pointed out that "the preservation of a functioning family system . . . is incompatible with complete 'equality of opportunity'" (p. 422). For the most extended treatment of this issue, see Fishkin (1983).

13. Davis and Moore (1945), Wrong (1970).

14. Walzer (1983).

15. Power, being relational and often specific to situations, is also by its nature less fungible than money, whose utility derives from the degree to which it can purchase goods in many spheres. Moreover, an antipathy to coercion usually leads us to try to restrict power by law or by fiat even more than it is already restricted by nature. For these reasons, power is usually not as efficient a reward as money.

16. Locke (1679–89/1965), section 4, p. 309.

17. Ibid.

18. Ibid., section 54, p. 346. Of course, Locke did not mean that the right of natural freedom, or equal power, in the state of nature entitled one to an equal vote in civil society. Universal manhood suffrage would be a radical proposal until the first half of the nineteenth century. Even the Levellers, who a century before Locke argued for a massive extension of the franchise, did not extend the franchise to servants, primarily on the grounds, I believe, that servants could not exercise a voice independent from their masters (see Maximillian Petty in the Putney debates. In this interpretation I differ from C. B. MacPherson (1962) and many others, e.g., Miller (1978), p. 84.

19. Hart (1958), Nozick (1974).
20. Rousseau (1762/1950), p. 50.
21. For example, Walzer, pp. 10–21.
22. Nagel (1975), p. 29. Nagel's definition improves on Dahl's (1957) "A getting B to do something that B would otherwise not do" as well as on the definitions of many others by including situations in which B anticipates what A will want in the absence of any specific signal from or conscious intention by A. It must, however, be understood to include stasis, or lack of external movement, among "outcomes." That is, if A exercises a certain amount of power in one direction, and B exercises the same amount in the opposite direction, resulting in stasis, I will say that both A and B are exercising power, indeed, that they are exercising equal power.

23. What area the political arena should cover is, of course, highly contested, particularly when there is prior agreement that "political" decisions should be made by "democratic" procedures. The analysis in this chapter does not depend on a resolution of the question.

24. Bachrach and Baratz (1963).

25. Friedrich (1958). See also Partridge's (1963) definition of influence as A affecting B without B subordinating his wishes to those of A.

26. In this analysis I will ignore the cases in which A exerts coercive power over B for B's own interest and the cases in which A influences B against B's interest. The first is an instance of paternalism, with its attendant problems. The second might be called "manipulation" and is not, as far as I know, legitimate in any version of democratic theory. See Lukes (1974) for more on this issue.

27. Mansbridge (1980/1983). The equal protection of interests is one of three reasons for equal power and the only one that logically requires what one might think of as quantitatively equal power. Though I endorse (Mansbridge 1980/1983) competition in conditions of equal power as a weak but appropriate normative model for situations of genuinely conflicting interest (not situations that can be resolved by the independently determined demands of justice), I also suggest a stronger model for meeting the demands of adversary democracy, a model of proportionate outcomes, or "taking turns." This purposely schematic division of common and conflicting interests does not, of course, adequately capture the way interests evolve under the impact of new experiences and of others' influence. Influence that changes another's interests must be judged legitimate or not in individual cases on the basis of arguments that draw on the nature of both humanity in general and the particular individual. These arguments will take into consideration, but will not ultimately depend on, the kinds of influence employed.

28. On the "equal power" side, Jack Lively (1975, p. 109) made political equality the "defining principle of democracy" and defined political equality as "actual equality in the ability to determine decisions" (p. 16). Carole Pateman (1970, p. 69; see also p. 43) argued that the participatory theory of democracy requires political equality, and she defined political equality as "equality of political power in determining the outcome of decisions." David Miller (1978)

wrote that "the general element [in "the notion of democracy"] is political equality. Each member of the society whose institutions are in question is to have an equal share in political power" (p. 77; see also p. 79). For similar definitions by Bertrand Russell, E. F. Carritt, Austin Ranney and Wilmoore Kendall, Elias Berg, Jack Nagel, and Giovanni Sartori, see Mansbridge (1980/ 1983) p. 334. On the "equal opportunity" side, Harold Lasswell and Abraham Kaplan (1950, p. 219) wrote that "a rule is defined to be equalitarian, not in the degree to which *power* is equally distributed, but rather *access* to power" (emphasis in original).

29. Bachrach (1967) and Dahl (1964), as reported in Bachrach (1967).

30. Dahl, 1961, p. 86. See also Dahl (1964), as reported in Bachrach (1967).

31. Dahl (1970). Robert Dahl vacillated over the years from defining the democratic ideal as what I call equal power (meaning preferences equally causing outcomes) (1956, pp. 32, 37; 1958, p. 466) to suggesting that equal power, an impossible ideal, should be replaced by the equal opportunity to exercise power (1961, pp. 79, 80, 86, 87; 1964), to defining the ideal only as equal opportunity (1970, p. 67; 1971, p. 2), and finally to defining the ideal again, as in his first works, as equal power, while adding the second criterion of equal opportunity of expression (1977, p. 11, 103; 1979, pp. 101–102; 1982, p. 6).

32. Barry (1980) defined power as the capacity to make a difference to the outcome overcoming resistance in the process. This definition is narrower than Nagel's definition of power but broader than my definition of coercive power. Since coercive power, a subset of Barry's power, is the subject of this section of the analysis, Barry's argument applies.

33. For the intensity problem, see Kendall and Carey (1968), Pennock (1979).

34. Note that the reasons for wanting to restrict distribution (and therefore to measure intensity) in situations of pure abundance may differ from the reasons for wanting to restrict distribution in scarcity. In situations of pure abundance (e.g., the vote), one may want to limit consumption to those who "really" desire it (desire it relatively intensely) in order to protect the larger system in ways that have nothing to do with depletion of resources. The same argument may be made for putting in a pet's trough a relatively unattractive but healthful food in order to discourage overeating. The usual reason for wanting to restrict distribution in situations of scarcity is, however, to limit depletion. Note also that measurements of intensity reflect only preferences, not necessarily underlying interests.

35. Verba and Nie (1972). Members of the middle class also have more information about politics, which tends to reduce the costs of voting. That information, though perhaps derived in part from more intense feelings about the outcome, also simply comes, without extra effort, as part of a more educated way of life. Mansbridge (1980/1983) indicated how the costs and benefits of different acts of political participation vary by geographical location and class even within relatively homogeneous groups like a New England town or a small "alternative" workplace.

36. Mansbridge (1981), p. 474. It is important to distinguish the costs and benefits of the participatory act itself (which should be equal) from the costs and benefits of the outcome that voting produces. The varying costs and benefits of the outcome generate the intensity that in this model it is legitimate to measure.

37. Verba and Nie (1972), Milbrath (1977). As a general rule, the harder the act, the greater the potential advantage of the rich or of any group that has some advantage in the participatory process. One cannot conclude simply from different rates of acting that an act is harder for the group with lower rates. But in every case except voting, the evidence is fairly clear that the poor have fewer verbal, social, and monetary resources for influencing the political process. Even with voting, the greater feelings of political efficacy and likelihood of talking about politics among the comparatively rich probably make the act easier for them.

38. Williams, p. 124. Goods, Williams pointed out, can also be limited "contingently" (not everyone satisfies the conditions of access, but there is no intrinsic limit to the numbers who might satisfy the conditions, as in a university education) or "fortuitously" (there is simply not enough of the good to go around) (pp. 124–125). Williams addressed only situations of "inequality of *merit*" (emphasis in original) (p. 239), not inequality of desire. One could, however, conceive of goods limited by their very nature (positional goods, like the best seats at a concert) that one wanted to distribute according to intensity of desire.

39. The problem of envy is a problem with any inequality (Mansbridge, 1983). Moreover, though any given act of influence in a context of common interests can be expected not to harm the influenced person, repeated acts of one-way influence can harm that person both by eroding the basis of equal respect that underlies civic friendship (leading both parties and onlookers to treat the source of greater influence as a being of greater intrinsic worth) and by reducing the likelihood that the recipient of influence will develop full capacities for autonomy (Mansbridge, 1980/1983).

40. Walzer (1983), p. 18, citing Karl Marx, *Economic and Philosophical Manuscript, in Early Writings,* ed. T. B. Bottomore (London, 1963), pp. 193–194.

41. Ibid., p. 19.

42. Walzer (1973), p. 405.

43. Walzer did not define merit in this passage, but the context, in which he compares "equality of results" to a "'just meritocracy' (the career open to talents)," suggests that he has in mind a merit measured by what Rawls called "fair equality of opportunity." He did not mean simply the intellectual merit of the ideas presented.

44. Walzer (1983), p. 304.

45. Ibid., pp. 305–309.

46. See, for example: "Power 'belongs to' persuasiveness" (p. 306); "Is [a push-button referendum] the exercise of power? I am inclined to say, instead, that it is only another example of its erosion of value—a false and ultimately degrading way of sharing in the making of decisions" (p. 307); "Democracy requires equal rights, not equal power" (p. 309).

47. Rawls (1971), p. 227. See also p. 222 on political parties addressing "a conception of the public good" and pp. 357–360 on legislative discussion "conceived not as a contest between interests, but as an attempt to find the best policy as defined by the principles of justice" (p. 357). Even in Rawls's most adversary passages, where he gave most weight to the need for political equality, he used the language of influence ("pleadings," p. 226) rather than that of coercive power. Rawls recognized the implications for equal power of the distinction between common and conflicting interests; in a discussion of J. S. Mill he pointed out that when a government is "assumed to aim at the common good," then even unequal voting can be perfectly just (pp. 232–233). This discussion of Mill leaves it unclear to what degree Rawls believed that a government based on common interests is possible.

48. Ibid., p. 221. This principle "requires that all citizens have the right to take part in, and to determine the outcome of, the constitutional process that establishes the laws with which they are to comply."

49. Ibid., p. 204.

50. Rawls's arguments for fair equal opportunity throughout *A Theory of Justice* assumed that with the right background conditions, fair equal opportunity will produce the greatest benefits for the least advantaged. His argument on the equal worth of liberty, though obscure, can be understood to follow the same logic. Accordingly, Rawls first pointed out that inequalities in the worth of liberty can be consonant with justice whenever the existence of those inequalities benefits the least advantaged (p. 204). He assumed, however, that with the right background conditions, fair equal opportunity will lead to the wisest having the most influence and thus producing decisions that are best for all.

51. Ibid., pp. 224–225.

52. Ibid., p. 225.

53. Ibid., pp. 225–226.

54. Ibid., p. 228.

55. Ibid., pp. 226–227.

56. Conversation with Rawls, 1972.

57. Rawls, p. 233. See note 46.

58. The influentials, if drawn more or less equally from all sectors of society, would constitute what James Wilson at the Constitutional Convention called "the most exact transcript of the whole society" (cited by Pitkin [1972], in her discussion of "descriptive representation").

59. Young (1958), p. 108.

60. Schaar (1967).

REFERENCES

Bachrach, Peter. *Theories of Democratic Elitism.* Boston: Little, Brown, 1967.

Bachrach, Peter, and Morton S. Baratz. "Decisions and Non-Decisions: An Analytical Framework." *American Political Science Review* (1963) 57:632–642.

Barry, Brian. "Is it Better to Be Powerful or Lucky?" *Political Studies* (1980) 28:183–194, 338–352.

Berlin, Isaiah. "Two Concepts of Liberty" [1958]. In Isaiah Berlin, *Four Essays on Liberty.* Oxford: Oxford University Press, 1969.

Dahl, Robert A. *A Preface to Democratic Theory.* New Haven: Yale University Press, 1956.

———. "The Concept of Power." *Behavioral Science* (1957) 2:201–215.

———. "A Critique of the Ruling Elite Model." *American Political Science Review* (1958) 52:463–469.

———. "Equality and Power in American Society." In William V. D'Antonio and Howard J. Ehrlich, eds., *Power and Democracy in America.* South Bend, Ind.: University of Notre Dame Press, 1961.

———. "Power, Pluralism and Democracy." Paper presented at the annual meeting of the American Political Science Association, Chicago, September 9–12, 1964.

———. *After the Revolution.* New Haven: Yale University Press, 1970.

———. *Polyarchy: Participation and Opposition.* New Haven: Yale University Press, 1971.

———. "On Removing Certain Impediments to Democracy." *Political Science Quarterly* (1977) 92:1–20.

———. "Procedural Democracy." In Peter Laslett and James Fishkin, eds., *Philosophy, Politics and Society,* fifth series. New Haven: Yale University Press, 1979.

———. *Dilemmas of Pluralist Democracy: Autonomy vs. Control.* New Haven: Yale University Press, 1982.

Davis, Kingsley, and Wilbert E. Moore. "Some Principles of Stratification." *American Sociological Review* (1945) 10:242–249.

Fishkin, James S. *Justice, Equal Opportunities and the Family.* New Haven: Yale University Press, 1983.

Friedrich, Carl J. "On Authority." In Carl J. Friedrich, ed., *Authority: Nomos I.* Cambridge: Harvard University Press, 1958.

Goodin, Robert E. "Negating Positive Desert Claims." *Political Theory* (1985) 4:575–598.

Hart, H.L.A. "Are There Any Natural Rights?" *Philosophical Review* (1958) 64:175–191.

Hobbes, Thomas. *Leviathan* (1651). New York: Dutton, 1950.

Kaplan, Abraham, and Harold Lasswell. *Power and Society.* New Haven: Yale University Press, 1950.

Kendall, Wilmoore, and George W. Carey. "The Intensity Problem and Democratic Theory." *American Political Science Review* (1968) 62:5–24.

Lively, Jack. *Democracy.* New York: Putnam/Capricorn, 1975.

Locke, John. "Second Treatise." In Peter Laslett, ed., *Two Treatises of Government* (1679–1689). New York: New American Library, 1965.

Lukes, Steven. *Power: A Radical View.* London: Macmillan, 1974.

MacPherson, C. B. *The Political Theory of Possessive Individualism.* Oxford: Oxford University Press, 1962.

Mansbridge, Jane. *Beyond Adversary Democracy* (1980). Chicago: University of Chicago Press, 1983.

————. "Living with Conflict: Representation in the Theory of Adversary Democracy." *Ethics* (1981) 91:466–476.

————. "Envy, Equal Respect and Egalitarianism." Paper presented to the annual meetings of the American Political Science Association, Chicago, September 1–4, 1983.

Milbrath, Lester W., and M. L. Goel. *Political Participation.* Chicago: Rand McNally, 1977.

Miller, David. "Democracy and Social Justice." *British Journal of Political Science* (1978) vol. 8. Reprinted in Pierre Birnbaum, Jack Lively, and Geraint Parry, *Democracy, Consensus and Social Contract.* Beverly Hills, Calif.: Sage, 1978, pp. 75–100.

Nagel, Jack. *The Descriptive Analysis of Power.* New Haven: Yale University Press, 1975.

Nozick, Robert. *Anarchy, State and Utopia.* New York: Basic Books, 1974.

Parsons, Talcott. "A Revised Analytical Approach to the Theory of Social Stratification." In Reinhold Bendix and Seymour M. Lipset, eds., *Class, Status and Power.* Glencoe, Ill.: Free Press, 1953. Reprinted in Parsons, ed., *Essays in Sociological Theory,* rev. ed. New York: Free Press of Glencoe, 1954, pp. 386–439.

Partridge, P. H. "Some Notes on the Concept of Power." *Political Studies* (1963) 2:107–125.

Pateman, Carole. *Participation and Democratic Theory.* Cambridge: Cambridge University Press, 1970.

Pennock, J. Roland. *Democratic Political Theory.* Princeton: Princeton University Press, 1979.

Pitkin, Hanna Fenichel. *The Concept of Representation.* Berkeley: University of California Press, 1972.

Rawls, John. *A Theory of Justice.* Cambridge, Mass.: Harvard University Press, 1971.

Rousseau, Jean Jacques. *The Social Contract,* G.D.H. Cole trans. (1762). New York: Dutton, 1950.

Schaar, John. "Equality of Opportunity, and Beyond." In J. Roland Pennock and John Chapman, eds., *Equality: Nomos IX.* New York: Atherton Press, 1967.

Spragens, Thomas A. *The Politics of Motion: The World of Thomas Hobbes.* Lexington, Ky.: University Press of Kentucky, 1973.

Verba, Sidney, and Norman H. Nie. *Participation in America.* New York: Harper and Row, 1972.

Walzer, Michael. "In Defense of Equality." *Dissent* (1973) 20:399–408.

————. *Spheres of Justice.* New York: Basic Books, 1983.

Williams, Bernard. "The Idea of Equality." In Peter Laslett and W. G. Runciman, eds., *Philosophy, Politics and Society.* Oxford: Blackwell, 1962, second series, pp. 111–131.

Woodhouse, A.S.P., ed. *Puritanism and Liberty.* Chicago: University of Chicago Press, 1951.

Wrong, Dennis H. "The Functional Theory of Stratification: Some Neglected Considerations." In Edward O. Laumann et al., eds., *The Logic of Social Hierarchies.* Chicago: Markham, 1970.

Young, Michael. *The Rise of the Meritocracy.* London: Thames and Hudson, 1958.

7

Equal Opportunity in Political Representation

CHARLES R. BEITZ

It is a matter of nearly unanimous agreement among contemporary theorists of democracy that democratic institutions should provide their citizens with equal opportunities to influence political decisions. However, it is not clear what this principle means or why we should accept it, and there is controversy about how it should be applied to institutions.

As with democratic theory, so with constitutional law. At least since the days of *Reynolds* v. *Sims,*[1] there has been little doubt that the Constitution embraces some requirement that citizens be treated equally in their capacity as participants in the political process. But there has been great uncertainty and continuing disagreement about the content of this requirement. These difficulties extend beyond the familiar areas of the distribution of the franchise and the weight of the vote, arising as well in the areas of criteria for the fair representation of parties and racial minorities, regulation of access to the ballot, procedures for candidate selection by political parties, and the system of political finance.[2]

Part of the problem is that we normally think of political equality as a simple univocal principle that is to be applied to the political system as a whole.[3] I believe that this view is a mistake. There are several kinds of institutional issues to which a theory of political equality should apply, but it is implausible (and in some cases senseless) to hold that they either can or should all be resolved by appeal to one sovereign principle.[4] To make progress in this area, the various institutional issues in which equality is implicated need to be explored separately, with the aim of constructing a theory of political equality with sufficient detail and complexity to apply plausibly to them all. My discussion of equal opportunity in representation is part of such a larger effort.[5]

In fact, I shall not even discuss the whole of the problem of equal representation. As it arises in systems of district representation, that problem has two parts, distinguished in U.S. constitutional litigation as the issues of "quantitative" and "qualitative" fairness.[6] Speaking roughly, the first of these involves adherence to the precept, "one person/one vote," or as I shall usually say, equality of voting power. In this chapter, I will only be incidentally concerned with this issue. For even if the requirement of equal voting power is assumed to be satisfied, there are important problems about representation that may remain unresolved. These involve such "qualitative" issues as partisan and racial gerrymandering and racial vote dilution. I would like to concentrate on these issues.

Although I shall be taking my illustrations from U.S. constitutional law, I shall consider qualitative fairness as a basic problem in the moral theory of democracy. One reason is that constitutional doctrine is ambiguous and the moral theory of democracy may help to resolve the ambiguity. But there is a further reason: Questions about qualitative fairness implicate a more general class of problems in democratic theory involving the choice of representation systems. Let me explain.

Let us say, provisionally, that voters have equal power within a voting system if the system provides each voter with equal procedural resources for affecting election outcomes (I shall say more about this later). This condition can be satisfied in many types of representation systems. For example, it is satisfied in all of the following, provided only that each person is allowed to cast one equally weighted vote: any system of single-member districts of equal size (no matter how absurdly gerrymandered); any system of multimember districts of equal size returning equal numbers of representatives (again, no matter how gerrymandered); any system of proportional representation employing the single transferable vote; and any system of at-large election.

Of course, this is well known to theorists of voting systems.[7] What is not clear is how (if at all) the principle of political equality bears on the choice of representation systems beyond the minimal requirement of equal voting weights. What is "qualitative" fairness in representation, and what (if anything) does it have to do with equality?

I pose the question this way because many have thought that equality applies rather obviously and uncontroversially to aspects of political representation beyond the minimal requirement of equal voting weights. John Stuart Mill, for example, characterized proportional representation as a necessary part of "a really equal democracy."[8] John Rawls thought it obvious that equality requires constitutional prohibition of gerrymandering.[9] These examples suggest that a main source of disagreement in connection with the practical issues of qualitative fairness is theoretical uncertainty about the meaning and rationale of political equality. Accordingly, we might hope that an analysis of equal opportunity in representation may not only shed light on practical problems of institutional reform but also deepen our understanding of political equality itself.

I will proceed in three steps. First, more needs to be said about the precise character of the issue at stake in controversies about qualitative fairness in representation, especially as it contrasts with the issue of quantitative fairness. We shall see that these controversies derive from an ambiguity in the concept of power; once this is recognized, it will become clear that quantitative and qualitative fairness are distinct ideas, raising different problems of political morality. Second, the connection of qualitative fairness with concerns about the representativeness of the legislature needs to be probed and these concerns examined in relation to the reasons why we take an interest in political equality in the first place. We must ask, What (if anything) is unfair about "qualitative unfairness"? Finally, I shall suggest—tentatively at this stage—the outline of a theory to guide our thinking about equality in representation.

I

A representation system can satisfy the precept, one person/one vote, but still appear to be "qualitatively" unfair. One need not grant that there is anything substantial behind this appearance in order to examine the ways in which it has arisen. Only then will we be in a position to decide whether, from the point of view of democratic theory, the appearance of qualitative unfairness is anything to worry about.

Qualitative unfairness has been alleged in constitutional litigation involving both partisan and racial gerrymandering, multimember districting, and at-large election systems.[10] The issue raised in these cases is clearly not a matter of quantitative equality: The systems challenged provided equal voting power to all voters.[11] Nevertheless, in all the cases, some sort of unfairness was alleged to have occurred in violation of the Equal Protection Clause. What kind of unfairness or unequal treatment can occur when equality of voting power is guaranteed?

Consider the following simple-minded example. A committee of three members operates according to a one person/one vote, majoritarian decision rule. Members A and B agree with each other and disagree with member C 80 percent of the time; the rest of the time, each one is as likely to agree as to disagree with C.

There is an obvious sense in which each member of this committee has equal voting power—indeed, this can be inferred directly from the symmetry with which the decision rule treats each member. But there is another sense in which member C seems to have substantially less power than A or B. What is the difference?

Let us say that power is the capacity to get what one wants despite resistance.[12] Then we may say, roughly, that the amount of one's power varies with the amount of resistance that one is in a position to overcome. If this is right, then we should say that all three members of the committee have equal power, since under the decision rule each is in a position to overcome the same amount of resistance—namely, that of (at most) one other member.

What, then, of the sense in which member C might be said to have less power than the others? Without claiming anything about conventional usage, I think things will be clearer if we say that what C has less of is not power but prospects of electoral success.[13] Considered as a capacity to overcome (some degree of) resistance, power is equally distributed on the committee. However, once the likely distribution of preferences is taken into account, we can see that not every member will do equally well; some will succeed (get the outcomes they want) more often than others.[14] The reason for resisting the temptation to say that power (or perhaps actual as distinct from a priori power) is distributed unequally is that what makes the difference among the members, once preferences are taken into account, is not the capacity of each member to overcome resistance (which would be the same under any distribution of preferences) but the amount of resistance that each is likely to face given some assumption about the distribution of preferences.

Henceforth I shall use the terms "power" and "prospects of success" in the senses just indicated. However, it is to be emphasized that nothing in the argument to follow depends on accepting the distinction between power and prospects of success as an accurate report of conventional usage. Moreover, I do not mean to hold that a theory of equal opportunity in politics should concern itself only with the former. Indeed, to anticipate, the theory I shall sketch at the end is concerned with both. The distinction is introduced only for the purposes of clarity. The weight to be attached to it from a normative point of view—that is, the degree to which the distribution of power or prospects of success should matter in a theory of political equality—is a separate question entirely.

The distinction reflects an important truth about power. As Brian Barry put it, whether one gets what one wants in a power-sharing situation depends on two factors, of which only one is power (considered as a capacity to overcome resistance); the other is luck in being supported by enough others to carry the day.[15] (Thus, in our committee, differences in luck rather than in power produced the asymmetry in the outcomes.) When the power-sharing group is at least moderately large, then from the point of view of any individual participant, the contribution of power to political success, as opposed to that of luck, will normally be vanishingly small: Whether one's preferences succeed or fail will almost always be determined by luck rather than power.[16]

The point of all this is that what is involved in controversies about qualitative fairness in representation is not the distribution of power but the prospects of electoral success. One might have suspected this all along, of course, simply because these controversies only appear when the likely distribution of political preferences across constituencies is taken into account. For example, a districting plan can be seen to present problems of partisan gerrymandering only when the plan itself is considered together with information about the geographical distribution of party strength, which provides a basis for predicting how voters will vote. Similarly, at-large election schemes will display problems of racial vote dilution only when the racial composition of the population is taken as indicative of the likely division of electoral preferences and it appears on that basis that the interests of racial minorities are unlikely to be adequately represented.

An apparently contrasting interpretation of qualitative fairness in representation regards it as an imbalance in voting power among groups rather than among individuals. For example, as Laurence Tribe formulates the Supreme Court's rule regarding qualitative fairness, "an apportionment scheme is unconstitutional, despite its compliance with the one person, one vote mandate, if it cancels or minimizes the *voting power* of cognizable population groups" (emphasis added).[17] As the analysis presented earlier suggests, this frames the contrast with quantitative fairness in a potentially misleading way. The contrast does not arise from a concentration on the voting power of individuals, in one case, and on that of groups, in the other (if, indeed, sense can be made of this distinction at all). In both cases the ultimate concern is the political status of individuals; however, different dimensions of political status are involved—power, in the first case, and prospects of success, in the second.

Nevertheless, reference to group membership is vital in identifying qualitative unfairness. To assess someone's prospects of success, it is necessary to know something about the likely political preferences of other voters so that the person's chances of success can be compared with those of others. When people are seen as members of cognizable groups, their group membership provides a basis (although perhaps not a very reliable one) for inferring their (and others') political interests, hence their likely political preferences, hence their prospects of success. Thus, in racial vote dilution cases—in which it is alleged that districting arrangements dilute the voting power of racial minorities without necessarily denying them equal individual voting power—what is really being claimed is that under the existing districting system members of the group are less likely to be successful than they would be under another possible system.[18] Why such a complaint should carry any weight as a matter of democratic theory is a further question, to which I now turn.

II

If the foregoing is correct, then the unfairness of qualitative unfairness cannot consist in an unequal distribution of voting power. There are several alternatives. Qualitative unfairness might consist in some type of formal inequality or violation of impartiality in the method by which districting systems are devised. Or it might be some kind of distributive inequality within the system of representation involving something other than power: most obviously, perhaps, inequality of prospects of success. Or it might reflect some distributive infirmity that does not directly involve political inequality at all. I shall argue for the last of these, mainly by arguing against the first two. Of course, it might also be that there is nothing unfair about what is called "qualitative unfairness"—perhaps any districting scheme satisfying equality of power is equally fair (although there might be other things wrong with some such schemes). I shall not say much here about this last possibility, although it will be clear why it seems implausible.

Consider first the idea that qualitative unfairness consists in a violation of impartial treatment in the design of districting systems. This is a generalization of a common complaint about gerrymandering, and I shall discuss it in that connection.[19] Traditionally, gerrymandering has been criticized for what may be called its formal features: unusual or complex district shapes, district boundaries that depart from those of established political subdivisions, and so on. These criticisms, in turn, have elicited a range of formal norms for acceptable districting practices, such as the precept that districts should be compact and contiguous.[20] What such norms have in common, and what might appear to recommend them, is a pretension to political neutrality; they are at least on the face impartial between parties and other aggregations of interest. The question, of course, is why this kind of impartiality or neutrality should be counted as a virtue.

A common view is that there is some sort of intrinsic fairness in the use of explicitly nonpolitical criteria, but two difficulties obstruct any effort to develop this idea persuasively. First, it is a mystery why this should recommend a districting plan at all. The idea may be that the use of nonpartisan districting criteria makes it more difficult to manipulate district boundaries in order to distort the outcomes of the political process, but this makes sense only if there is some baseline in terms of which distortions can be identified, and it is not clear where the baseline could come from. A natural thought is that the baseline should be the pattern of political outcomes that would occur under some randomly chosen districting system. But this will not do. For one thing, it is indeterminate: Many districting systems might be randomly chosen, each of which would yield a different pattern of political outcomes, and there would be no way of saying which should be preferred.[21] And in any case, any "preferred" pattern of outcomes would reflect the geographic distribution of political preferences as these were filtered through the districting system, and there is no reason to treat this distribution itself as anything but arbitrary.

The other obstacle is this. Even if some sense could be given to the idea that facially impartial districting criteria are preferable on grounds of intrinsic fairness, one must recognize that the choice of districting systems unavoidably has political results. As Robert Dixon reminded us, "all districting is gerrymandering" in the sense that "whether or not there is a gerrymander in *design,* there normally will be some gerrymander in *result* as a concomitant of all district systems of legislative election."[22] Whatever criteria are used to construct a district system, some interests will be advantaged and others disadvantaged in comparison to what their prospects would have been in a system constructed according to different criteria. If there is any point of view from which outcomes matter—as obviously there is—and if the political circumstances warrant any definite predictions about the relationship between districting arrangements and outcomes, then this is not something to which one can be indifferent.

Of course, one need not maintain that impartial or neutral districting criteria are intrinsically fair in order to advocate their use. One might believe, instead, that the use of such criteria, perhaps in conjunction with some nonpartisan (or bipartisan) scheme for making apportionment decisions, is the best way to avoid the substantive evils associated with gerrymandering.[23] It is a further and independent question of democratic theory why the "evils" of gerrymandering are in fact evil. But any answer to this question will carry us back to a concern about results, so that, on this view, the neutrality or impartiality of the criteria will have only derivative significance. Their moral importance will be parasitic on the value attached to the political effects produced when districting systems are constructed in accord with them.

I will not pause to generalize these remarks about partisan gerry-mandering to the idea that qualitative fairness in representation involves some sort of formal neutrality or impartiality in the construction of districting systems. It is enough to point out that there is no plausible alternative, in analyzing qualitative unfairness, to a consideration of the political results—for example, of the distribution of prospects for electoral success—anticipated from the districting arrangements in question. Thus, if there is a general principle of qualitative fairness, it must specify the kind of outcomes that fairness requires. And if qualitative fairness is to be brought within a theory of political equality, it must be shown how equality bears on this requirement.

The most obvious outcome-oriented view regards qualitative unfair-ness as a deviation from equality of prospects of success, just as quantitative unfairness is a deviation from equality of voting power. This thought gains plausibility from the analogy with proportional representation, whose claim to embody a special kind of fairness stems precisely from the fact that it confers on nearly every voter an equal chance of voting for a winning candidate.[24] However, it is difficult to see why we should care about equality of prospects of success in the first place. What may appear to be the obvious answer—that equal prospects of success at the ballot box lead to equal prospects of satisfaction in the legislature—rests on a simple misunderstanding. Recall that the prospects in question are chances of casting a winning vote for a candidate for the legislature, not chances of getting the legislation one wants. There is no guarantee that in a regime of equal prospects of electoral success voters will have equal chances of seeing their policy preferences satisfied. All that is promised is that the legislature will mirror in some sense the political preferences of the electorate as the voters themselves identify them. Popular minorities will be represented, but their representatives will constitute legislative minorities, unable except through compromise to effect their constit-uents' will. Although proportional representation may have other virtues, it cannot be said a priori that minorities will do better under such a system than under some alternative system satisfying equal power but not equal prospects of success (such as a competitive party system).

Even if equal prospects of success were thought worth pursuing, a special problem arises when it is sought within a system of district, rather than proportional, representation. The difficulty derives from the different ways in which constituencies are composed in these systems.

In true proportional representation, constituencies define themselves through the voting process; it is up to individual voters to decide how to rank their political interests and which candidates are most likely to serve those interests effectively. By contrast, in district representation constituencies are established by the politicians and judges who apportion the population among districts. If their goal is some sort of proportionality between the electorate and the membership of the legislature, they must first adopt a criterion of proportionality—for example, party affiliation, race, religion. Then, by taking population data into account, they must draw district lines accordingly—they must engage in gerrymandering calculated to maximize the probability that each group identified by the criterion will be represented in proportion to its size.

It follows from this contrast that whereas proportional representation can almost completely equalize chances of electoral success, district representation, no matter how subtly gerrymandered, usually cannot. In proportional representation, because each winning candidate has a unanimous constituency, nearly every voter is represented by a legislator for whom he or she voted. But the same cannot be said of the kind of gerrymandering efforts in question here; given geographical constituencies, there will virtually always be voters who voted for losers. To seek equality of success within a system of district representation is to seek a goal that cannot normally be attained. So the egalitarian argument for proportional representation, whatever its strength in that case, is much weaker when applied to efforts to manipulate districting systems to secure proportional representation for groups identified independent of the voters' own expressed preferences. As I suggest in the following, there may be other good reasons to undertake such efforts in some cases, but they do not derive their force from egalitarian considerations of the kind that might be thought to make proportional representation a desirable ideal.

There is a further point about the contrast between proportional representation and district representation that has been gerrymandered to achieve some sort of proportionality. Here I can only put the point very roughly. In addition to its association with equal prospects of electoral success, true proportional representation might be thought desirable because it reproduces in the legislature the same balance of political interests that exists in the electorate at large. As a result, legislative compromise and accommodation will generate coalitions (and corresponding legislative outcomes) that replicate those that would arise if the entire electorate were somehow able to meet as a legislative assembly. Let us call this "interest proportionality." Its linchpin is that the system allows voters to vote for the candidate whose program most closely reflects their own interests as they themselves rank order them. Now, whatever the significance of this aspect of proportional representation, gerrymandered district representation yields at best a pale imitation. The reason is that the proportionality achieved in the legislature under such a system will not necessarily reflect the voters' own identification and ranking of their interests but rather that presumed by the designers of the district system. The degree of fit between the latter and the former is an empirical question, but it will be approximate at best.

Consider, for example, district systems designed to produce legislative representation proportional to party strength.[25] Party strength proportionality will have the same legislative effects as interest proportionality only if it mimics it; but it will mimic it only if the rank-ordered political interests of a party's voters are accurately reflected in the party's program (and if every voter is a member of a party). This, of course, is highly unlikely. Large parties necessarily formulate their programs in ways intended to attract the support of coalitions of voters with differing interests and differing views about their relative importance. This coalition-building activity will yield a legislative party whose program may not be accepted by any individual voter as his or her most-preferred legislative agenda; accordingly, the process of legislative compromise and accommodation will begin from a different balance of interests than that found in the electorate at large and may have correspondingly different outcomes. Again, there may be reasons to strive for party strength proportionality in the design of representation systems, but those reasons must be different from those that make interest proportionality seem to be a desirable objective. (Much the same could be said about other kinds of proportionality that might be sought in districting, such as race proportionality.)

I observed earlier that equal prospects of electoral success, even if it could be attained, will not necessarily lead to equal prospects of political satisfaction. I meant to discredit the idea that qualitative fairness should be analysed in terms of prospects of electoral success. It might be thought, in consequence, that a more plausible analysis of qualitative fairness would be couched instead in terms of prospects of political satisfaction. Perhaps a system is qualitatively fair to the extent that it yields political decisions that satisfy everyone's political preferences equally often. Qualitative unfairness, then, would arise when a structural bias tended systematically to produce inequalities in the distribution of preference satisfaction. This is the third view of qualitative fairness that I want to examine. As stated, it suffers from grave defects, but I believe that it points in the right direction.

The view derives from a familiar theory of the justification of democracy and from the conception of political equality associated with it. It is worth looking more closely at this conception and at the way it seems to support the view of qualitative fairness just sketched. The conception holds that everyone has an equal right to have his or her political preferences satisfied; but since it will normally be impossible to satisfy all political preferences simultaneously, some compromise is necessary, and the only compromise consistent with equality is that political decisions should satisfy the preferences of each member of the population an equal proportion of the time.[26]

It seems plausible that a conception of this general kind animated the normative political theory of many American pluralists. However this may be, the point to note—as critics of pluralist theory often insist—is that a representation system satisfying equal power will yield equal preference satisfaction only if various empirical conditions are met in society. For example, there must be neither intense nor permanent minorities.[27] Obviously these conditions need not hold. When they do not, preference satisfaction will likely be distributed unequally; in particular, minorities may be disproportionately disadvantaged and in the extreme case may be excluded altogether. Even when the conditions are satisfied, cleverly constructed districting arrangements could lead to distortions in the distribution of preference satisfaction. To maximize the probability that political outcomes will yield equal satisfaction over time, equal power must therefore be supplemented by a further pro-cedural requirement. Such a requirement would correspond to a principle of qualitative fairness and would mandate manipulation of the districting system to compensate for the predictable inequalities in preference satisfaction that would otherwise be produced.

This interpretation of qualitative fairness seems initially to meet the desiderata that have emerged in the foregoing discussion: It is outcome oriented and it clearly embodies an egalitarian principle. It has particular appeal because it provides a plausible rationale for objecting to the types of irregularities in representation most frequently challenged in recent constitutional litigation, namely, those involving "dilution" of the votes of blacks and other minorities.

Nevertheless, the interpretation is flawed as it stands. The critical defect lies in the premise that people have equal rights to have their political preferences satisfied. This is simply not a principle that one should accept. Why, after all, should the political system be arranged so that everyone is equally advantaged or disadvantaged in the long run? Like its cousin in the welfare economic injunction to move toward the Pareto frontier, this principle will appeal only if the prior distribution of preference satisfaction has some independent justification. If not—

if the economic system tends to produce unwarranted inequalities in the overall distribution of goods, for example—then a representation system that was egalitarian in the present sense might succeed only in perpetuating unwarranted inequalities. Since there is no reason in the general case to assume that the status quo distribution has any special warrant, the principle cannot stand.[28]

This is a fairly obvious objection, so it is worth asking why the principle of equal satisfaction might seem even initially plausible. I believe that the answer has to do with the point of view from which a justification of representative democracy—and, relatedly, a conception of political equality—is sought. Suppose we approach the question of justification from the point of view of a self-interested citizen. Then we shall be led to consider what reasons exist for such a citizen to obey the laws and in particular whether the fact that the laws issued from representative institutions provides any special reason for obeying them.[29] If the pragmatic necessity of compromise is accepted, then the view of fairness in representation that I have sketched is the natural result.

Although it is not without interest to consider why a self-interested citizen should obey the laws of a democracy, I do not believe that this question provides an appropriate formulation of the problem of justification, or, consequently, of the point of view from which a doctrine of fairness in representation should be worked out. Because it takes the actual interests of citizens as its starting point, the approach reproduces (albeit in a less obvious way) the mistake of presupposing the legitimacy of the existing distribution of goods. If this presupposition cannot be supported, then the "justification" will not necessarily yield moral reasons for obedience, much less a moral justification of democracy. (Indeed, it is not even clear that the justification can supply reasons of self-interest to everyone concerned. Why should it matter, to someone in the bottom half of the income distribution, that the representation system gives everyone an equal chance of having their policy preferences satisfied? Why shouldn't they expect more?)

I will not say more here about the defects of the justification of democracy we are considering or about the conception of equality of political opportunity associated with it.[30] The important point is that the resulting doctrine of qualitative fairness is defective in its conception of equality but not necessarily in its structure. I would like to conclude by exploring whether a more satisfactory doctrine of qualitative fairness can be constructed by accepting the instrumentalism of the view I have been criticizing while substituting a more appropriate conception of the equality to which democratic systems should aspire.

III

Theorizing about equality in representation is made difficult by the fact that any satisfactory doctrine of political equality must simultaneously address several different kinds of concerns. These correspond to three aspects of the democratic ideal, which describes a method of decisionmaking about public policy that has value by virtue of its characteristics as a public cooperative enterprise, the content of the legislation it tends to produce, and its contribution to the political education of citizens. These sources of value do not fully overlap. Of course, procedures matter partly because they tend to produce certain kinds of results rather than others; but they matter also because they define the terms on which citizens recognize each other as participants in a public process of political choice and because they give structure to the process whereby contending views are presented for public consideration. Equality bears on all three aspects of democracy, but it bears in different ways.

Now it is primarily the first two values that are implicated in issues involving representation. Citizens must be treated as persons entitled to equal status as participants in politics ("equal recognition"), but they must also be treated equally as the subjects of public policy ("equal consideration"). A theory of equality in representation should be sensitive to both aspects of the democratic egalitarian ideal, even though this may require some theoretical compromises. I would like to present a sketch (indeed, a crude sketch) of such a theory.

I believe that the first concern—for equal recognition—can be satisfied within systems of district representation by ensuring that everyone has equal power to affect the outcomes of the legislative process. A necessary (although not a sufficient) condition for equal power is that each person be entitled to cast an equally weighted vote for a representative who will be entitled, in turn, to cast an equally weighted vote in the legislature. (A full theory of equal political opportunity would spell out further conditions as well, specifying the meaning of equality in the preelection stages of political competition, including campaign activity and competition for a place on the final election ballot; here I limit myself to the structure of representation.) I have already noted that equal power, even if fully realized, may not guarantee very much about the likely distribution of prospects of electoral success or of political preference satisfaction; but because it requires that each citizen be given procedural opportunities to overcome the same amount of resistance, there is a clear sense in which equal power gives public recognition to the equal status of democratic citizens as participants in political decisionmaking. For this reason, equal power is an important requirement independent of its effects on electoral and legislative outcomes.

The second concern—that people be treated equally as subjects of public policy—is more complex. The complexity has both a philosophical and a pragmatic dimension. I have already mentioned the philosophical problem: Equal treatment must not be interpreted simply as equal satisfaction of preferences or interests because this would presuppose without warrant the acceptability of the existing distribution of goods. I see no alternative to bringing in a theory of just legislation to give content to the requirement of equal treatment of interests.[31] Legislation can be said to treat people equally in a morally significant sense when, over time, it promotes a distribution of benefits and burdens that accords with the requirements of justice, which are themselves to be worked out from a point of view in which each person's prospects are taken equally into account.[32]

As will have become obvious, I am going to suggest that whereas the aim of quantitative fairness in representation is to give public recognition to the equal political status of democratic citizens, the aim of qualitative fairness is the promotion of just legislation. The function of equality of power is primarily (although of course not exclusively) expressive, while that of efforts to influence the distribution of prospects of success is more instrumental. But it would be too simple, or at least too unhelpful, to say only that the choice among quantitatively fair representation systems should be guided by the aim of promoting distributive justice. The reason involves the pragmatic complexity referred to earlier. The direction of legislation is determined jointly by a great variety of factors, among which the structural features of the system of representation play at best a subordinate role. But it does not necessarily follow that an instrumental approach to qualitative fairness is either a hopeless or a pointless venture. Although it may be too much to expect that by manipulating the structure of representation just legislation can be systematically promoted, it may at least be possible to minimize some of the familiar dangers to which representation schemes have historically been prone. These include in particular the danger of majority tyranny—that is, the danger that the majority in the legislature will pay too little attention to the interests and rights of popular minorities.

A variety of strategies might be employed to give the interests of minorities some degree of protection in the structure of representation. Here, I shall discuss two that might be implemented in systems based on single-member districts.[33] First, the system can be organized so as to promote party competition, on the assumption that the more competitive the parties, the more likely they are to orient their programs to attract the support of disaffected minorities.[34] Second, when minorities are geographically concentrated and politically isolated, and when it is unlikely that their interests would be taken into account by the established parties even under the pressures of normal party competition, the system can be adjusted to increase the chance that these minorities will at least have a legislative voice.[35]

Both strategies for protecting minority interests may require the use of gerrymandering techniques to achieve their objectives. Operationally, both strategies may seek some sort of proportionality between a party or group's share of the electorate and the portion of the constituencies it controls. But in neither case is the fundamental underlying aim to promote proportional representation overall. Rather, it is to promote just legislation. The choice of procedures is directly conditioned on the goal of securing a desirable pattern of substantive legislative results.

This aspect of the theory I am proposing gives rise to two kinds of objections, which I will consider briefly. The assumption in connection with both strategies for protecting minority interests is that otherwise the minorities in question would fail to be treated justly—for example, by being denied their just distributive share or by having their rights infringed by an indifferent or hostile majority. This is plainly a historical assumption, whose validity in any particular case depends on the facts of that case. It is a further assumption that manipulation of the districting system will in fact avoid or help remedy the injustices at which they are aimed, and the validity of this assumption also depends on empirical judgments about particular historical situations. But someone might object that the application of fundamental principles of democratic theory should not be so dependent on the contingencies of social and political life. For one thing, this means that the institutional requirements of democratic theory will be relative to particular social situations, and this seems to conflict with the idea that the value of democracy (and hence its basic institutional requirements) is not relativistic. For another, it means that questions of institutional design will turn on empirical judgments that are both subject to significant error and (perhaps for that reason) inherently controversial, and this might undermine the perceived legitimacy of democratic legislation.[36]

In reply to the concern about relativism, it can only be said that the application of any substantive principle to particular situations will unavoidably involve some degree of empirical judgment. But we do not in general regard this as a compelling reason for rejecting substantive principles of political morality. The kind of "relativism" involved is benign: Nothing follows about the moral basis or value of democracy.

The concern about error and controversiality is not so easily dismissed. It is, at least, not crazy to speculate that the popular legitimacy of a

representation system might be undermined by the widespread per-
ception that its structure was open to frequent revision to produce
legislation that runs counter to the desires of the majority (especially
where the structural revisions come about as a result of judicial
intervention). However, the force of this concern must be kept in
perspective. There are two points. First, it is easy to overestimate the
possibilities for popular disaffection. A general belief that the system
yields legislation that is acceptable on the whole is a powerful antidote
to disaffection flowing from countermajoritarian procedural arrangements
or from particular instances of unpopular legislation. (Consider, for
example, the extraordinary uncontroversiality of such a patently anti-
egalitarian arrangement as the apportionment of the U.S. Senate.)
Second, the kinds of manipulation that I have suggested have a limited
potential for producing legislation at odds with the desires of the
majority. There is no threat to majoritarianism in efforts to ensure
proportional representation for parties; indeed, the opposite will more
often be the case. And gerrymandering to give a legislative voice to
disadvantaged minorities will accomplish only that—it will enable those
minorities, through their representatives, to put their case to the
legislative majority and to play a part in the process of legislative
compromise, but it can hardly guarantee them the legislation they want
regardless of the desires of others.

The other objection is this. The doctrine of qualitative fairness that
I have outlined allows choices about procedures to be conditioned on
the probability that some procedures more than others will encourage
patterns of legislative results that can be recognized as desirable from
the point of view of a substantive theory of justice. But result-oriented
considerations of this kind may seem to have no place in matters of
procedural choice. Democracy is rule by the people, and this implies
that the people may be—indeed, have a right to be—wrong on the
merits. The manipulation of procedures to avoid or minimize this
possibility may therefore appear to be an unwarranted interference in
the process of self-government.[37]

As a general matter, I believe that this objection rests on an implausible
view of the moral basis of democracy.[38] But a more specific reply is
possible. The idea of "rule by the people" (or, what amounts to the
same thing, the ideal of democratic equality) is ambiguous and vague.
Surely its minimal content is equal power in the sense distinguished
earlier; but beyond this, the idea is simply too general to provide much
guidance in matters of procedural design. It is an illusion fostered by
the undiscerning rhetoric of "rule by the people" that the protean idea
of procedural equality will by itself settle controversy about qualitative
fairness. As no system of legislative districting can be neutral in its

results, some further basis is needed for choosing among those alternative feasible arrangements that are consistent with the minimal requirement of equal power. The suggestion that the choice should be guided by the aim of protecting minorities against injustice therefore cannot be disposed of merely by pointing out that it involves appeal to substantive principles.

I observed at the beginning that it is a mistake to regard political equality as a simple principle of democratic theory in the sense of being a univocal principle capable of being applied directly in the definition of democratic procedures. If my remarks about qualitative fairness are correct, then they will illustrate this observation. Political equality is a complex ideal—not necessarily in the sense recently set forth by Michael Walzer,[39] but rather in the sense that the ideal is sufficiently abstract that its application to problems of institutional design requires a good deal of interpretation and adaptation to political and historical circumstance. If equality of political opportunity is regarded as a fundamental organizing principle of democratic theory, then although it normally demands that citizens have equal power over political decisions, this is better understood as one among many implications of the principle than as the content of the principle itself. The egalitarian commitment that animates democratic aspirations is richer and more substantial than this.

ACKNOWLEDGMENTS

An earlier version of this chapter was presented at the 1984 Annual Meeting of the American Political Science Association. For helpful criticisms of that version, I am especially grateful to Ronald Rogowski and Ian Shapiro.

NOTES

1. 377 U.S. 533 (1964).

2. Writing in 1964, Martin Shapiro noted the absence from constitutional doctrine of a coherent democratic philosophy that would provide guidance in interpreting the idea of "equal opportunity for every individual to participate in governing." After more than twenty years of subsequent litigation concerning nearly every aspect of political representation, one has to say that constitutional doctrine is not obviously more coherent. For Shapiro's comments, see *Law and Politics in the Supreme Court* (New York: Free Press, 1964), p. 219.

3. Thus many writers, when addressing the subject of political equality, are satisfied simply to repeat some version of the slogan that democratic institutions satisfy the requirement of equality if they give every citizen an equal opportunity

to influence political decisions. For several variations, see Carole Pateman, *Participation and Democratic Theory* (Cambridge: Cambridge University Press, 1970), p. 43; John Rawls, *A Theory of Justice* (Cambridge, Mass.: Harvard University Press, 1971), p. 221; Jack Lively, *Democracy* (Oxford: Basil Blackwell, 1975), pp. 8, 16; Amy Gutmann, *Liberal Equality* (Cambridge: Cambridge University Press, 1980), pp. 180–181.

4. The main institutional issues include the following: (1) the distribution of power over election outcomes; (2) the structure of districting systems; (3) access to the ballot (including the question of structural bias in favor of major parties and their procedures for selecting nominees); and (4) the distribution of campaign resources.

5. I have considered other aspects of political equality in "Procedural Equality in Democratic Theory: A Preliminary Examination," in *Liberal Democracy: Nomos XXV,* J. Roland Pennock and John W. Chapman, eds. (New York: New York University Press, 1983), pp. 69–91; and "Political Finance in the United States," *Ethics* 95, no. 1 (October 1984):129–148.

6. *Reynolds* v. *Sims,* 377 U.S. 533 (1964), at 565–566; Laurence H. Tribe, *American Constitutional Law* (Mineola, N.Y.: Foundation Press, 1978), p. 749.

7. In particular, see Ronald W. Rogowski, "Representation in Political Theory and in Law," *Ethics* 91 (1981):395–430.

8. *Considerations on Representative Government* (1861) (Indianapolis: Liberal Arts Press, 1958), ch. 7, p. 102. For a more recent endorsement of proportional representation on egalitarian grounds, see Joshua Cohen and Joel Rogers, *On Democracy* (Harmondsworth, Middlesex: Penguin, 1983), pp. 156–157.

9. Rawls, *A Theory of Justice,* p. 223.

10. The leading cases are *Gaffney* v. *Cummings,* 412 U.S. 735 (1973) (partisan gerrymandering); *United Jewish Organizations* v. *Carey,* 430 U.S. 144 (1977) (affirmative or racial gerrymandering); *White* v. *Regester,* 412 U.S. 755 (1973) (multimember districting); *Mobile* v. *Bolden,* 446 U.S. 55 (1980) and *Rogers* v. *Lodge,* 458 U.S. 613 (1982) (at-large elections).

11. Or could have been altered so that equal power would be realized without curing the qualitative defect. For example, in *Gaffney,* one of the issues was the degree of permissible deviation from precise mathematical equality in district size that could be justified by the aims of maintaining the integrity of local boundaries and of producing proportional legislative representation for parties. But in considering the constitutionality of the second of these aims, the court clearly assumed that, taken on its own, proportional representation for parties would not necessarily require any variation from precise mathematical equality (412 U.S., at 751–754).

12. Influential sources of this conception of power include Max Weber, *The Theory of Economic and Social Organization,* A. M. Henderson and Talcott Parsons, trans. (New York: Free Press, 1947), pp. 152ff; Robert Dahl, "The Concept of Power," *Behavioral Science* 2 (1957):201–215. The discussion that follows is particularly informed by two papers by Alvin Goldman: "Toward a Theory of Social Power," *Philosophical Studies* 23 (1972):221–268, and "On the Measurement of Power," *Journal of Philosophy* 71 (1974):231–252, and one

by Brian Barry, "Is It Better to Be Powerful or Lucky?" *Political Studies* 28 (1980):183–194, 338–352.

13. Others differ on this point. For example, Rogowski refers to the interpretation of equality in representation that I will call "equal prospects of success" as "equally powerful representation" ("Representation in Political Theory and in Law," p. 399).

14. It is plain that C will succeed—will get the outcome he or she favors—whenever at least one other member of the committee supports him or her. Otherwise C will fail. Given our assumptions, C will certainly fail the 80 percent of the time when jointly opposed by A and B and will succeed on three-quarters of the remaining votes (since on each of them, A and B each have an equal [and independent] probability of agreeing or disagreeing with C). Thus, overall, C's probability of success on a randomly chosen issue is $(80\% \times 0) + (20\% \times 75\%) = 15\%$.

15. "Is It Better to Be Powerful or Lucky?" pp. 338ff.

16. My remarks here are confined to voting and similar types of decision procedures that come into action after everyone's preferences have been established. A different kind of power—and in democracies at least as important a kind—is the power to influence the formation of preferences (for example, through persuasion). The nature of this kind of power and the sense in which its distribution can be gauged require a different analysis than that presented here.

17. Tribe, *American Constitutional Law*, p. 750; see also Owen M. Fiss, "Groups and the Equal Protection Clause," *Philosophy and Public Affairs* 5 (1976):151–154.

18. See, for example, *Wright* v. *Rockefeller*, 376 U.S. 52 (1964).

19. Such a view is briefly suggested in Rawls, *A Theory of Justice*, p. 223. It is given ambiguous but more extended expression in the Common Cause report, *Toward a System of 'Fair and Effective Representation'* (Washington, D.C.: Common Cause, 1977), esp. pp. 12–30.

20. See, for example, William Vickery, "On the Prevention of Gerrymandering," *Political Science Quarterly* 76 (1961):105–110.

21. See Edward Tufte, "The Relationship Between Seats and Votes in Two-Party Systems," *American Political Science Review* 67 (1973):540–554.

22. Robert G. Dixon, *Democratic Representation* (New York: Oxford University Press, 1968), p. 462.

23. Such a view was held by Robert Dixon. See his prepared statement in U.S. Senate, Committee on Governmental Affairs, *Congressional Anti-Gerrymandering Act of 1979 [S. 596]: Hearings* (Washington, D.C.: Government Printing Office, 1979), pp. 218–244.

24. I say "nearly every voter" because, strictly speaking, everyone may not have an equal chance of voting for a winner. Even in a perfectly constructed scheme of proportional representation (one based on the single transferable vote rather than on party lists and containing no bias in favor of major parties), a voter might be unlucky enough to vote only for candidates who turn out to accumulate fewer votes than the quota required for election. The classical

source on the single transferable vote is Thomas Hare, *The Election of Representatives: Parliamentary and Municipal,* 3rd ed. (London: Longman, Green, Longman, Roberts, and Green, 1865). See also Enid Lakeman, *Power to Elect: The Case for Proportional Representation* (London: Heinemann, 1982), pp. 45ff.

25. Such a system was at issue in *Gaffney* v. *Cummings,* 412 U.S. 735 (1973).

26. Something like this idea seems to have been suggested by Brian Barry in "Is Democracy Special?" *Philosophy, Politics and Society,* 5th series, Peter Laslett and James Fishkin, eds. (New Haven, Conn.: Yale University Press, 1979), pp. 176ff. The version of the view presented in the text owes much to Peter Singer's discussion of procedural fairness in *Democracy and Disobedience* (New York: Oxford University Press, 1973), pp. 30–41.

27. For a helpful discussion of these conditions, see Barry, "Is Democracy Special?" pp. 176–177.

28. It is worth noting that even if the prior distribution were acceptable, the possibility that political decisions could give rise to external benefits and costs means that the desirable features of the prior distribution might not be preserved through subsequent reallocations of relative satisfaction.

29. This is how Barry formulates the problem of justification in "Is Democracy Special?"

30. I have criticized this justification at greater length in "Procedural Equality in Democratic Theory," pp. 81–83.

31. As William Nelson argued (*On Justifying Democracy* [London: Routledge and Kegan Paul, 1980], ch. 6).

32. I shall resist the temptation to explore the many possible interpretations of this ambiguous idea. An illuminating discussion can be found in Ronald Dworkin, "What Is Equality?" *Philosophy and Public Affairs* 10 (1981):185–246 and 283–345.

33. For alternatives based on multimember districts, see note, "Alternative Voting Systems as Remedies for Unlawful At-Large Systems," *Yale Law Journal* 92 (1982):244–260.

34. For an exploration of the difficulties in doing so, see Richard G. Niemi and John Deegan, Jr., "A Theory of Political Districting," *American Political Science Review* 72 (1978):1304–1323.

35. A similar result would be reached by applying to districting questions Fiss's theory of equal protection for "specially disadvantaged groups," of which blacks are the most prominent example ("Groups and the Equal Protection Clause," passim). An application of such a theory to the issue of racial vote dilution may be found in note [Howard M. Shapiro], "Geometry and Geography: Racial Gerrymandering and the Voting Rights Act," *Yale Law Journal* 94 (1984):189–208.

36. Justice Brennan expressed this fear in his opinion concurring in part in *United Jewish Organizations* v. *Carey,* 430 U.S. 144 (1977), at 174.

37. This objection was suggested to me by Michael Walzer's remarks in "Philosophy and Democracy," *Political Theory* 9 (1981):379–399. But I am not sure that Walzer would endorse the objection as formulated in the text.

38. As I have argued in "Procedural Equality in Democratic Theory."

39. In his book, *Spheres of Justice* (New York: Basic Books, 1983).

8

Free Speech and Social Structure

OWEN M. FISS

Freedom of speech is one of the most remarkable and celebrated aspects of American constitutional law. It helps define who we are as a nation. The principle is rooted in the text of the Constitution itself, but it has been the decisions of the Supreme Court over the last half century or so that have, in my view, nurtured that principle, given it much of its present shape and accounts for much of its energy and sweep. These decisions have given rise to what Harry Kalven has called a Free Speech Tradition.

In speaking of a Tradition, Kalven, and before him, Karl Llewellyn[1] and T. S. Eliot[2] (talking about the shoulders of giants), aspire to an all-embracing perspective. Everything is included—nothing is left out, not the dissents, not even the decisions overruled. Every encounter between the Court and the First Amendment is included. There is, however, a shape or direction or point to the Tradition. It is not an encyclopedia or dictionary, but more in the nature of a shared understanding. Those who speak of a Free Speech Tradition try to see all the decisions and to abstract from them an understanding of what free speech means—what lies at the core and what at the periphery, what lies beyond the protection of the First Amendment and what is included, where the law is headed, etc. The whole has a shape. The shape is not fixed for all time, since each new decision or opinion is included within the Tradition and thus contributes to refiguring the meaning of the whole, but the Tradition also acts as a constraining force on present and future decisions. The Tradition is the background against which every judge writes. It defines the issues, provides the resources by which the judge can confront those issues, and also creates the obstacles that must be surmounted. It orients the judge.

I believe it is useful to view the free speech decisions of the Supreme Court as a Tradition, and I am also tempted to celebrate that Tradition in much the way that Kalven does. The title of his (still unpublished) manuscript is *A Worthy Tradition*.[3] But for me that is only half the story. It also seems that the Tradition is flawed in some important respects—so much so that it might be necessary to begin again (if that is even possible).

I

My concerns first arose in the 1970s—one of the few periods when America wondered out loud whether capitalism and democracy were compatible. In the political world these doubts were linked to Watergate and the eventual resignation of President Richard Nixon. The precipitating event was the break-in at the Democratic National Headquarters, but by the time the impeachment process had run its course, we realized how thoroughly economic power had begun to corrupt our politics. Congress responded with the Campaign Reform Act of 1974,[4] imposing limits on contributions and expenditures and establishing a scheme for the public funding of elections. The tension between capitalism and democracy was also a special subject of concern to the academic world, as evidenced by the excitement and controversy generated by the publication in 1977 of Charles E. Lindblom's book *Politics and Markets*.[5] Lindblom tried to show that, contrary to classical democratic theory, politics was not an autonomous sphere of activity, but was indeed shaped and controlled by the dominant economic interests. As a consequence of this "circularity," the most important issues of economic and social structure—what Lindblom called the "grand issues"—remained at the margins of politics. Voters were not actually considering the continued viability of capitalism, the justness of market distributions, or the structure within which organized labor was allowed to act, because, Lindblom hypothesized, of the control exercised by corporate interests over the political agenda.[6]

While academics were reading and debating Lindblom's book and while politicians were trying to make sense of Watergate, the Supreme Court was faced with a number of cases that required it to examine the relationship of political and economic power. The Court was asked whether it was permissible for a state to extend the fairness doctrine to the print media,[7] and whether the Federal Communications Commission (FCC) was obliged to provide critics of our efforts in Vietnam access to the TV networks.[8] In another case the Campaign Reform Act of 1974 was attacked;[9] and in still another a challenge was raised to a Massachusetts statute limiting corporate expenditures in a referendum on the income tax.[10] Political activists, lacking funds to purchase space or time in the mass media, sought access to the shopping centers to get their message across to the public, and they also turned to the courts for this purpose.[11] Admittedly, issues of this character had been presented to the Court before, but in the seventies they arose with greater frequency and urgency, and they seemed to dominate the Court's First Amendment docket.

These cases presented the Court with extremely difficult issues, perhaps the most difficult of all First Amendment issues, and thus one would fairly predict divisions. One could also predict some false turns. What startled me, however, was the pattern of decisions: Capitalism almost always won. The Court decided that a statute that granted access to the print media to those who wished to present differing views was invalid; that the FCC did not have to grant access to the electronic media for editorial advertisements; that the political expenditures of the wealthy could not be curbed; and that the owners of the large shopping centers and malls that constitute the civic centers of suburban America need not provide access to pamphleteers. Democracy promises collective self-determination—a freedom to the people to decide their own fate—and presupposes a debate on public issues that is (to use Justice Brennan's now classic formula) "uninhibited, robust, and wide-open."[12] The free speech decisions of the seventies, however, seemed to impoverish, rather than enrich, public debate and thus threatened one of the essential preconditions for an effective democracy. And they seemed to do so in a rather systematic way.

My first inclination was to see these decisions as embodying a conflict between liberty and equality—as another phase in the struggle between the Warren and Burger Courts. I saw the decisions of the seventies as part of the program of the Court, largely (and now, it seems, ironically) constituted by President Nixon, to establish a new priority for liberty and to bring an end to the egalitarian crusade of the Warren Court. The idea was that in these free speech cases, as in the school financing area,[13] the Burger Court was not willing to empower the poor or less advantaged if that meant sacrificing the liberty of anyone. On reflection, however, the problem seemed deeper and more complicated. I saw that at issue was not simply a conflict between equality and liberty, but also and more importantly, a conflict between two conceptions of liberty. The battle being fought was not just Liberty v. Equality, but Liberty v. Liberty, or to put the point another way, not just between the First Amendment and the Equal Protection Clause, but a battle *within* the First Amendment itself. I also came to understand that the Court was not advancing an idiosyncratic or perverted conception of liberty, but was in fact working well within the Free Speech Tradition. The Court was not crudely substituting entrepreneurial liberty (or property) for political liberty;[14] the rich or owners of capital in fact won, but only because they had advanced claims of political liberty that easily fit within the received Tradition. Money is speech—just as much as picketing is.

In time I became convinced that the difficulties the Court encountered in the free speech cases of the seventies could ultimately be traced to inadequacies in the Free Speech Tradition itself. The problem was the Tradition not the Court. The Tradition did not *compel* the results— as though any body of precedent could. Arguably, there was room for a nimble and determined craftsman working within the Tradition to come out differently in one or two of these cases, or maybe in all of them. But, on balance, it seemed that the Tradition oriented the justices in the wrong direction and provided ample basis for those who formed the majority to claim, quite genuinely, that they were protecting free speech when, in fact, they were doing something of a different, far more ambiguous, character altogether. This meant that criticism would have to be directed not simply at the Burger Court but at something larger: at a powerfully entrenched, but finally inadequate body of doctrine.

II

For the most part, the Free Speech Tradition can be understood as a protection of the street corner speaker. An individual mounts a soapbox on a corner in some large city, starts to criticize governmental policy, and then is arrested for breach of the peace. In this setting the First Amendment is conceived of as a shield, as a means of protecting the individual speaker from being silenced by the state.

First Amendment litigation first began to occupy the Supreme Court's attention during World War I, a time when the constitutional shield was rather weak. The street corner speaker could be arrested on the slightest provocation. Those early decisions were openly criticized, most notably in the dissents of Brandeis and Holmes, but that criticism— eloquent and at times heroic—stayed within the established framework and sought only to expand the frontiers of freedom incrementally; it sought to place more restrictions on the policeman and to give more and more protection to the street corner speaker. In this incremental quality, the criticism took on the character of the progressive movement in general, and also shared its fate. The progressive critique achieved its first successes during the thirties, at the hands of the Hughes Court, but its final vindication awaited the Warren Court: It was only then that the shield around the speaker became worthy of a democracy.

What largely emerged from this historical process is a rule against content regulation—it now stands as the cornerstone of the Free Speech Tradition. The policeman cannot arrest the speaker just because he does not like what is being said. Time, place, and manner regulations are permitted—the speaker must not stand in the middle of the roadway—but the intervention must not be based on the content of the speech, or a desire to favor one set of ideas over another. To be sure, the Court has allowed the policeman to intervene in certain circumstances on the basis of content, as when the speaker is about to incite a mob. But even then the Court has sought to make certain that the policeman intervenes only at the last possible moment, that is, before the mob is unleashed. In fact, for most of this century First Amendment scholarship has largely consisted of a debate over the clear and present danger test and the so-called incitement test, in an effort to find a verbal formula that best identifies the last possible moment.[15] The common assumption of all those who participated in that debate— finally made explicit in the 1969 decision of *Brandenburg* v. *Ohio*,[16] perhaps the culmination of these debates and in many respects the final utterance of the Warren Court on this subject—is that the policeman should not step in when the speaker is only engaged in the general expression of ideas, however unpopular those ideas may be.[17] *Brandenburg* involved a rally of the Ku Klux Klan, and in it the Supreme Court held unconstitutional a state statute that prohibited the advocacy of violence as a method of political reform.

I would be the first to acknowledge that there has been something noble and inspiring about the fifty-year journey that culminated in *Brandenburg*. A body of doctrine that fully protects the street corner speaker is of course an accomplishment of some note; the battles to secure that protection were hard fought and their outcome was far from certain. *Brandenburg* is one of the blessings of our liberty. The problem, however, is that today there are no street corners, and the doctrinal edifice that seems to Kalven and others so glorious when they have the street corner speaker in mind is largely unresponsive to conditions of modern society.

Under the Tradition extolled by Kalven, the freedom of speech guaranteed by the First Amendment amounts to a protection of autonomy—it is the shield around the speaker. The theory that animates this protection, and that inspired Kalven,[18] and before him Alexander Meiklejohn,[19] and that now dominates the field,[20] casts the underlying purpose of the First Amendment in social or political terms: The purpose of free speech is not individual self-actualization, but rather the preservation of democracy, and the right of a people, as a people, to decide what kind of life it wishes to live. Autonomy is protected not because of its intrinsic value, as a Kantian might insist, but rather as a means or instrument of collective self-determination. We allow people to speak so others can vote. Speech allows people to vote intelligently and freely, aware of all the options and in possession of all the relevant information.

The crucial assumption in this theory is that the protection of autonomy will produce a public debate that will be, to use the talismanic phrase once again, "uninhibited, robust and wide-open." The Tradition assumes that by leaving individuals alone, free from the menacing arm of the policeman, a full and fair consideration of all the issues will emerge. The premise is that autonomy will lead to rich public debate. From the perspective of the street corner, that assumption might seem plausible enough. But when our perspective shifts, as I insist it must, from the street corner to, say, CBS, this assumption becomes highly problematic. Autonomy and rich public debate—the two free speech values—might diverge and become antagonistic.[21] Under CBS, autonomy may be *insufficient* to ensure a rich public debate. Oddly enough, it might even become *destructive* of that goal.[22]

III

Some acknowledge the shift of paradigms, and the obsolescence of the street corner, but would nonetheless view CBS as a forum—an electronic street corner.[23] They would demand access to the network as though it were but another forum and insist that the right of access should not follow the incidence of ownership. This view moves us closer to a true understanding of the problem of free speech in modern society, for it reveals how the freedom to speak depends on the resources at one's disposal, and it reminds us that more is required these days than a soapbox, a good voice, and the talent to hold an audience. On the other hand, this view is incomplete: It ignores the fact that CBS is not only a forum, but also a speaker, and thus understates the challenge that is posed to the received Tradition by the shift in paradigms. For me CBS is a speaker and in that capacity renders the Tradition most problematic. As speaker, CBS can claim the protection of autonomy held out by the Tradition, and yet the exercise of that autonomy might not enrich, but rather impoverish, public debate and thus frustrate the democratic aspirations of the Tradition.

In thinking of CBS as a speaker, and claiming for it the benefit of the Tradition, I assume that the autonomy protected by the Tradition need not be confined to individuals. It can extend to institutions. Autonomy is not valued by Meiklejohn and his followers because of what it does for a person's development (self-actualization), but rather because of the contribution it makes to our political life, and that contribution can be made by either individuals or organizations. The NAACP, the Nazi Party, CBS, and the First National Bank of Boston are as entitled to the autonomy guaranteed by the Tradition as is an individual, and no useful purpose would be served by reducing this idea of institutional autonomy to the autonomy of the various individuals who (at any one point of time) manage or work within the organization.

Implicit in this commitment to protecting institutional autonomy is the understanding that organizations have viewpoints and that these viewpoints are no less worthy of First Amendment protection than those of individuals. An organization's viewpoint is not reducible to the views of any single individual, but is instead the product of a complex interaction between individual personalities, internal organizational structures, the environment in which the organization operates, etc. The viewpoint of an organization such as CBS or First National Bank of Boston might not have as sharp a profile as that of the NAACP or Nazi Party (that is probably one reason why we think of a network as a forum rather than a speaker), but that viewpoint is nonetheless real, pervasive, and communicated almost endlessly. It is not confined to the announced "Editorial Message," but extends to the broadcast of "Love Boat" as well. In the ordinary show or commercial a view of the world is projected, which in turn tends to define and order our options and choices.

From this perspective, the protection of CBS's autonomy through the no-content-regulation rule appears as a good. The freedom of CBS to say what it wishes can enrich public debate (understood generously) and thus contribute to the fulfillment of the democratic aspirations of the First Amendment. The trouble, however, is that it can work out the other way too, for when CBS adds something to public debate, something is also taken away. What is said determines what is not said. The decision to fill a prime hour of television with "Love Boat" necessarily entails a decision not to broadcast a critique of Reagan's foreign policy or a documentary on one of Lindblom's "grand issues" during the same hour. We can thus see that the key to fulfilling the ultimate purposes of the First Amendment is not autonomy, which has a most uncertain or double-edged relationship to public debate, but rather the actual effect of a broadcast: On the whole does it enrich public debate? Speech is protected when (and only when) it does, and precisely because it does, not because it is an exercise of autonomy. In fact, autonomy adds nothing and, if need be, might have to be sacrificed to make certain that public debate is sufficiently rich to permit true collective self-determination. What the phrase "the freedom of speech" in the First Amendment refers to is a social state of affairs, not the action of an individual or institution.

The risk posed to freedom of speech by autonomy is not confined to situations when it is exercised by CBS, or by the other media, but occurs whenever speech takes place under conditions of scarcity, that is, whenever the opportunity for communication is limited. In such situations, one utterance will necessarily displace another. With the street corner, the element of scarcity tends to be masked; when we think of the street corner we ordinarily assume that every speaker will have his or her turn, and that the attention of the audience is virtually unlimited. Indeed, that is why it is such an appealing story. But in politics, scarcity is the rule rather than the exception. The opportunities for speech tend to be limited, either by the time or space available for communicating or by our capacity to digest or process information. This is clear and obvious in the case of the mass media, which play such a decisive role in determining which issues are debated and how, but it is true in other contexts as well. In a referendum or election, for example, there is every reason to be concerned with the campaign mounted by the rich or powerful, because the resources at their disposal enable them to fill all the available space for public discourse with their message. Playing Muzak on the public address system of a shopping mall fills the minds of those who congregate there. Or consider the purchase of books by a library, or the design of a school curriculum. The decision to acquire one book or to include one course necessarily entails the exclusion of another.

Of course, if one has some clear view of what should be included in the public debate, as does a Marcuse,[24] one has a basis for determining whether the public debate that will result from the exercise of autonomy will permit true collective self-determination. Such a substantive baseline makes life easier but it is not essential. Even without it, there is every reason to be concerned with the quality of public discourse under a regime of autonomy. For the protection of autonomy will result in a debate that bears the imprint of those forces that dominate social structure. In the world of Thomas Jefferson, made up of individuals who stand equal to one another, this might not be a matter of great concern, for it can be said that the social structure, as well as the formal political process, is itself democratic. But today we have every reason to be concerned, for we live in a world farther removed from the democracy Jefferson contemplated than it is from the world of the street corner speaker.

The fear I have about the distortion of public debate under a regime of autonomy is not in any way tied to capitalism. It arises whenever social power is distributed unequally: Capitalism just happens to be one among many social systems that distribute power unequally. I also think it wrong, even in a capitalist context, to reduce social power to economic power and to attribute the skew of public debate wholly to economic factors. Bureaucratic structures, personalities, social cleavages, and cultural norms all have a role to play in shaping the character of public debate. But I think it fair to say that in a capitalist society, the protection of autonomy will on the whole produce a public debate dominated by those who are economically powerful. The market— even one that operates smoothly and efficiently—does not assure that all relevant views will be heard, but only those advocated by the rich, by those who can borrow from others, or by those who can put together a product that will attract sufficient advertisers or subscribers to sustain the enterprise.

CBS is not a monopoly, and competes with a few other networks (and less powerful media) for the public's attention. The fact that CBS's managers are (to some indeterminate degree) governed by market considerations does not in any way lessen the risk that the protection of autonomy—staying the hand of the policeman—will not produce the kind of debate presupposed by democratic theory. The market is itself a structure of constraint that tends to channel, guide and shape how that autonomy will be exercised. From the perspective of a free and open debate, the choice between "Love Boat" and "Fantasy Island" is trivial. In this respect, CBS and the rest of the broadcast media illustrate, by example, not exception, the condition of all media in a capitalist society. True, CBS and the other networks operate under a license from the government or under conditions of spectrum scarcity. But the dangers I speak of are not confined to such cases, for distortions of public debate arise from social, rather than legal or technical, factors.

Individuals might be "free" to start a newspaper in a way that they are not "free" to start a TV station, because in the latter case they need both capital and government approval, while for the newspaper they need only capital. But that fact will not close the gap between autonomy and public debate; it will not guarantee that under autonomy principles the public will hear all that it must. Licensing may distort the market in some special way, but even the market dreamt of by economists will leave its imprint on public debate, not only on issues that directly affect the continued existence of the market, but on a much wider range of issues (though with such issues it is often difficult to predict the shape and direction of the skew). No wonder we tend to identify the Free Speech Tradition with the protection of "the marketplace of ideas."[25]

IV

Classical liberalism presupposes a sharp dichotomy between state and citizen. It teaches us to be wary of the state and equates liberty with limited government. The Free Speech Tradition builds on this view of the world when it reduces free speech to autonomy and defines autonomy to mean the absence of government interference. Liberalism's distrust of the state is represented by the antagonism between the policeman and soap box orator and by the assumption that the policeman is the enemy of speech. Under the received Tradition, free speech becomes one strand—perhaps the only left[26]—of a more general plea for limited government. Its appeal has been greatly enhanced by our historical commitment to liberalism.

Nothing I have said is meant to destroy the distinction presupposed by classical liberalism between state and citizen, or between the public and private. Rather, in asking that we shift our focus from the street corner to CBS, I mean to suggest only that we are not dealing with hermetically sealed spheres. CBS is privately owned and its employees do not receive their checks directly from the state treasury. It is also true, however, that CBS's central property—the license—has been created and conferred by the government. It gives CBS the right to exclude others from its segment of the air waves. In addition, CBS draws upon advantages conferred by the state in a more general way, through, for example, the laws of incorporation and taxation. CBS can also be said to perform a public function: education. CBS is thus a composite of the public and private. The same is true of the print media, as it is of all corporations, unions, universities, and political organizations. Today the social world is largely constituted by entities that partake of both the public and private.

A shift from the street corner to CBS compels us to recognize the hybrid character of major social institutions; it begins to break down some of the dichotomies between public and private presupposed by classical liberalism. It also renders pointless the classificatory game of deciding whether CBS is "really" private or "really" public, for it invites a reevaluation of stereotypical roles portrayed in the Tradition's little drama. No longer can we identify the policeman with evil and the citizen with good. The state of affairs protected by the First Amendment can just as easily be threatened by a private citizen as by an agency of the state. A corporation operating on private capital can be as much a threat to the richness of public debate as a government agency, for each is subject to constraints that limit what it says or what it will allow others to say. The state has a monopoly on the *legitimate* use of violence, but this peculiar kind of power is not needed to curb and restrict public debate. A program manager need not arrest someone (lawfully or otherwise) to have this effect, but only choose one program over another, and although that choice is not wholly free, but constrained by the market, that does not limit the threat that it poses to the integrity of public debate. It is instead the source of the problem. All the so-called private media operate within the same structure of constraint, the market, which tends to restrict and confine the issues that are publicly aired.

Just as it is no longer possible to assume that the private sector is all freedom, we can no longer assume that the state is all censorship. That too is one of the lessons of the shift from the street corner orator to CBS. It reminds us that in the modern world the state can enrich as much as it constricts public debate: It can do this, in part, through the provision of subsidies and other benefits. Here I am thinking not just of the government's role in licensing CBS, but also and more significantly of government appropriations to public television and radio, public and private universities, public libraries, and public educational systems. These institutions bring before the public issues and perspectives otherwise likely to be ignored or slighted by institutions that are privately owned and constrained by the market. They make an enormous contribution to public discourse, and should enjoy the very same privileges that we afford those institutions that rest on private capital (and, of course, should be subject to the same limitations).

We can also look beyond the provision of subsidies, and consider whether the state might enrich public debate by regulating in a manner similar to the policeman. CBS teaches that this kind of governmental action—once again based on content—might be needed to protect our freedom. The power of the media to decide what is on its program must be regulated because, as we saw through an understanding of the dynamic of displacement, this power always has a double edge: It subtracts from public debate at the very moment that it adds to it. Similarly, expenditures of political actors might have to be curbed, to make certain all views are heard. To date we have ambivalently recognized the value of state regulation of this character on behalf of speech—we have a fairness doctrine for the broadcast media and limited campaign financing laws. But these regulatory measures are today embattled, and in any event, more, not less, is needed. For example, there should also be laws requiring the owners of the new public arenas—the shopping centers—to allow access for political pamphleteers. A commitment to rich public debate will allow, and sometimes even require the state to act in these ways, however elemental and repressive they might at first seem. Autonomy will be sacrificed, and content regulation sometimes allowed, but only on the assumption that public debate might be enriched and our capacity for collective self-determination enhanced. The risks of this approach cannot be ignored, and at moments they seem alarming, but we can only begin to evaluate them when we weigh in the balance the hidden costs of an unrestricted regime of autonomy.

At the core of my approach is a belief that contemporary social structure is as much an enemy of free speech as is the policeman. Some might move from this premise to an attack upon social structure itself—concentrations of power should be smashed into atoms and scattered in a way that would have pleased Jefferson. Such an approach proposes a remedy that goes directly to the source of the problem, but surely is beyond our reach, as a social or legal matter, and maybe even as an ethical matter. The First Amendment does not require a revolution. It may, however, allow and even require a change in our attitude about the state. We should learn to recognize the state not only as an enemy, but as a friend of speech; like any social actor, it has the potential to act in both capacities, and, using the enrichment of public debate as the touchstone and avoiding the traditional liberal assumption against the state, we must begin to discriminate between the various ways the state can act. When the state impoverishes public debate it should be stopped. But when the state acts to enhance the quality of public debate, its actions should be upheld as consistent with the First Amendment. What is more, when on occasions it fails to take measures to enrich public debate, we can with confidence demand that the state so act. The duty of the state is to preserve the integrity of public discourse—much the same way as a great teacher— not to indoctrinate, not to advance the "Truth," but to safeguard the conditions for true and free collective self-determination. It should constantly act to correct the skew of social structure, if only to make certain that the status quo is embraced because we believe it the best, not because it is the only thing we know or are allowed to know.

A question can be raised whether the (faint-hearted) structural approach I am advocating really represents a break with the Free Speech Tradition, for some traces of a welcoming attitude toward the state can be found within the Tradition. One is *Red Lion,* which upheld the fairness doctrine and the regulation of content of a speaker such as CBS.[27] This decision does not fit into the overall structure of the Tradition taken as a whole, and never has been sufficiently rationalized. It has been something of a freak, excused, but never justified, on the ground that broadcasters are licensed by the government. It has never grown, as an adequately justified precedent might, to allow a state to impose a similar fairness obligation on a newspaper or to allow the fairness doctrine and all that it implies to become obligatory rather than just permissible. It is of no small significance to me that Kalven (and a number of the other First Amendment scholars working within the Tradition) signed briefs in *Red Lion* on the side of the media.[28] There is, however, one other branch of First Amendment doctrine that evinces a welcoming attitude toward the state and that is more firmly entrenched and more adequately justified. I am now referring to what Kalven called the "heckler's veto."[29]

This doctrine has its roots in Justice Black's dissent in *Feiner* v. *New York*,[30] but it is now an established part of the Tradition. It recognizes that when a mob is angered by a speaker and jeopardizes the public order by threatening the speaker, the policeman must act to preserve the opportunity for an individual to speak. The duty of the policeman is to restrain the mob. In such a situation, strong action by the state is welcomed, and the doctrine of the heckler's veto might thus appear as an opening wedge for my plea for a change in our attitudes about the state, but one that would allow the Court to work within the Tradition. Upon closer inspection, however, this seems to me wishful thinking, and that a more radical break with the past is called for.

First, the heckler's veto does not require an abandonment of the view that free speech is autonomy, but explains that the state intervention is necessary to make the speaker's autonomy "real" or "effective." The person on the soap box should be given a *real* chance to speak. In contrast, the approach I am advocating is not concerned with the speaker's autonomy, real or otherwise, but with the quality of public debate. It is listener oriented. Intervention is based on a desire to enrich public debate, and though the concept of "real" or "effective" autonomy might be so stretched as to embrace the full range of interventions needed to enrich the public debate, the manipulative quality of such a strategy will soon become apparent once the extensiveness and pervasiveness of the intervention are acknowledged. It is also hard to see what is to be gained by such a strategy: Autonomy, in its inflated version, would remain as the key value, but while in the received Tradition it operated as a response to government intervention, under this strategy it would serve as a justification of such intervention. Autonomy would be saved, but be put to a different use.

Second, although the doctrine of the heckler's veto welcomes the strong arm of the law, it does so only on rare occasions—when violence is about to break out, and then only to divert the police action away from the speaker and toward the mob. The general rule is that the state should not intervene, but when it must, it should go after someone other than the speaker. In contrast, the structural approach contemplates state intervention on a much more regular and systematic basis. A prime example of such intervention is, once again, the fairness doctrine, a varied and elaborate set of regulations and institutional arrangements that have evolved over several decades. Other instances of this sort of intervention can be found in federal and state laws regulating campaign contributions and expenditures, or in the laws of some states creating access to privately owned shopping centers for political activities. These laws entail a form of state intervention that is more regular and more pervasive than that contemplated by the occasional arrest of the heckler.

Third, when the policeman arrests the heckler, no interests of any great significance seem to be jeopardized. The government is interfering with the heckler's freedom, but the heckler is not an object of much sympathy. He is an obstructionist, who is not so much conveying an idea as preventing someone else from doing so. The heckler is defined rather two-dimensionally, as someone who refuses to respect the rights of others. Yes, he will have his chance on the soap box, if that is what he wants, but he must wait his turn. The issue appears to be one of timing. But the laws that have divided the Supreme Court over the past decade, and that the structural approach seeks to defend, jeopardize interests that are more substantial than those represented by the heckler.

At the very least, the laws in question involve a compromise of the rights we often believe are attached to private property—the right to exclude people from the land you own, or to use the money you earn in any way that you see fit. In some cases the stakes are even greater: free speech itself. The laws in question threaten the freedom of an individual or institution to say what it wants and to do so precisely because of the content of what is being said. One branch of the fairness doctrine requires a network to cover "public issues," and another requires a "balanced presentation." In either case, a judgment is required by government agency as to what constitutes a "public issue" and whether the presentation is "balanced." By necessity, attention must be paid to what is being said, and what is not being said. Similarly, laws that regulate political expenditures to prevent the rich from completely dominating debate also require some judgment as to which views should be heard. The same is true even if the state acts through affirmative strategies, such as when it grants subsidies to candidates or purchases books or sets a curriculum.

From the perspective of autonomy these dangers are especially acute, and present what is perhaps a decisive reason against intervention. However, even if we shift the perspective, and rich public debate is substituted for autonomy as the controlling First Amendment value, there is good reason to be concerned, and to a greater degree than we are when the heckler is silenced. The stated purpose of the government intervention and content regulation might be to enrich debate, but it might have precisely the opposite effect. It might tend to narrow the choices and information available to the public and thus to aggravate the skew of debate caused by the social structure. In fact, there is good reason to suspect that this might be the case, for, as suggested by Lindblom's idea of circularity, the social structure is as likely to leave its imprint on government action (especially of a legislative or administrative character) as it is to leave its mark on the quality of public debate.

V

The presence of the dangers to First Amendment values and other social interests is sufficient to distinguish the approach I am advocating from the heckler's veto, and the general Tradition of which it is part, but a question still remains—perhaps the ultimate one—whether these dangers are sufficient to reject the structural approach altogether and turn back to the received Tradition and the protection of autonomy. Are the dangers just too great?

When the government intervention threatens what might be regarded as an ordinary value, signified by the interference with property rights, then the answer seems clearly "no." Free speech is no luxury. Sacrifices are required, and though there are limits to the sacrifice (as Justice Jackson put it, the Constitution is no "suicide pact"[31]), free speech lies so close to the core of our constitutional structure to warrant tipping the scales in its favor. In this regard, the structuralist can confidently borrow the weighted balancing process used by progressives to protect speech in the interest of autonomy. Traditionally, speech is protected even if it causes inconvenience, a congestion, etc., and I see no reason why the same rule could not be applied to further public debate, when the state appears as a friend rather than an enemy of speech.

This perspective could help in a number of the cases that stymied the Court in the seventies. A law creating access to a shopping center might interfere with the property rights of the owners and cause a loss of sales (by keeping away those who do not like to be bothered by politics), but those interests may have to be sacrificed in order to fulfill the democratic aspirations that underlie the First Amendment. To use one of the phrases that inspired the progressives of the fifties and sixties and that gave the Tradition much of its vitality, freedom of speech is a "preferred freedom."[32] The only difference is that under the structural approach the enrichment of public debate is substituted for the protection of autonomy, and free speech operates as a justification rather than as a limit on state action. The same process of weighted balancing, with the hierarchy of values that it implies, is used, though the traditional perspective on the relationships between the state and freedom is reversed. The notion of "preferred freedoms" or weighted balancing is, however, of little help when the interests sacrificed or threatened by state action are not "ordinary" ones, like convenience or expense, but are also grounded in the First Amendment itself. Then, so to speak, the First Amendment appears on both sides of the equation: The state may be seeking to enrich public debate but might in fact be impoverishing it.

This danger is presented by the fairness doctrine and that—not the talk about infringement of institutional autonomy—is what makes the doctrine so problematic. The doctrine seeks to enhance public debate by forcing the broadcasters to cover public events and to present opposing sides of an issue; but it simultaneously restricts debate by preventing the media from saying what it otherwise might (in response to market pressures, or to advance the political views of the managers or financial sponsors, etc.). The hope is that public debate will be enriched, but the fear is that it might work in the opposite direction, either directly by forcing the networks to cover issues that are not important, or indirectly by discouraging them from taking chances and by undermining norms of professional independence. Federal and state laws that restrict political expenditures by the rich or corporations also might be counterproductive. These laws seek to enhance the public debate by allowing the full range of voices to be heard, by ensuring that the ideas of the less wealthy are also heard. But at the same time these laws might over-correct, slanting the debate in favor of one view or position, and in that way violate the democratic aspirations of the First Amendment.

I do not believe that this danger of First Amendment counter-productivity arises in every single instance in which the state intervenes to enhance public debate, as is evident from my discussion of the shopping center cases (I put the displacement of Muzak by the songs of protest to one side). Nevertheless, believing as I do that scarcity is the rule rather than the exception in political discourse, and that in such situations one communicative act displaces another, I must acknowledge that this danger of counterproductivity is almost always present. I also acknowledge how real a danger this truly is, for as Lindblom teaches, the state is not autonomous. We turn to the state because it is the only hope, the only institution that has the power needed to correct the distorting influence of social structure on public debate and that has the necessary public commitments. Yet there is every reason in the world to fear that the state is not as "public" as it appears but is in fact under the control of the very same forces that dominate the social structure.

The burden of guarding against the danger of First Amendment counterproductivity will largely fall to the judiciary. Judges are the ultimate guardians of constitutional values, and due to institutional arrangements that govern tenure and salary and due to professional norms that insulate them from politics, they are likely to be more independent of the forces that dominate contemporary social structure (the market) than other government officials. The burden is theirs, and it is likely to be an excruciating one. Judges are accustomed to weighing conflicting values, but the conflict here is especially troublesome because the values seem to be of similar import and character. We cannot casually insist that the courts allow the political agencies to experiment or to take a risk, as we do when something like productive efficiency or administrative convenience is at stake, for the evils to be suffered are qualitatively equal to the benefits to be gained. Nor can we take comfort in doctrines of deference that generally ask courts to respect the prerogatives of legislative or administrative agencies. Those agencies might be as captive to the forces that dominate social structure as is public discourse itself. And I see no more reason in this context than I do in the discrimination area[33] to revert to an approach that emphasizes the motives or "good faith" of the state agency involved: From democracy's standpoint, what matters is not what the agency is trying to do but what it has in fact done. To assess the validity of the state intervention the reviewing court must ask, directly and unequivocally, whether the intervention in fact enriches rather than impoverishes public debate.

This is no easy question, especially when we proceed, as we must, without Marcuse's guidance as to what kind of views are to be allowed in a democracy. The democratic aspirations of the First Amendment require robust debate about issues of public importance, and as such, call for process norms, betrayed as much by the imposition of particular outcomes, as by the failure to secure meaningful conditions of debate. In constructing the required norms, we may find help in the old notion that it is easier to identify an injustice than to explain what is justice. In the racial area,[34] we have proceeded in this negative fashion, trying to identify impermissible effects ("group disadvantaging," "disproportionate impact," etc.), without a commitment to a particular end state. I suspect that is how we must proceed in the First Amendment domain as well. In fact, the notions of "drowning out"[35] or "domination,"[36] used by Justice White on various occasions to explain how social or economic power under a regime of autonomy might distort public debate strike me as gestures in this direction. They are, of course, only a beginning, and perhaps a small one at that, and we should have no illusion about how long and how difficult a journey lies ahead.

Realism is not, however, the same as pessimism, and in these matters I tend to be optimistic. I believe in reason and in the deliberate and incremental methods of the law: I see no reason why the courts are more disabled from giving content to the enrichment of public debate idea than to any other (including autonomy). I am also sustained by my belief in the importance—no, the urgency—of the journey that the structuralist has invited us to take. Unless we stop the by now quite tiresome incantation of Brennan's formula, and begin to explain precisely what we mean when we speak of a debate that is "uninhibited, robust and wide-open," and to assess various interventions and strategies in light of their contribution toward that end, we will never establish the effective precondition of a true democracy.

VI

I do not expect everyone to share my optimism. I can understand someone who acknowledges how social structure and the protection of autonomy might skew public debate, but believes (for some reason) that the inquiries called for by another approach are too difficult, or too dangerous. I would argue with that position, but I would understand it. It would be an acknowledgment of the tragic condition in which we live—we know what freedom requires, but find it too difficult or too dangerous to act on its behalf. But that has not been the posture of the controlling bloc of the Burger Court in the free speech cases of the seventies, and that is why I believe a reaction stronger than mere disagreement is appropriate. The Court did not present its decision to invalidate the Massachusetts law limiting corporate political expenditures as a tragedy, where, on the one hand, it acknowledged how the "domination" that Justice White described might interfere with First Amendment values, but on the other, explained that it might be too dangerous or too difficult even to entertain the possibility of corrective measures by the state. Rather, Justice Powell announced the Court's decision as a full and triumphant vindication of First Amendment values. It is this stance, above all, that I find most troubling and that has led me to wonder whether the real source of the problem is not the justices but rather the Tradition.

Some of the justices have recognized the divergence between autonomy and rich public debate, and have been prepared to honor and further the public debate value at the expense of autonomy. Now and then they are prepared to work in patient and disciplined ways to make certain that the intervention in question will actually enrich rather than impoverish public debate. They are attentive to questions of institutional design and the danger of First Amendment counter-productivity. Here I am thinking especially of Justices White and Brennan. The method of the prevailing majority, perhaps best typified by the work of Justice Powell but by no means confined to him, is, however, of another character entirely. For them, it is all autonomy—as though we were back on the street corner and that the function of the First Amendment were simply to stop the policeman. Their method *is* the Tradition.

One part of their method is to see a threat to autonomy almost everywhere. For example, Powell feared that a law requiring access to a shopping center might compromise the free speech rights of the owners[37]—the Fourteenth Amendment may not enact the *Social Statics* of Mr. Herbert Spencer, but maybe the First Amendment does. The autonomy of the owners will be compromised, Justice Powell argues, because there is a risk that views of the political activists will be attributed to them. Faced with the fact that the activists gained access by force of law and under conditions that provide access to all, and that in any event, the owners could protect against the risk of attribution by posting signs disclaiming support for the views espoused, Justice Powell moves his search for autonomy to an even more absurd level. He insists that being forced to post a disclaimer might itself be a violation of the autonomy guaranteed by the First Amendment.[38]

Another part of the method of the prevailing majority is to treat autonomy as a near absolute and as the only First Amendment value. The enrichment of public debate would be an agreeable by-product of a regime of autonomy (they too quote the Brennan formula), but what the First Amendment commands is the protection of autonomy—individual or institutional—and if that protection does not enrich public debate, or somehow distorts it, so be it. To be sure, the fairness doctrine is tolerated, but largely out of respect for precedent, or a deference to the legislative or administrative will, and is distinguished on rather fatuous grounds. The Court has made clear that the FCC is free to abandon it, and in any event, the doctrine and the regulation of content that it implies are not to be extended to the print media (and presumably other electronic media that do not require an allocation of the scarce electromagnetic spectrum). Curbs on financial contributions to candidates are permitted once again out of deference to precedent, and as a way of curbing corruption, but curbs on expenditures are invalidated as interference with the autonomy supposedly guaranteed by the First Amendment. These are the decisions that gave the seventies its special character. Reflecting the full power of the received Tradition, time and time again, the Court has declared: "[T]he concept that government may restrict the speech of some elements of our society in order to enhance the relative voice of others is wholly foreign to the First Amendment. . . . "[39]

Autonomy is an idea especially geared to the state acting in a regulatory manner—it is the shield against the policeman. When the state has so acted, the Court has been on its guard. When the state acted affirmatively, however, say through the provisions of subsidies or benefits, the Tradition does not have much to say and as a result, the Burger Court has been, much to my relief, more tolerant of such state intervention. But that tolerance has been achieved at a price of coherence. The Court has no standard to guide its review. Rather than asking whether the action in question enriches debate, the justices have tried to reformulate the issue in terms of the received Tradition. In a school library case Justice Brennan found himself obliged to cast the censorship—a transparent attempt to narrow debate—into an infringement of autonomy and a violation of the rule against content regulation.[40] This led him to make an untenable distinction between the removal and acquisition of books, and to look into the motives of the school board—a type of inquiry for which, as he demonstrated in other contexts, he has no taste whatsoever. Even then, he was unable to secure a majority.

In this case, and in others that involved the state in some capacity other than policeman, Justice Brennan and his allies faced a high-pitched dissent by Justice Rehnquist, in which he made explicit the distinction between when the state acts as sovereign (policeman) and when it acts in other capacities (e.g., as educator, employer, financier).[41] For the latter category, Rehnquist argued for a standard that leaves the state with almost total discretion. In this regard he speaks for others, and in one case,[42] he secured a majority and wrote the prevailing opinion (which Brennan joined—a fact he later regretted[43]). It seems to me, however, that what the First Amendment requires in these cases is not indifference, but a commitment on the part of the Court to do all that it can possibly do to support and encourage the state in efforts to enrich public debate, to eliminate those restrictions of its subsidy programs that would narrow and restrict public debate, and if need be, even to require the state to continue and embark on programs that enrich debate.[44] The problem of remedies and the limits on institutional competence may, in the last instance cause the justices to retreat from such an ambitious undertaking, but such a failure of nerve, or exercise in prudence, should be recognized for what it is: a compromise, not a vindication of the First Amendment, and its deepest democratic aspirations.

When subsidies are involved, the state is allowed to act—the Court is torn, and the opinions incoherent, but the First Amendment is not viewed as a bar to state action. When confronted with regulatory measures, however, such as ceilings and limits on political expenditures, the justices see a threat to autonomy as defined by the Tradition and react in a much more straightforward and much more restricted way. They strike out at the state. In so doing the justices give expression to the Tradition and to our long-standing commitment to the tenets of classical liberalism and its plea for limited government. They also give expression to the political mood of the day, which is defined by its hostility to the activist state. Abolition of the fairness doctrine can be passed off as just one more instance of "deregulation."[45] It seems to me, however, that there is much to regret in this stance of the Court and the Tradition upon which it rests.

The received Tradition presupposes a world that no longer exists and that is beyond our capacity to recall—a world in which the principal political forum is the street corner. The Tradition ignores the manifold ways that the state participates in the construction of all things social and how contemporary social structure will, if left to itself, skew public debate. It also makes the choices that we confront seem all too easy. The received Tradition takes no account of the fact that to serve the ultimate purpose of the First Amendment we may sometimes find it necessary to "restrict the speech of some elements of our society in order to enhance the relative voice of others," and that unless the Court allows, and sometimes even requires, the state to do so, we as a people will never truly be free.

NOTES

1. Karl N. Llewellyn, *The Common Law Tradition: Deciding Appeals* (Boston: Little, Brown, 1960).

2. T. S. Eliot, "Tradition and the Individual Talent," in *Selected Prose of T. S. Eliot* (New York: Harcourt Brace Jovanovich, 1975; first published 1919), p. 37.

3. The manuscript is in the possession of Jamie Kalven and myself and will be published by Harper and Row in January 1988.

4. Federal Election Campaign Act Amendments of 1974, Pub. L. No. 93-443, 88 Stat. 1263 (codified at 2 U.S.C. §§ 431–434, 437–439, 453, 455, 5 U.S.C. §§ 1501–1503, 26 U.S.C. §§ 2766, 6012, 9001–12, 9031–9042 (1982)).

5. Charles E. Lindblom, *Politics and Markets: The World's Political-Economic Systems* (New York: Basic Books, 1977).

6. Ibid., pp. 201–221.

7. *Miami Herald Publishing Co.* v. *Tornillo,* 418 U.S. 241 (1974).

8. *Columbia Broadcasting Sys.* v. *Democratic Nat'l Comm.,* 412 U.S. 94 (1973).

9. *Buckley* v. *Valeo,* 424 U.S. 1 (1976).

10. *First Nat'l Bank of Boston* v. *Bellotti,* 435 U.S. 765 (1978).

11. *Lloyd Corp.* v. *Tanner,* 407 U.S. 551 (1972).

12. *New York Times Co.* v. *Sullivan,* 376 U.S. 254, 270 (1964).

13. *San Antonio Indep. School Dist.* v. *Rodriguez,* 411 U.S. 1 (1973).

14. But see Norman Dorsen and Joel Gora, "Free Speech, Property, and the Burger Court: Old Values, New Balances," *Supreme Court Review* (1982):195.

15. See, for example, Gerald Gunther, "Learned Hand and the Origins of Modern First Amendment Doctrine: Some Fragments of History," *Stanford Law Review* 27 (1975):719; Harry Kalven, Jr., "Professor Ernst Freund and *Debs* v. *United States,*" *Univ. Chicago Law Review* 40 (1973):235.

16. 395 U.S. 444 (1969).

17. Ibid. at 447–449.

18. Harry Kalven, Jr., "The *New York Times* Case: A Note on 'The Central Meaning of the First Amendment,'" *Supreme Court Review* (1964):191.

19. See Alexander Meiklejohn, "The First Amendment Is an Absolute," *Supreme Court Review* (1961):245; see also William J. Brennan, "The Supreme Court and the Meiklejohn Interpretation of the First Amendment," *Harvard Law Review* 79 (1965):1.

20. See, for example, Lee C. Bollinger, "Free Speech and Intellectual Values," *Yale Law Journal* 92 (1983):438. The breadth of the support is indicated by adherents as diverse as Kalven and Bork. See Robert H. Bork, "Neutral Principles and Some First Amendment Problems," *Indiana Law Journal* 47 (1971):1.

21. On the two free speech values, see Justice Brennan's remarks in "Address," *Rutgers Law Review* 32 (1979):173. For an opinion informed by this perspective, see *Richmond Newspapers* v. *Virginia,* 448 U.S. 555, 584–589 (1980) (Brennan, J., concurring in judgment). See also Jeffrey M. Blum, "The Divisible First Amendment: A Critical Functionalist Approach to Freedom of Speech and Electoral Campaign Spending," *N.Y.U. Law Review* 58 (1983):1273.

22. For a parallel but antecedent intellectual process in the domain of equality, see Owen M. Fiss, "Why the State?" *Harvard Law Review* 100 (1987):781, 783–785.

23. See, for example, Jerome A. Barron, *Freedom of the Press for Whom? The Right of Access to Mass Media* (Bloomington: Indiana University Press, 1973).

24. Herbert Marcuse, "Repressive Tolerance," in Robert P. Wolff et al., *A Critique of Pure Tolerance* (Boston: Beacon Press, 1969), p. 81.

25. The metaphor stems from Holmes's famous dissent in *Abrams* v. *United States,* 250 U.S. 616, 630 (1919) ("But when men have realized that time has upset many fighting faiths, they may come to believe even more than they believe the very foundations of their own conduct that the ultimate good desired is better reached by free trade in ideas—that the best test of truth is the power of the thought to get itself accepted in the competition of the

market"). The actual phrase "marketplace of ideas" is, oddly enough, Brennan's. *Lamont* v. *Postmaster General,* 381 U.S. 301, 308 (Brennan, J., concurring). The deliberative element in Brennan's thinking about the First Amendment can ultimately be traced to Brandeis, who is often linked to Holmes in his use of the clear and present danger test, but who in fact had no taste for the market metaphor. On the poetics of the Tradition, see David Cole, "Agon at Agora: Creative Misreading in the First Amendment Tradition," *Yale Law Journal* 95 (1986):857.

26. See Ronald H. Coase, "The Market for Goods and the Market for Ideas," *American Economic Review Proceedings* 64 (1974):384. Aaron Director, "The Parity of the Economic Market Place," *Journal of Law and Economics* 7 (1964):1.

27. *Red Lion Broadcasting Co.* v. *FCC,* 395 U.S. 367 (1969).

28. Included are Archibald Cox and Herbert Wechsler (the lawyer for the *New York Times* in *New York Times Co.* v. *Sullivan*). See Brief for Respondents Radio Television News Directors Association, *Red Lion Broadcasting Co.* v. *FCC,* 395 U.S. 367 (1969); Brief for Respondent Columbia Broadcasting System, *Red Lion Broadcasting Co.* v. *FCC,* 395 U.S. 367 (1969).

29. Harry Kalven, Jr., *The Negro and the First Amendment* (Chicago: University of Chicago Press, 1965), pp. 123–160.

30. 340 U.S. 315 (1951).

31. *Terminiello* v. *Chicago,* 337 U.S. 1, 37 (1949) (Jackson, J., dissenting) ("[I]f the Court does not temper its doctrinaire logic with a little practical wisdom, it will convert the constitutional Bill of Rights into a suicide pact").

32. See Robert B. McKay, "The Preference for Freedom," *N.Y.U. Law Review* 34 (1959):1182.

33. See Owen M. Fiss, "Inappropriateness of the Intent Test in Equal Protection Cases," 74 F.R.D. 276 (1977) (remarks presented at the Annual Judicial Conference, Second Judicial Circuit of the United States, September 11, 1976).

34. See Owen M. Fiss, "Groups and the Equal Protection Clause," *Philosophy and Public Affairs* 5 (1976):107.

35. *Red Lion Broadcasting Co.* v. *FCC,* supra n. 27, at 387.

36. *First Nat'l Bank of Boston* v. *Bellotti,* 435 U.S. 765, 809–812 (1978) (White, J., dissenting).

37. *PruneYard Shopping Center* v. *Robins,* 447 U.S. 74, 96–101 (1980) (Powell, J., concurring in part and in the judgment).

38. Ibid., at 99.

39. See, for example, *First Nat'l Bank of Boston* v. *Bellotti,* 435 U.S. 765, 790–791 (1978) (quoting *Buckley* v. *Valeo,* 424 U.S. 1, 48–49 (1976)).

40. *Board of Educ.* v. *Pico,* 457 U.S. 853 (1982).

41. Ibid. at 908–910 (Rehnquist, J., dissenting).

42. *Regan* v. *Taxation With Representation of Washington,* 461 U.S. 540 (1983).

43. See *FCC* v. *League of Women Voters,* 468 U.S. 364 (1984).

44. See *Columbia Broadcasting Sys.* v. *Democratic Nat'l Comm.,* 412 U.S. 94, 170–204 (1973) (Brennan, J., dissenting).

45. For the current challenge to the fairness doctrine, see "In re Inquiry into Section 73-1910 of the Commission's Rules and Regulations Concerning the General Fairness Doctrine Obligations of Broadcast Licensees," 102 F.C.C. 2d 143 (1985); *Action Center* v. *FCC,* 801 F.2d 501 (D.C. Cir. 1986); *Radio-Television News Directors Association* v. *FCC,* 809 F.2d 860 (D.C. Cir. 1987); *Meredith Corp.* v. *FCC,* 809 F.2d 863 (D.C. Cir. 1987); and Syracuse Peace Council, FCC Decision 87-266, released August 6, 1987. For President Reagan's veto of legislation trying to give the fairness doctrine a more secure statutory basis, see 23 weekly Comp. Pres. DOL. 25, 715–716 (June 19, 1987).

About the Contributors

Brian Barry is professor of political science at the London School of Economics and Political Science. He is the author of *Political Argument; Sociologists, Economists and Democracy; The Liberal Theory of Justice;* and *Theories of Social Justice* (forthcoming).

Charles R. Beitz teaches political theory at Swarthmore College. He is the author of *Political Theory and International Relations* (1979) and *Political Fairness* (forthcoming) and of articles on democratic theory.

Norman E. Bowie is professor of philosophy and director of the Center for the Study of Values at the University of Delaware. He is the past executive director of the American Philosophical Association, the author of *Business Ethics* (1982), as well as the editor or coauthor of books on ethics, business ethics, and political philosophy.

James S. Fishkin is professor of government and philosophy at the University of Texas at Austin. He is the author of *Tyranny and Legitimacy* (1979), *The Limits of Obligation* (1981), *Justice, Equal Opportunity and the Family* (1982), and *Beyond Subjective Morality* (1984). The last book won the Erik Erikson Prize from the International Society of Political Psychology in 1985. During 1987–1988 Fishkin is a fellow of the Center for Advanced Study in the Behavioral Sciences at Stanford University.

Owen M. Fiss is professor of public law at Yale Law School. He is the author of *The Civil Rights Injunction* (1978) as well as numerous articles in legal journals.

Jennifer L. Hochschild is a professor of politics and public affairs at Princeton University. She is the author of *What's Fair: American Beliefs about Distributive Justice* (1981) and *The New American Dilemma: Liberal Democracy and School Desegregation* (1984) and a coauthor of *Equalities* (1981). She is a panelist on the National Academy of Sciences Committee on the Status of Black Americans and a 1987–1988 fellow at the Center for Advanced Study in the Behavioral Sciences.

Christopher Jencks is professor of sociology and urban affairs at Northwestern University. He is the principal author of three books— *The Academic Revolution, Inequality,* and *Who Gets Ahead?*—and is currently working on a book about changes in the standard of living among the poor.

Jane Mansbridge teaches political theory at Northwestern University. She is the author of *Beyond Adversary Democracy* (1983) and *Why We Lost the ERA* (1986). Her current research includes a study of envy and equal respect.

George Sher is professor of philosophy at the University of Vermont. He is the author of *Desert* (1987) and of numerous essays in metaphysics and moral and social philosophy.